WHAT THE CHILDREN TOLD US

THE UNTOLD STORY OF THE FAMOUS "DOLL TEST" AND THE BLACK PSYCHOLOGISTS WHO CHANGED THE WORLD

TIM SPOFFORD

sourcebooks

Published by Sourcebooks
P.O. Box 4410, Naperville, Illinois 60567-4410
(630) 961-3900
sourcebooks.com

Library of Congress Cataloging-in-Publication Data

Names: Spofford, Tim, author.
Title: What the children told us : the untold story of the famous "doll
    test" and the Black psychologists who changed the world / Tim Spofford.
Description: Naperville, Illinois : Sourcebooks, [2022] | Includes
    bibliographical references and index. | Summary: "For readers of The
    Immortal Life of Henrietta Lacks and Hidden Figures, WHAT THE CHILDREN
    TOLD US tells the story of the towering intellectual and emotional
    partnership between the two Black psychologists who pioneered the
    groundbreaking "doll test," paving the way for the landmark Brown v.
    Board of Education case and decades of impactful civil rights
    activism"-- Provided by publisher.
Identifiers: LCCN 2021055924 (print) | LCCN 2021055925 (ebook) | (hardcover) | (epub)
Subjects: LCSH: Clark, Mamie Phipps. | Clark, Kenneth Bancroft, 1914-2005.
    | Psychologists--United States--Biography. | African American
    psychologists--Biography. | African Americans--Civil rights. | Child
    psychology.
Classification: LCC BF109.A1 S66 2022 (print) | LCC BF109.A1 (ebook) |
    DDC 150.92/2 [B]--dc23/eng/20220224
LC record available at https://lccn.loc.gov/2021055924

LC ebook record available at https://lccn.loc.gov/2021055925

Printed and bound in the United States of America.
LSC 10 9 8 7 6 5 4 3 2 1

For three wonderful women:

Kate Harris, the late Russia Hughes, and as always, for Barbara

It is easier to build strong children than to repair broken men.

— ATTRIBUTED TO FREDERICK DOUGLASS[1]

THE DOLL TEST

One's reputation, whether true or false, cannot be
hammered, hammered, hammered, into one's head
without doing something to one's character.

—PSYCHOLOGIST GORDON ALLPORT[1]

Young Dr. Kenneth Clark walked into a Harlem Woolworth store
to look at dolls—not for the new baby that he and his wife,
Mamie, were expecting but for a psychology experiment they were
planning together. It was 1940, near the end of the Great Depression,
and Dr. Clark spotted on the shelves just what he needed: four baby
dolls in diapers, two of them brown-skinned with hair painted black
and two of them white with hair painted yellow. Cast from identical
molds, the four dolls were otherwise the same.

A short, thin, brown-skinned man with close-cropped hair and
wire-rimmed glasses, Dr. Clark, in his midtwenties, had just finished

his PhD at Columbia University. But because of his race, no white college would hire him. So with a baby on the way, he and Mamie got grants to start a new enterprise: a psychology experiment that one day would touch the hearts of millions and change the way we think about racial identity. The Clarks would use the four dolls to study how Black children regarded themselves and others on the subject of race. The Rosenwald Fund provided the cash to test Black pupils in both the nominally integrated North and the strictly segregated South. Julius Rosenwald, the retailer who'd built the Sears empire and new Black schools across the South, funded the grants. His goal was to encourage Black people to cultivate their talents and realize the aspirations of their race.

The Clarks' experiment with dolls was an offshoot of Mamie's master's degree thesis at Howard University, where she'd been an A student, popular, and regarded as a hot catch by the fellows on her historically Black campus. Mamie's ambitious thesis had used drawings instead of dolls and was not chiefly concerned with race. By this point, however, she was way too busy to do the testing. She'd just started her doctoral studies at Columbia and, at age twenty-three, was caring for her first baby. Rising at six every morning, Mamie breastfed and burped their first child, little Kate, before laying her in the crib to sleep until the baby's 9:00 a.m. bath. Not till about midnight did the feeding, burping, and diapering cease. The routine had to be exhausting for Mamie—balancing all that nursing, wiping, and washing with her schoolwork.

So Kenneth packed his clothes and dolls, left their apartment in Harlem, and traveled alone 150 miles north to Springfield,

Massachusetts, to kick-start the testing on a chilly Thursday. A New England mill town of 150,000, Springfield was a thriving but gritty little city of narrow streets and rumbling factories, chief among them the national armory, home of the Springfield rifle, and the Indian motorcycle plant nearby that put the nation's police on two wheels. With scores of other plants churning out auto parts, machine tools, board games, and glossy magazines, Springfield was better off than most cities in the Depression. Workers with lunchboxes filled the streets each morning on their way to punch in for the first shift, most of them Irish, Greek, Italian, and French-Canadian men struggling to feed their families.

Blacks, too, were attracted by the factory jobs, though their forebears had been here long before the white ethnics arrived. A hotbed of abolitionism in the nineteenth century, Springfield had served as a station on the Underground Railroad, and Primus Mason, a Black farmer and real estate investor, was among the agents helping fugitive slaves make it to freedom. Abolitionist John Brown had lived among the town's Black population and organized his League of Gileadites to stop slave catchers from snatching the fugitives in town and dragging them back to Dixie in chains.

Much had changed here by the time Kenneth arrived. Many Blacks worked alongside whites in the factories, and their kids played together on the same streets. Springfield's public schools were racially integrated by state law; still, slurs and rocks often flew between Black and white pupils heading home from school. Parents of both races warned their kids to steer clear of the bad ones on the other side of the color line, just as they had in Hot Springs, Arkansas, when

Mamie was growing up. And this was the whole point of choosing Springfield for the Clarks' experiment: beneath the cellophane-thin veneer of Northern integration, Springfield was not unlike Mamie's hometown of Hot Springs, where Kenneth would begin the Southern, rigidly segregated portion of his testing. Like Hot Springs, Springfield had never scraped the rural mud from its boots. The stench of hog farms still wafted through its neighborhoods, and it was home to thirty-two hundred Black people, about 2 percent of the population. Kenneth's goal was to test every Black child, two through eight years old, about 120 in all, starting at the Barrows School and the Works Progress Administration (WPA) Nursery in Springfield's city hall.

Among the first he tested was little KJ, a shy, eight-year-old boy who showed up in the schoolroom in a blue suit. To set him at ease, Kenneth chatted a while before showing KJ four dolls in a staggered, integrated lineup, no white doll separate from a brown one. "Give me the doll that looks like a white child," he told the boy, just as he would tell all the other pupils.[2] The eight-year-old chose a white doll. Asked to indicate which doll was "colored" or a "Negro," KJ picked a brown doll, proving his familiarity with racial terms. "Give me the doll you like to play with, the doll that you like best," Kenneth then asked. The dark-skinned boy overlooked the two brown dolls to choose a white one. "Give me the doll that is a nice doll." KJ selected the same white doll. "Give me the doll that looks bad." This time, the boy picked a brown doll. Asked to show the doll "that is a nice color," KJ again selected a white doll. Kenneth's toughest request always came last: "Give me the doll that looks like you." Dark-skinned KJ hesitated, looked embarrassed, and this time chose a brown doll. Kenneth asked if he liked the doll? "No—I don't like that one," KJ answered.

Seven-year-old Helen N., however, seemed more at ease with her racial identity. Though fidgety and nervous, Helen picked a brown doll as best, saying she had a white doll at home but it was broken and now she wanted a brown doll.

KENNETH AND A BLACK CHILD
SIMULATE DOLL TESTS IN 1947

Asked to choose a doll that looked bad, she selected a white one, and then she pointed out a brown doll as good looking. "That's a nice color," she said.[3] Asked about white people, Helen made it clear that race was a topic at home: "My mother told me not to play with them because they get me in trouble."

Kenneth returned about three days a week for the rest of October to finish his testing in Springfield. Most of the kids answered his questions the way little KJ did, preferring white dolls to one of their own race. To Kenneth, the children had internalized the low opinion of their race that prevailed in a white nation. Clearly, their preference for white dolls was not a matter of chance, for in many instances, the kids had told him what was on their minds. Some even denied their racial identity. "I look brown because I got a suntan," said Edward D., who was nearly age eight and preferred the white dolls.[4] "I look brown and they always call me a nigger but I'm not—I'm a white boy." Phyllis J., nearly four and light-skinned, also denied her race.

"No—I'm a white girl," she said.[5] "I don't like the colored children because they don't look better." A few acknowledged wishing they were white. "Yes, I would like to be white," said brown-skinned Joan W., age six, who preferred white dolls.[6] "I don't know why." But dark-skinned Juanita R. had her reasons. "Because people call me black and I don't like that," the six-year-old said.[7] "My mother call me black, father call me black, and sister."

Nonetheless, most of the children seemed to enjoy the test as a game, and some begged to retake it. But it pained Kenneth to see others squirm when he asked which doll looked most like themselves. A few seemed so unraveled by choosing between the dolls that they wept. Caleb D., a seven-year-old who was dark but denied being "black,"[8] cried so hard that Kenneth had to postpone the testing and give the boy a penny to cheer him up. Another who wept was Kermit L., who was light-skinned and nearly age seven. He picked a white doll as best and looking "sumpin' like me."[9] Starting to weep, Kermit stammered, "My mother—said I wasn't a Negro."

In all, Kenneth tested 119 pupils in Springfield by the end of October. In January, he'd resume his work in Hot Springs, Mamie's segregated hometown. The time-consuming task of compiling, calculating, and charting all this data would fall to Mamie, who would prepare the final report for the Rosenwald Fund. Only then would the Clarks know for sure whether the Southern results differed from the data gathered in Springfield. The Clarks' findings would be hotly disputed by lawyers, scholars, and pundits of both races for years to come. Newspapers, journals, and books would fuel the controversy. In 1954, nine black-robed justices in the U.S. Supreme Court would hear some of these arguments in *Brown v. Board of Education*, and their ruling on state-sanctioned school segregation would alter the course of history.

The Clarks' role in these historic events was only their opening act in a lifetime of activism in Harlem and on the national stage. Unyielding integrationists, they were determined to use disciplined intelligence to rock the foundations of segregation so that all Americans, especially the children, could live, learn, and work together. In the face of fierce white resistance that lingers even today, the Clarks would hold America to its creed that all its children were created equal. And they would continue the struggle as long as health would allow.

PART ONE
COMING OF AGE

ONE

THE DOCTOR'S DAUGHTER

Black folks aren't born expecting segregation, prepared from day one to follow its confining rules. Nobody presents you with a handbook when you're teething, and says, "Here's how you must behave as a second-class citizen."

—MELBA PATTILLO BEALS[1]

Young Mamie Phipps boarded her train, walked down the narrow aisle of a Jim Crow car, and entered a private compartment. It was a mid-September day in 1934, and her father, Dr. Harold Phipps, had found the compartment and a companion to watch over Mamie on her three-day trip east to Washington. Brown-skinned, svelte, and only sixteen, Mamie was eager to leave segregated Hot Springs to study at Howard, a Black university. Her Arkansas hometown was too small and too slow to change for her liking: its train station with the "colored" waiting room, for instance, its city library for whites only, and all-white Central School, on her own street, where she could not enroll as a child. Hot Springs offered few professional jobs, especially for Blacks, and not a single college. Mamie's closest friends were leaving too.

Still, she was sad to leave, for most of what she prized in life was here: her friends, close-knit family, and her tiny church, St. Mary's Episcopal, where she played the organ. Seated near the window in her compartment, Mamie was nervous. Her father, a former Pullman porter, had warned that it was dangerous for a Black girl to travel alone through the South. He told her to keep the window shades down and stay in her compartment. He asked the porters to keep an eye on Mamie and keep her and her companion fed. As the hissing, clanging train pulled slowly from the depot and lumbered down the tracks, it belched black smoke that wafted over Mamie's neighborhood. As the green mountains of town receded, her train gathered speed, clacking down the rails.

Three days later, shy, soft-spoken Mamie arrived tired but safe when her train pulled into Union Station in Washington. It was cool, in the sixties, and upperclassmen flocked about her and the other freshman ladies to lug their baggage and drive them to the campus. Once in her dormitory, Mamie unpacked and learned that she had a roommate. An intensely private person, she didn't like the arrangement. She also resented the second-class status of Howard women, especially in their first term, with a 9:00 p.m. curfew most nights and the bans on makeup, dating, and joining in the footraces, so unladylike, during fall orientation.

After days without a word from his daughter, Dr. Phipps asked about Mamie in a letter to her uncle Alfred Smith, a savvy fellow in Washington who served in President Roosevelt's Black Cabinet. "My only fear for her is the fact that the ground work done here at Langston [School] was rather superficial and poor," Phipps wrote.[2] "But she has the brain and with steady application she should overcome the handicap." Mamie's uncle would keep an eye on her.

One day, she walked into a room full of buzzing freshmen at a fall orientation session. A short, thin, bespectacled senior in charge called them all to order, but the freshmen kept yakking and yakking. Frustrated, the senior shouted, "Shut up!"[3] He seemed haughty and humorless to Mamie, and she asked someone his name. Kenneth Clark, a woman hater, she was told. So this was the same Clark who had sent her a welcome-to-Howard letter over the summer. Well, he was not so welcoming now.

The story of how that letter landed in Mamie's mailbox takes us back to October 18, 1917, in the middle of the Great War, when her mother went into labor with her. Dr. Phipps delivered his daughter at home that day, and they named her after her grandmother, Mamie Smith. Dr. Phipps could have afforded a hospital bed for his wife, but whites set a low priority on health care for Blacks, and every hospital in town barred them. That was why two big Black hotels in town, the Pythian and Woodmen of the Union, offered wards for patient care. Both hotels were owned by fraternal groups that sold insurance. Dr. Phipps, a big wheel in Black medical associations and the

Colored Knights of Pythias, worked two jobs at the Pythian Hotel: as its manager and as a physician with a private practice.

Mamie was raised with her brother, Harold, in the big brick bungalow their father had built at 320 Garden Street in a segregated, middle-class neighborhood in the popular resort town of Hot Springs, fifty miles south of the state capital at Little Rock. A native of the Caribbean island of St. Kitts, her father was a tall, dark, solemn man and a pillar of his community. Truth be told, Dr. Phipps was an aloof and humorless fellow with a deep voice and British accent, a formidable figure to Mamie and Harold. But he was a tireless and excellent provider. The home he'd built for his family had five bedrooms, a music room, and a porte cochere for his Cadillac. When the Pythian Hotel filled for conferences in town, his house served as an elite inn absorbing the overflow. The Phippses served lavish dinners for Black guests and friends from across the nation: Chicago, New York, Washington, Indianapolis, and other cities. By the standards of their caste and class, the Phippses were rich.

In quest for a better life, young Harold Phipps had left St. Kitts and his job as a schoolmaster to start medical school in America with $160 dollars in his wallet. He worked as a Pullman porter to put himself through Meharry, the medical school for Blacks in Tennessee, and in 1908, he hung his shingle on Hot Springs' Malvern Avenue, the Black business district. Hot Springs was ideal for a new doctor on the make. It was a resort town of fourteen thousand, a quarter of them Blacks with decent jobs. Hot Springs touted its scalding, health-giving springs and drew ailing pilgrims of both races from across the nation. Central Avenue, the town's main thoroughfare and white business district, was tucked between two mountains downtown. Down the middle of the avenue coursed its electric streetcars, and looming over one side of the street was West Mountain with the storefronts of druggists, barbers, and merchants, along with saloons, cafés, and gambling dens at its rocky base. On the opposite side of the street were the stately, mansion-like spas of Bathhouse Row, and rising behind them was Hot Springs Mountain, where its thermal waters streamed through pipes and into the elite spas with names like Ozark, Magnesia, and Horseshoe. Both the afflicted and sybaritic steeped their limbs in tubs filled with the warm waters. Black attendants in white uniforms scrubbed, toweled, and massaged the bathers, who afterward took a seat on the veranda or strolled arm in

arm with a partner along the Government Promenade. White gentlemen and ladies from the poshest hotels—the Arlington, the Eastman, and the Majestic—were there to see and be seen, to enjoy the dances and concerts, especially in the winter high season. Spacious dining rooms in the best hotels offered dinner and drinks second to none. But as a Black man, Dr. Phipps was not welcome.

YOUNG HAROLD PHIPPS WITH HIS MOTHER, MARGARET, BEFORE LEAVING ST. KITTS TO BECOME A DOCTOR

The town had a seedier side as well. By the 1920s, notorious mobsters were drawn to its casinos and bordellos: Al Capone, Bugsy Siegel, Lucky Luciano, and Pretty Boy Floyd among them. Mayor Leo McLaughlin and his police chief welcomed them all and fended off FBI agents and state troopers trying to arrest the gangsters. Malvern Avenue, the Black business district in Mamie's neighborhood, flourished in the free and easy times. The dives there sold moonshine. "It was a hot street," resident Hilda Martin recalled. [4] "It was wide open." Liquor flowed citywide, Prohibition be damned. Cops and cabdrivers directed tourists to the brothels. The bathhouses were bubbling and the bellhops hopping at the hotels, and Mayor McLaughlin got envelopes stuffed with casino cash. In Bible-Belt Arkansas, Hot Springs was Sodom. A roulette wheel, a jug of white lightning, and a brothel's red lamp belonged on the city seal.

But for the average tourist, it was a gawker's paradise with zoos, shooting galleries, burro rides, hiking trails, and spring-training games for Major League Baseball teams like the Pittsburgh Pirates. Spring-fed fountains let visitors quaff the beneficial waters downtown, but Dr. Phipps could not partake. Blacks had to buy their own water in bottles.

Dr. Phipps met the love of his life on Malvern Avenue. Katie Smith did clerical work at the Crystal Hotel less than a block from his office. The hotel was run by her parents—manager Jesse Rufus Smith, who'd been enslaved before the Civil War, and his wife, Mamie, the bookkeeper. Their charming, red-haired daughter, Katie, could pass for white. "She was vibrant, had a good mind, and was very good looking," actress Billie Allen, a family friend, recalled.[5] Katie, who was fond of people and loved to dance, had gone to Spelman College in Atlanta for a time before returning to her hometown. She stole the heart of Dr. Phipps, a terribly sober, rigid man ten years her senior. She tried to loosen him up, and they clicked. Nine months after their wedding, Katie bore their first child, Harold Jr. Her mother's namesake, little Mamie, arrived a year later.

Dr. Phipps wanted a quality education for his children so they could support themselves, find suitable spouses, and advance the Black race. Without kindergartens in Hot Springs, he sent Mamie and little Harold to St. Gabriel's, a rare little integrated school run by Catholic nuns on the outskirts. Black parents gave high marks to the white nuns. "The sisters were real kind," recalled Ida Fort Thompson, a lifelong resident.[6] Mamie had to notice the white kids scampering up the dirt road in front of her house on their way to all-white Central School on her street. Would she join them there someday? She must have asked her parents that, and the answer had to be no. Explaining segregation to a little girl could not have been easy. "I would say I learned most of it from my parents, because we had to be prepared before we

MAMIE AND HER BROTHER HAROLD PHIPPS
OUTSIDE HOT SPRINGS, ARKANSAS

9

were sent out, you know, on our own," Mamie recalled.[7] "I was never surprised."

Her childhood coincided with the rebirth of the Ku Klux Klan, and she would never forget the day the white hoods rode into town and gave her neighborhood a fright. Another was August 1, 1922, when she was four. Blacks ran and shouted through her neighborhood, warning that a white mob was about to lynch a Black man nearby. Gilbert Harris, age twenty-eight, was accused of killing a white man. White terrorists tossed Harris onto a truck and dragged him downtown to the same light pole used in the town's last lynching in 1913. Hundreds of men, women, and children watched as Harris, with a noose around his neck, screamed that he was not the killer. "Harris was hoisted about 20 feet in the air while the great crowd yelled and cheered," the city's *New Era* newspaper reported.[8] The mob tried to drag his corpse through the streets, but police stopped them. Mamie recalled an eerie quiet falling on her neighborhood: "It takes days after a thing like that, you know, before people even venture out."[9]

She learned at an early age that she belonged to a despised caste. Streetcar conductors required her to take a back seat, and some theaters would not sell her a ticket. She learned to avoid eye contact whenever a white stranger passed her. "Well," Mamie once said, "you were very wary of anybody white." Growing up in a segregated society shapes the personality, said Evelyn Boyer, a psychologist and Mamie's niece. "It wears on you. You become more reserved, perhaps, more careful, cautious—which one sees in Mamie."[10]

By the fourth grade, Mamie had followed her brother to a segregated public school closer to home, Langston, a two-story brick building with fourteen classrooms. The grade school was on the first floor and the high school upstairs. Langston School was named for John Mercer Langston, a Reconstruction-era congressman from Virginia who later served as acting president of Howard University. Along with the three R's, Mamie learned things at Langston she'd never pick up in a white school: African American history and the words to "Lift Every Voice and Sing," the Black national anthem. "The teachers were really patient with us," graduate Thomas Anderson recalled.[11] "They were interested in our learning." Even so, they were never paid as much as white teachers.

Langston had its shortcomings. Forty-four pupils packed Mamie's fourth-grade classroom. Her school had no gym or playing field, and her tattered schoolbooks were all hand-me-downs from the white schools. Even so, Langston stood out in Arkansas. Most rural areas had no high school at all for Blacks, and their schoolhouses were often drafty, termite-ridden shacks with leaking roofs, potbellied stoves, and the woods for a latrine. The state's Black teachers were dedicated but poorly trained; 14 percent never attended high school, and 77 percent had never gone to college. Summing up her Langston years, Mamie once said, "The school was poor, and later I realized how much we didn't learn."[12]

Dr. Phipps tried to compensate for this, demanding that his children speak standard English and no slang. He bought books for a home library and quizzed the kids to boost their vocabulary, asking Mamie, for instance, to define a word like *acerbic*. If she failed, she had to look it up and recite the meaning to him. If she made a wild claim at the dinner table, her father debunked it and lectured her on getting her facts straight. "You had to be right with Granddaddy," recalled his niece Evelyn Boyer.[13] "You had to know your stuff." He loathed pretension and tolerated no bragging. Always on the spot, Mamie became a perfectionist and learned to choose her words carefully. Whenever she had to speak in public, she was terrified—a phobia that would plague her for life.

Progressing through the grades, Mamie moved upstairs to the high school where she became an A student, a cheerleader, the senior class president, and a leader of school clubs. She organized a dance to raise money for school library books, "something that has never happened during the history of Langston," reported the *Maveric*, her school newspaper.[14] Katie Phipps had her daughter take piano lessons and at thirteen perform in her first recital at Roanoke Baptist, her mother's church. Facing an ambitious program of eight classical pieces, Mamie glided through the first, Burgmüller's Fantaisie Brillante. The *Hot Springs Echo*, a Black newsweekly, observed, "Displaying a versatility in different execution, remarkable technique and a charming stage presence, and poise expected with one far beyond her years, Miss Phipps immediately won her audience and charmed throughout the brilliant program."[15]

Mamie's mother was in many ways her husband's opposite: outgoing, fun-loving, and dedicated to making her home a happy place. She played her baby grand piano for the family and took Mamie for drives in the country and on visits to see friends or bring free food and medicine to church members in need, kindling a humanitarian impulse in her daughter. She and her husband were active in Black civic groups and the NAACP. Katie Phipps was impeccably turned out with perfume, makeup, jewelry, and dresses from the best shops. To ensure that her children looked smart for church, school, and social events, she brought them to white stores on Central Avenue where most Blacks felt unwelcome. Many merchants were glad to see her, because Katie Phipps had money. "We had certain access to certain kinds of things, like merchandise stores, drug stores, variety stores, that other people didn't have, or that other people didn't take advantage of," Mamie recalled.[16] "So you knew there was a real chasm, really, between the races." As aristocrats of color, the Phippses were resented by members of both races, and Mamie would become wary of anyone but those closest to her.

To cultivate Mamie's feminine side, her mother sent her to a charm school where Mamie learned to set a table, walk smartly, talk with confidence, and sit discreetly in a dress. She attended a ball for subdebutantes in town and traveled to dances and proms for the young social set up in Little Rock, where there were more middle-class Blacks and the Phippses had friends. The *Echo* newsweekly touted her social life: "Miss Mamie Katherine Phipps, the talented and attractive daughter of Dr. and Mrs. H. H. Phipps, and one of the season's most charming sub-debs, held open house following the Langston-Dunbar football game, for members of Little Rock's younger Smart Set, who attended the game and dance at 'The Casino Beautiful.'"[17] With no shortage of suitors, Mamie pasted their pictures in her scrapbook, some in snappy suits with hats at a rakish angle and hailing from Little Rock and even Tuskegee, Alabama. One fellow sent her a special February 14 telegram: "JUST DROP ME A LINE AND SAY YOULL BE MINE SWEET VALENTINE."[18]

Mamie's male admirers had to feel uneasy in Dr. Phipps's lair on Garden Street. He warily regarded each boy and fretted whenever she went out at night with girlfriends. He was no populist or democrat. He looked askance at Blacks with poor hygiene, ragged clothes, or loose ways. He would not tolerate such things from Mamie or Harold. They were Phippses, and he expected them to rise, to join in uplifting the race. He never spanked Mamie; a scolding in his inner sanctum, the bedroom, had the proper effect. And there was that stare of his, the stare of utter disapproval. "He had to be one of the most difficult persons to approach," granddaughter Kate Clark Harris recalled.[19] "A very formidable and formal guy."

Yet Mamie was no goody-two-shoes, for she had a mischievous streak. On one report card, she got a D for deportment and was twice cited for tardiness. Her flirtations with boys were grist for the school paper's gossip column. And she organized a dance troupe at Langston that included girls who were wild, woolly, and working class, the Junior Buddies, and asked the Princess Theatre to let them perform on stage between movies. "They did little dances, tap dances," recalled Dorothy Logan, then a teenager who watched from the theater's balcony for Blacks.[20] "That was the funny thing about her," Logan said of Mamie and her fellow hoofers. "My parents probably wouldn't have wanted me to be in with one or two of them."

When it was time to consider colleges, Mamie and her mother traveled to Washington in cherry blossom time. Her uncle Alfred Smith, a Howard University graduate and booster, likely showed them around the campus. A hot family debate ensued. Mamie wanted to go to Howard, but her father preferred Spelman, the women's college in Atlanta that her mother had attended. Raised to join the ranks of the best and brightest, Mamie knew that Howard was the capstone of Black education. Her father, on the other hand, feared she would fall in love and marry before graduating. He insisted on single-sex Spelman, but Mamie held her ground. "And I'm telling you," daughter Kate recalled, "my grandfather was a formidable obstacle."[21]

Nonetheless, Dr. Phipps caved to Mamie's demands, and when Howard accepted her in the spring of 1934, she was thrilled. Designated as one of two Langston seniors to graduate with honors, she was cited on her class night as the "Most Popular" and "Best All-Around" senior as well as the most talented and studious.[22] According to family lore, Mamie was the valedictorian of her tiny class of thirty-two students, but the graduation program took no notice of it—probably because her problem with stage fright made a valedictory address impossible. Instead, she played Chopin's Scherzo No. 2 at commencement.

After a lively summer of senior-class parties, dances, and picnics, a letter from Howard University regarding freshman orientation arrived for Mamie in the front-porch mailbox.

Because we want better spirit than we have ever had we are trying to make this the best Freshman Week we have ever had. To this end, the Student Council is requiring a Freshman Fee of One dollar ($1.00), which will cover all expenses of Freshman Week: the Freshman cap, Freshman reception, and a sightseeing tour of the Nation's Capital.[23]

Mamie studied the signature and wondered why a Howard student, even if he *was* in charge of fall orientation, was asking her for money. She mailed him the dollar anyway and thought little more of it. But as it would turn out, she would long recall this first letter from Kenneth Clark.

A twenty-year-old Howard senior from Harlem, Kenneth was the son of a seamstress and single mom who emigrated from Panama. In spite of his humble origins, he was a big wheel at Howard and looking for a new flame. For two years, he had dated Bernice Early, a classmate from Washington, before they amicably broke up. Kenneth was popular and had his hand in almost everything on campus as publicist for Kappa Alpha Psi fraternity, editor of the *Hilltop* newspaper, director of freshman orientation, and now scribe, or editor, of the prestigious *Stylus* literary magazine. He worked with its two renowned advisers: poet Sterling Brown and philosopher Alain Locke. But Kenneth was short and scrawny and felt uneasy about his looks and his chances with the ladies. "He was not the best-looking dude," recalled Leighla Wheeler, the social butterfly he had tried and failed to woo in his freshman year.[24] But as Leighla would learn, there was more to Kenneth than his looks.

In the fall term of his senior year, all the guys were raving about a bewitching freshman from Arkansas with an aristocratic air. "Have you seen Mamie Phipps?" they asked Kenneth.[25] She'd made quite a splash, getting elected to the student council and joining the Ivy Leaf Club for aspirants of Alpha Kappa Alpha, the most popular sorority.

Unimpressed by her newfound celebrity, Kenneth stopped her coming down a stairway one day and asked if she was Miss Phipps. Yes, she answered. "I don't think you're so hot," he jabbed.[26] Shy but confident, Mamie shrugged him off and moved on. Actually, he *did* think she was hot—that's why he'd challenged her—but he also figured that anyone *that* poised and *that* well-dressed was a snob.

At a formal dance on campus one night, Mamie looked up and spotted Kenneth in a tuxedo by the balcony spotlight. He stood smoking, his left hand tucked into his jacket and his gaze fixed on the dance floor below—the big shot surveying his domain. Mamie was impressed by campus leaders like Kenneth, so when he asked her to dance, she was perplexed but willing. As they locked hands and glided across the dance floor, she addressed him coolly as Mr. Clark, recalling the day that he yelled "Shut up!" at the freshmen. Silently vowing to avenge her class, especially the women, she counted his invitation to dance as point number one toward his defeat. Maybe she'd charm him into falling in love and then break his heart.

Clearly, she cast a spell on him, because after the dance, Kenneth sang the praises of beautiful Mamie Phipps as he sat with his pals over beers that night. The fellows all nodded in agreement. He liked that she didn't jabber on about silly stuff, as so many girls did, and there was that quiet self-assurance about her. And yet there were too many suitors fluttering about her for Kenneth's comfort. They were like vultures, and he was afraid to woo her.

So Mamie took the initiative, approaching him on campus one day and asking him to phone her. When his call came, she chalked it up as point number two in her contest to cut him down to size.

Between calls, they met covertly at night in the psychology department office where he worked as a clerical assistant to his professors. Kenneth knew that Mamie was seeing other fellows. He hated it but bided his time. He was intimidated by her beauty and feared that she'd pose an insurmountable challenge.

By the spring term, Kenneth summoned the courage he needed to go beyond chats, notes, and phone calls to Mamie. He invited her to his fraternity's annual dawn dance, and she accepted, chalking it up to point number three toward his humiliation. Then she upped the ante by inviting him to the freshmen prom, which came before the dawn dance, even though she suspected he already had a date. Kenneth said yes, broke his other date, and showed up at Mamie's dormitory in a tuxedo. At first, she scored this as point number four, but Kenneth was fun to be with and charmed her at the prom. True, he was a bit full of himself, but he wasn't the starchy psychology scholar she'd expected, and he treated her like a queen. So Mamie dropped her plot to humiliate him. Kenneth formed a better impression of her as well. She seemed brainy and brash, not just a prim or frivolous Southern belle. He was sold.

Mamie embodied much that he hoped for in a partner: beauty, brains, and an ability to hold her own in a conversation, which was important to Kenneth, who talked all the time. More than just a lover, he needed a partner to challenge his mind. Supersmart Mamie needed much the same, though looks were not as important to her. She wanted someone bright, loyal, and on his way up. Feckless playboys need not apply; after all, she was a Phipps.

One midnight in April, the first night of spring break after school had closed, Kenneth showed up in a tuxedo again to take Mamie to his fraternity dawn dance. They had the hours before sunrise to take each other's measure. She liked that he cracked jokes and enjoyed teasing her. Her reservations? His fingernails were a mess, and he had a superior attitude toward women. Kenneth noticed that she was a velvet-voiced introvert. Even so, she was self-assured and unusually well read. His reservations? She was awfully young, with too many wooers.

And yet they had plenty in common, including a love of books, jazz, and dancing. Both were Episcopalian with a parent from the Caribbean. Whirling across the dance floor that night, they giggled and chatted till dawn. It was a magical night, and tired of sharing Mamie with other guys, Kenneth abruptly asked her to stop seeing them. Flummoxed, she impulsively agreed. He pledged to write her from home during spring break, but cautious, guarded Mamie stayed silent on that count.

Right after the dawn dance, with the morning sun still rising, Kenneth boarded a train and headed home to Harlem a happy man. His mother's six-story apartment building was at 880 St. Nicholas Place, but Kenneth arrived in another dimension. He was dizzily, delightfully in love, and his mother and sister, Beulah, were astonished to see him in such a euphoric state that he could barely wait to write Mamie.

Fountain pen in hand, he tried not to sound like a smug upperclassman from the Big Apple. "There isn't very much going on here in this glorified country town," Kenneth began.[27] But he lifted the veil and revealed his ego when he mentioned seeing Roland Hayes, the great Black tenor, at Carnegie Hall. A budding leftist, Kenneth joked about spring in New York City: "Today is the type of day that makes a pauper the equal of either a Morgan or Rockefeller. So far no crafty capitalist has found a way of creating a monopoly on the weather." He told her he hoped to become a psychiatrist someday and closed his long letter with a jest fit for a physician's daughter: "I guess that this is a large enough initial dose. It has probably made you sick long ago—so I suppose that I shall be a good doctor and know when to stop giving medicine."

Mamie never responded. While Kenneth was away in New York, she was at play in Washington, already breaking her pledge of fidelity by taking car rides and going dancing with another fellow. But once her favorite psychology major was back on campus, she stopped seeing the other suitor. Mamie had just one steady boyfriend now, Kenneth Clark.

They took long, romantic rambles in hilly, verdant Rock Creek Park and around the reservoir near Howard. They went to the student council banquet together, made a trip to Baltimore, and devoured sundaes at the University Grill. On student council nights, they trysted in the psychology office. The more Mamie saw of Kenneth, the more she appreciated that he was mature and serious, unlike so many fellows who goofed off instead of studying. She told him that he'd make a great psychiatrist someday. He mused that Mamie was amazingly confident for a shy person and easy to get along with. They were together constantly. "He and Mamie fit like a shoe," Leroy Weekes, a fraternity brother, recalled.[28] "Clark had position, stability. Those were the things girls were looking for back then."

After final exams, Mamie stayed in town for Kenneth's graduation and met his mother, Miriam Clark, and his fun-loving Harlem pal Victor Carter. Victor told Kenneth that Mamie was gorgeous, peerless. At commencement, Kenneth's mother beamed with pride. All her hard work to pay his tuition and all her prodding for his homework over the years had paid off. She approved of his returning to Howard in the fall for a master's degree in psychology.

After a day of celebrating, Kenneth and Mamie went together to Union Station before parting for the summer. Aboard the night train, they had one more hug and kiss and vowed again to write, though both worried their feelings for each other might cool over the summer. After Kenneth stepped off Mamie's train, it rolled down the track and took her and his spirits with it. He was glum the next day on his own train back to New York. Usually, he swapped small talk with the conductor, but on this trip home, he never said a word. He worried that Mamie's ardor, stoked in the spring, would never last till the fall.

A marriage of minds and the requirements of American history would depend upon it.

TWO

THE SON OF A SEAMSTRESS

De ole sheep, dey know de road,
De young lambs must find de way.

—NEGRO SPIRITUAL[1]

Arriving at Howard for the fall term in 1935, Kenneth and Mamie threw their arms around each other. After a long summer apart, they resumed their walks on the leafy paths of Rock Creek Park and held hands in Black movie theaters like the Lincoln and Booker T. Mamie wore his fraternity pin, and they frequented Harrison's Café, Gerry's, and other Howard haunts. Drawing on her allowance from home, she often picked up the tab. A graduate student now, Kenneth was usually broke.

Instead of renewing her scholarship for her sophomore year, as her father preferred, Mamie took Kenneth's advice and started a clerical job in the psychology department—the same tuition-paid job he held before graduating. The professors appreciated her typing skills, and she got an insider's view of their work. Unhappy with her math grades, Mamie no longer hoped to teach, and Kenneth pressed her to major in psychology, which he said jibed with her interest in children. Regarding romance as a transient thing, he believed that marriage with a bright, beautiful psychologist was a stride toward the good life. So Mamie switched majors, and unlike her math professors, the psychologists welcomed her.

Kenneth's career path was also taking shape. Dr. Sumner, the department chairman, promised that if he completed his master's degree on time, Kenneth could teach for a professor on leave next fall. Kenneth remained immersed in campus activities, living in the Kappa frat house, writing for the school paper and literary magazine, and going to proms with Mamie. They ran to her dormitory at night to comply with her curfew, and sometimes she had to sneak indoors. But their romance was not all sweetness and light. After Christmas, they broke up often, and Mamie left him a note: "Frankly these two months of 1936 have been a crisis for me. It's not over yet and whether things turn out for the better or worse when it is over I do not know—and it makes me afraid."[2] The problem was Kenneth's insecurity about poverty and his looks. She had cash; he had none. She dismissed her many suitors with aplomb, but no one lined up to date Kenneth, who was awkward with women. Intensely jealous, he suspected Mamie of being unfaithful and threw a fit when she went to a dance with girlfriends. Still, she carried a torch for him. Like her beloved father, Kenneth was serious, smart, and ambitious. She had no interest in handsome playboys.

KENNETH KEPT THIS
PHOTO OF HIS GIRLFRIEND,
MAMIE PHIPPS, ON HIS DESK

A young man of his times, Kenneth felt superior to Mamie, and whenever he crossed the line, which was often, she warned him to back off, which he always did, because he needed her as a lover and colleague to challenge him intellectually. Playing Pygmalion to her Galatea, he honed her critical thinking skills and shaped her career. He showed her the ropes in their department and coached her on books to read and courses to take. Mamie burned to be as intellectually sophisticated as he was and even picked up his tobacco habit—two or three cigarettes a day at first.

She typed his term papers and helped with his master's thesis, a study of Howard students' attitudes toward parents. Enamored of his mother but not his father, Kenneth wondered what other students thought of their own parents and developed a questionnaire on parental traits such as intelligence and moral character. He asked students which of their parents they preferred. At fifty-seven pages, his thesis was impeccably typed by Mamie and stuffed with tables and charts she probably helped him compile. His thesis showed that Howard students, especially the men, preferred their mothers to their fathers, just as Kenneth did. He concluded that "some degree of Oedipus [complex] exists among the male subjects."[3] Mamie had been a great help—"our thesis," she called it[4]—and he thanked her in his acknowledgments section. His thesis was unremarkable but on time, and it made the grade, clearing his path to teach at Howard in the fall.

To explore Kenneth's wobbly, uphill path to Howard and a career in psychology, we go back to July 14, 1914, in the port city of Colón days before the new Panama Canal opened its gates there. He was born in the warm and muggy wet season when tropical rains came in cataracts, rattling the tin roofs of homes and spawning clouds of mosquitoes. Panama was an independent, Spanish-speaking nation, but the baby boy's parents were of colonial Jamaican descent, and he was a British subject. At age nineteen, his mother, Miriam, was the daughter of shopkeepers, and his father, Arthurton Clark, twenty-nine, was a supervisor on the docks. Fathering a son was a point of pride with Arthurton, and Miriam was determined that this wriggling mass of boyhood would thrive.

Their home was close to the wharves where Arthurton worked. Thanks to its harbor on the coast, Colón was a boomtown where only a narrow, fifty-mile-wide patch of swamp, hills, and jungle separated the Caribbean Sea from the waves of the Pacific. This was the crossroads of Central America, gateway to the great new canal, a shortcut to save ships thousands of miles through treacherous seas.

Along Front Street in Colón was a line of three-story wooden buildings that looked like a Wild West stage set of saloons, hotels, and storefronts catering to whites arriving with ready cash—the canal's engineers, contractors, and managers. "From the moment of landing the stranger is beset by a howling crowd of nondescripts who contend with one another for the privilege of fleecing him," author Logan Marshall wrote in 1913.[5] Horse-drawn carts and carriages hurried by under searing sun or torrential rains and headed to the wharves nearby. Along the tracks on the opposite side of the street were the trains that whisked supplies and laborers to the canal's work camps. Colón was a rugged town of bars, whorehouses, and gambling dens. Men who dug channels or lugged crates of dynamite all week, many of them Black laborers from West Indies islands like Jamaica, flocked to these dives on pay day. Arthurton was not one of them. Like his Jamaican-born father, he supervised workers on the wharves.

Miriam Clark's parents, the Hansons, had quarreled and separated in Kingston, Jamaica. Her strict, churchgoing mother had left a philandering husband behind to start a new life with her three daughters as a baker in Colón. Miriam, the oldest, was only six years old then. By her early teens, her mother warned her, "Don't dance and let a man touch you."[6] But Miriam met often on the beach with her beau, Arthurton. Soon she was married and diapering little Kenneth. Rewarding the toddler with bread and jam, she taught him his numbers and the alphabet. He sat with her in a horse-drawn carriage one day, crying out the numbers of houses they passed. As the neighbors stared, his mother beamed with pride. At three, he went to an Anglican nursery school where the morning's lessons were in English and the afternoon's in Spanish. Soon, he could read and recite from memory, and he greeted the audience at a school pageant:

"Kind friends and dear parents, we welcome you here to our dear school."[7]

But at home, his family life was crumbling. Kenneth's strong-willed mother complained that Arthurton was imperious and had a yen for other women. Like her own mother before her, Miriam dreamed of building a new life abroad without her spouse. But first she asked Arthurton to move with her to America, arguing that Kenneth and his new baby sister, Beulah, were stuck in the class of their birth in Panama. Arthurton shot back that the Black man had no chance in the United States.

So they separated, and in May 1918, Miriam clambered into a horse-drawn carriage with her baby girl and left Kenneth at age three with strong, big-boned Grandma Bea Hanson. He looked up sadly at Mama in the carriage with little Beulah in her arms. Promising to send for him, his mother said goodbye. Kenneth sobbed, and as her carriage rattled down the street toward the harbor, he went into the house and wept.

Two years later, on August 4, 1920, he and his beloved Grandma Bea stepped off the SS *Siboney* at Ellis Island in New York Harbor and walked into the Great Hall. They stood in line with others eager to set foot in America. Clerks, doctors, and immigration officers checked their paperwork as the two inched through the building amid the bustle and babble of languages. Seeing little Kenneth's sad eyes, reddish hair, and elfin ears, a white man in uniform smiled and gave the boy a friendly pat. "What a fine young man," he said.[8] Examining his papers and finding them in order, Inspector Leger admitted Kenneth and his grandmother to the United States.

YOUNG KENNETH

Arriving that day on 141st Street in Harlem, Kenneth and Grandma Bea found the tenement where his mother had a narrow railroad flat with five open rooms, front to back. Kenneth hugged Mama and saw that Beulah was a toddler now. Grandma Bea would cook and care for them all while Miriam worked as a seamstress in the garment district.

Kenneth found Harlem exciting. There were canyons of brick buildings with people on the stoops out front and kids playing in the streets. "We did a lot of stickball and a lot of roller skating," John Moseley, a 141st Street neighbor, recalled.[9] The kids dodged horse-drawn wagons and pushcarts, and the mischievous stole fruit from Italian grocers. There were children of all races and classes, but most were Irish. Others were Black with parents fleeing segregation, lynching, and share-cropping in the South. A great migration was funneling the Black masses into Northern cities, and some, like the Clarks, had come by boat from the Caribbean. "Some of them looked like whites, some of them looked like Blacks, some of them looked like Indians," Moseley recalled.[10]

Parades were big in Harlem, and one day, Kenneth saw a Black man in a uniform and plumed hat marching with his followers on Seventh Avenue. It was orator Marcus Garvey, promoter of Black pride and enterprise, who founded Black businesses that Kenneth's mother invested in. Garvey also promoted the manufacture of Black dolls: "Mothers! Give your children dolls that look like them to play with and cuddle."[11] Kenneth's mother made sure that his sister had a Black doll.

Miriam Clark enrolled her son in the first grade at Public School 5 on 140th Street, minutes from home. Most pupils were white, though a few were Black. All the teachers were white, but one day, Kenneth heard about a new Black teacher in school. The boy asked for a bathroom pass, scurried down the hall, and peered through a classroom window at a tall brown-skinned man in a suit coat and tie, Mr. Hubert Delaney, who was doing his practice teaching. Kenneth was thrilled the day his own teacher was out and Mr. Delaney substituted. But Kenneth was not thrilled the day his mother spotted bloodstains on his shirt and learned that his tormentor was a white teacher. Furious, his mother took the stained shirt to school. "Don't ever let this happen again," Miriam told the culprit.[12] "I come here like a lady now; don't let me come like a nigger next time."

Miriam was a stickler for rules: Kenneth's playmates had to meet her, and she had to know where he was at all times. On weeknights, he had to show her his homework, and she told him never to use his race as an alibi for low grades or bad behavior. She did not want him to "have race"[13]—turn bitter over minor slights.

Twice a week, she brought him and Beulah to St. Luke's, a Black Episcopal church in Harlem, where she taught Sunday school. Hers was a practical faith: "God has no hands but our hands and no feet but our feet," she said.[14] That is, God's people better roll up their sleeves and help themselves. Hoping that Kenneth might become a priest, she had him train as an altar boy, and to keep him on the right path, she had him take violin lessons. He disliked church and loathed practicing on the violin but had no say in these matters. A cross word could earn him a slap or a belt strapping.

Kenneth managed to skip a grade before moving on to PS 139, a new junior high for boys that was named for Frederick Douglass. Harlem had turned increasingly Black by then, so few of the pupils were white. Kenneth's homework proved harder now, but his mother helped, thanks to the night classes she'd taken at George Washington High in subjects like algebra to earn a diploma. Kenneth watched her study hard for tests, yet his own grades were not stellar, a sore point with his mother. He spent hours reading the books he loved but daydreamed in his classes. Some of his PS 139 teachers were Black, including Mr. Dixon, who taught speech and music and liked one of Kenneth's speeches so much he suggested that he enter the Bond Bread essay contest. Kenneth beamed at a school assembly when he collected the Bond gold medal.

With the Harlem Renaissance in full flower, Kenneth's teachers praised Black writers who lived or worked nearby, including Jessie Fauset, James Weldon Johnson, and Jamaican Claude McKay. Their writing reflected the Black experience—from the streets and speakeasies to the salon and university. As editor Alain Locke put it, "The pulse of the Negro world has begun to beat in Harlem."[15]

Short, skinny, and no pugilist, Kenneth found a safe harbor from bullies in the public library on 135th Street. One day at age twelve, he left the children's section and nervously climbed the stairs to the quiet third floor where he saw a Black man in glasses with his hair parted down the center. Instead of ordering the boy downstairs, the man put his arm on Kenneth's shoulder and introduced him to works that featured people of color: a portrait of tragedian Ira Aldridge, for example, and books about ancient Africa. Renowned bibliophile Arthur Schomburg soon had Kenneth poring over books about Black troops in the Civil War and Haitian rebel Toussaint Louverture. As Kenneth matured, Schomburg tutored him in the printing process: in the typefaces and the kinds and qualities of paper.

When junior high was drawing to a close, Kenneth was summoned to the guidance office, where his counselor opened a folder and asked why he'd applied for an academic high school. "I don't think you should," she said, recommending a vocational school to learn a trade[16]—advice white counselors often gave to Black students. Kenneth didn't object, but his mother did and brought him to the office the next day. When the counselor argued that Kenneth's grades were weak and trade school was the right choice, his mother stood up, her eyes glaring and voice rising. "You can send your son to vocational school if you want to. He is going to George Washington High School." She stormed out with Kenneth and sat for days on a hallway bench to meet the principal, who finally came out and told her that Kenneth could not handle rigorous courses like Latin. "He can manage it," Miriam said. "I want Latin."

In September, Kenneth took a bus to George Washington High in Washington Heights, a neoclassical schoolhouse with huge concrete columns and a cupola. He was intimidated by the school, where all the teachers and most students were white. He seldom spoke in class but studied hard enough to earn passing grades. The dances and proms seemed for white kids only, so he met with Black friends and classmates in Harlem for fun.

Church and neighborhood were the center of his life. He served Mass with his buddy Dean Dixon, a Black violinist who'd become an acclaimed international conductor. The two boys practiced, performed at recitals, went to concerts, and attended church socials together. Kenneth met his first girlfriend at St. Luke's: Audrey McNeil, the sister of his pal Jim. Kenneth lacked broad shoulders, but he was all boy. He played handball, joined a club called the Ashantis, and sneaked onto rooftops to leap from roof to roof. One day, a playmate failed to clear the gap and plunged several stories to the courtyard below. Kenneth stopped, looked down at the body, and kept right on leaping.

In his first year at Washington High, the stock market collapsed. "People were sleeping in subways and on newspapers in office doors, because they had no homes," Langston Hughes wrote, "and in every block a beggar appeared."[17] Beverly Smith of the *Herald Tribune* wrote of Harlem, "The fact is that this community of 220,000 Negroes is the poorest, the unhealthiest, the unhappiest and the most crowded single large section of New York City."[18] Kenneth's mother scrimped or did without whenever her work hours were cut. Taller and thinner in his teens, Kenneth took odd jobs for cash: sweeping up and shining shoes at a barber shop, pouring medicine into bottles and running deliveries for a drugstore. One day, he asked his mother about the Depression and her plans for him in college. "Kenneth, this won't bother us a bit," she said.[19] "We're poor now and we'll continue to be poor." One summer, he had a crush on a Howard University medical student who taught him in a city art class. She said that Howard's president and faculty were Black and she loved it there. So Kenneth told his mother that he wanted to go too and become a doctor. She bought him a big trunk and began filling it with new clothes.

Only a so-so student at Washington High, Kenneth counted English and history as his favorite subjects, but in his senior year, he took a shine to economics. His teacher, Mr. Gottesman, became his idol. Amid the Depression, Gottesman was skeptical of the "natural" laws of economics—laws shaped by the elite for their own benefit. Kenneth spoke often in class and burned to win the economics prize at graduation.

He'd faced the occasional racial slight from whites in school, and to deal with them, he put on a smile and withdrew into a bubble of "protective insensitivity," as he later put it.[20] If others looked down on him because of his race, that was their problem, not his. But in the spring of 1931, his protective bubble burst. Classmates had predicted that he'd win the economics prize at graduation, but in the end, it went to a white youth—all because of his race, Kenneth believed. He loathed Gottesman after that, and losing the award put him in a funk for the summer. He was fed up with high school, serving Mass for priests, and practicing the violin for his mother.

Shortly before departing for college, a burglar broke into Kenneth's home and stole all the new clothes in his trunk. Fearing the worst, he asked if he was still going to Howard. "Yes, you're going," his mother said and replaced most of the items at once.[21]

Soon Kenneth was packing his bags and heading for the bus station, his days as the childhood darling of his mother and Grandma Bea behind him. At seventeen, he'd be free in Washington, DC: no violin lessons to take, no priests to serve.

As his bus left Manhattan and lumbered down the highway toward Washington, Kenneth was bug-eyed, his face glued to the window. At age seventeen, he'd never been south of the Mason-Dixon line, and he was thrilled by his first glimpses of Philadelphia and Baltimore at bus stops. Arriving in Washington, he looked for a restroom and was shocked to find one marked "Colored." He was in Dixie now.

Grabbing his luggage, Kenneth headed for the home of a dentist who boarded medical students from Howard. Kenneth moved into a room there, and he found the university nearby on a hilltop behind gates of wrought iron, a campus with neoclassical buildings of brick and concrete columns, including the four-story Main Building overlooking the broad, tree-lined commons. Kenneth was in awe: all this for Black students, some in medicine, law, and dentistry—seventeen hundred in all.

Nearby on Georgia Avenue and U Street were the storefronts of businesses: the University Grill, the Howard Theater, and the Bison Cab Company—the latter a tip of the hat to the school mascot. There were bars and nightclubs, none of them legal, for Prohibition was the law of the land. Tidy brick row houses lined the narrow, hilly side streets where students, professors, and others lived. But much of Black Washington was steeped in Depression-era misery, with the homeless wandering the streets and barefoot kids playing in alleys that festered with trash and human waste.

Kenneth had landed on the one campus in America dedicated to an assault on segregation. Founded in 1867 by white Congregational Church leaders, Howard University opened with a radical mission: to educate people of all races, including women, to study law, medicine, teaching, and the ministry. The new school would bear the name of General Otis Howard, the white Civil War hero from Maine who headed the Freedmen's Bureau to aid former slaves. But contrary to the founders' plan, once segregation gripped the nation, the school named for Howard admitted only Blacks.

In the 1920s, Mordecai Johnson became Howard's first full-time Black president. He slashed support for varsity football, raised faculty pay, and wangled an annual appropriation from Congress that sparked a building boom and drew the cream of the nation's Black academic elite, scholars such as attorney Charles Hamilton Houston, who would lead a legal assault on segregated schooling; Charles Drew, a pioneer in blood banking; and Ralph Bunche, Kenneth's political mentor, who one day would win the Nobel Peace Prize. Under Johnson, Howard practically functioned as an integrationist think tank.

Kenneth blossomed and soon joined the staff of the *Hilltop*, the school newspaper. Never one to grub for grades, he studied just enough to keep pace. He liked his courses and professors, but chemistry, crucial to his premed major, bored him. He preferred English with Miss Coleman, who had high standards and abhorred his rambling sentences. To halt the sprawl, she scolded, "Put a period there, Mr. Clark."[22]

Howard's well-heeled students were often snooty and dressed to the nines, the men in suits and ties and the ladies in fur coats. "We use artificial proms, fabulous displays of wardrobes and cars and frigid stares to our less fortunate classmates as outward expressions of our sophistication," one student wrote in the *Hilltop*.[23] Kenneth was among those who had to pinch pennies. "Those were tight times," recalled Leroy Weekes, then a student leader.[24] "Most of us were there on a very short margin."

Kenneth discussed sex with the medical students who boarded with him. Snickering at his virginal musings, they recruited a female friend to tutor him in the arts of love. "They made fun of me" afterward, Kenneth recalled, "and rightly so."[25]

He was also initiated into the Southern way of life. As Professor Bunche once put it, "Living in the nation's capital is like serving out a sentence."[26] Weeks before Christmas, Kenneth and a fellow student found night jobs sorting mail at the central post office near the Capitol. Taking a meal break their first night, they crossed the street to a café for hamburgers. Few seats were left, so Kenneth snatched one and sat down, but his friend hesitated. A tall white counterman screamed, "Get up, get up!"[27] They could buy food, he yelled, but take it outdoors. Why? Kenneth demanded, and the counterman shouted, "Get out of here—we don't serve niggers in here!"[28] Kenneth unleashed a stream of profanity, and his friend pressed him to leave, but Kenneth kept cursing as white customers stared. Slamming the door behind him, Kenneth glared at the Capitol's lighted white dome etched against the dark sky, and he cursed again.

Kenneth proved an average premed student that first term,

eking out a C in chemistry. But after a fun-filled second term in Kappa Alpha Psi fraternity, he drew a D in chemistry and an F in freshman lectures. To stoke interest in his studies, his fellow boarders showed him around their medical school one night, but the dissected cadavers he saw dampened his enthusiasm for becoming a doctor. In his sophomore year, he was far more interested in activities like the *Bison* yearbook, the *Stylus* magazine, and serving as publicist for his fraternity and assignment editor for the *Hilltop*. He churned out news stories and a column titled "Big Shots in Miniature," with brief and breezy profiles of campus leaders like Rietta May Hines, a campus feminist: "A gift of Providence—yes, she is from Providence. Rhode Island."[29]

Trying to cover a meeting of the student council one day, Kenneth was turned away for violating its ban on reporters. Outraged, he skewered the leadership for "laboring under the delusion that the Student Council is a secret organization."[30] His sunshine crusade in the *Hilltop* helped him win the editor in chief's job in a campus-wide election. Nearly breathless, he wrote his mother: "I am just coming from elections and am I happy & excited. Still a baby you know but I have responsibility now. I wonder what it's going to feel like. Your loving son, Kenneth."[31]

He had an epiphany one day in a psychology class taught by short, barrel-chested Dr. Francis Sumner, renowned today as the father of Black psychology and the nation's first Black PhD in the field, but at Howard back then, he was notorious for dull lectures that acted like a narcotic on students. So Kenneth was daydreaming during the lecture this day and peering out the classroom window at two birds about to mate. Once they flew off, he tuned in to Sumner's lecture, which finally struck a chord, though Kenneth could not recall why. He later said that he kept listening to Sumner for the rest of his life, but the change wasn't all that sudden. Kenneth had yet to switch his major or boost his grade above a C. Gradually, however, he became Sumner's protégé, even adopting his cigarette habit and growing a mustache.

Kenneth also grew as a social critic and activist under Howard's radical integrationist scholars such as political scientist Bunche and economist Abram Harris. Kenneth raised mugs of beer in their homes and attended conferences and other meetings with them. Men of Marxist leanings, they discussed the great issues of the day: war, poverty, and segregation. It made sense for a budding journalist or political activist to spend his time this way, but not for a struggling premed major like Kenneth.

As the *Hilltop* editor in chief, Kenneth wrote columns that were the bane of Howard administrators. He attacked their cuts to journalism courses and skewered Dean Kelly Miller for an essay calling on Blacks to shun communists. Kenneth likened Miller to one of "our old school Negro leaders."[32] Whenever President Johnson objected to his editorials, Kenneth listened politely but wrote what he pleased. Soon, the administration sliced the *Hilltop*'s budget by nearly half. Kenneth objected that other campus groups had gotten increases in tight times, but his crusade for the independence of the student press came to naught. A purist, he resigned in protest, and the *Hilltop* closed shop.

This was a salutary outcome for Kenneth, who needed time to

find his true calling and focus on his studies. He changed his major to psychology, though he still fantasized about medical school and training in psychiatry. Obsessed with psychology now, he haunted Sumner's office, and his mentor protested, "There must be room for breathing, and you can't have a friend who suffocates you."[33] Even so, Sumner plied him with articles to read and ideas to consider, and before long, Kenneth was tutoring novice psychology students.

But segregation, not his major, was on his mind on St. Patrick's Day in 1934. A waiter in the Capitol had raised a ruckus by turning away a Black customer in the House of Representatives restaurant. Soon, integrated groups of diners were testing the color line at the restaurant, among them Professor Bunche, who was light skinned and got served, and Howard historian Charles Wesley, who was turned away.

After a "For Members Only" sign went up at the restaurant, Kenneth arrived with about thirty Howard students in a House corridor.[34] Capitol police blocked their way, and a student retorted, "We are citizens and we can go wherever we want in the Capitol of the United States."[35] Shoving one of them, the restaurant manager jeered, "You are the damned n—who was down here yesterday."[36] The police ejected Kenneth and his comrades from the Capitol, but they regrouped to face the officers again. This time, the cops arrested one student, and Kenneth's group followed him to the First Precinct station. All, including Kenneth, were arrested on the station's sidewalk and told to remove their ties to be booked. But a sympathetic police captain emerged from his office to halt the charade. "Take their names off the books!" he ordered. "Let them go!"[37]

Still, Kenneth and his friends awoke the next morning in very hot water. The *New York Times* had put their protest on the front page: "Negro Students Rush Congress Restaurant in Vain Effort to Test Rule Barring Race."[38] U.S. Senator Thomas Blanton of Texas demanded that Howard expel the radicals or lose federal aid. "Unless we can weed Communism out of that institution," Blanton warned, "we ought to close it up and not give it further sanction and support by this government."[39]

Kenneth and his group faced the wrath of President Johnson, a faculty disciplinary committee, and the prospect of expulsion. But Bunche and two other professors broke ranks and backed the students. With his ear pressed to the conference room door, Kenneth heard Bunche tell the committee, "We ought to be giving these young men medals." Kenneth and the others were free to go.[40]

Along with dodging expulsion that spring, Kenneth had gained two good jobs on campus: as psychology department assistant and director of freshman orientation. At home in Harlem that summer, he drafted a letter welcoming new freshmen as their orientation director: He typed out, "MY DEAR FELLOW STUDENT."[41] And so began his first letter to find its way to Arkansas and into the mailbox of sixteen-year-old Mamie Phipps, who would sail the same progressive, intellectual currents that Kenneth navigated at Howard.

Two years later in the fall of 1936, having won Mamie's heart, Kenneth found that he liked teaching so much it seemed wrong to accept a Howard paycheck. The challenge of gaining students' attention and answering their questions excited him. Dr. Sumner served as his pedagogical model: dry, formal, yet kind and with a command of his subject. Kenneth addressed each student with a courtesy title: Miss, Mister, or Missus. Butterflies roiled his stomach before every lecture, and to Dr. Sumner, Kenneth seemed terribly stressed—not uncommon for a new instructor.

As a college junior, Mamie still lived in a dormitory and worked in the psychology department. She was active in Alpha Kappa Alpha sorority, was elected again to the student council, and elected as scribe, or editor, of the *Stylus* literary magazine. The latter role suited Mamie, a capable administrator with a gift for narrative writing.

As a college lecturer, Kenneth finally put his frat house days behind him to live with a classmate in a row house near Meridian Hill Park. He and Mamie picnicked in the park on hot dogs, Coke, and ice cream. They studied together at the Library of Congress, and Kenneth steered their dates off campus to avoid accusations of a faculty-student romance. The couple met in the homes of married friends such as sociologist Hylan Lewis and his wife, Leighla. One afternoon, Hylan and Kenneth were chatting in Hylan's office and watching Mamie outdoors as she walked by their window. Enraptured by the vision, Kenneth sang her praises. "Marry the girl," Hylan advised him. "Marry the girl."[42]

Despite Kenneth's best efforts to separate romance from his teaching, Mamie upset him by signing up for one of his courses. She sat in the front row where the sight of her practically unraveled Kenneth. Though she seldom spoke in class, she often snapped back with a terse answer to one of his questions, and it sounded to him like heckling. To avoid accusations of favoritism, he'd warned her that she'd never get an A, but Mamie aced nearly every course she took, and his class would be no exception.

As scribe of the *Stylus*, she charted an ambitious new course for the magazine and organized a violin recital for one of its events. Terrified of public speaking, she tapped her uncle Alfred Smith as the master of ceremonies. Kenneth helped her by promoting the magazine, and the *Hilltop* agreed to dedicate one of its editions to the *Stylus* and include new pieces by the magazine's staff. Kenneth contributed "Lament in Ebony," a tongue-in-cheek blues lyric probably inspired by his spats with Mamie:

> *Ma' gal's done lef' me*
> *An' she ain' gwine see me no mo'*
> *Ma' gal's done lef' me*
> *'Cause she sez I'se too dam po'*
> *To give her the things she crave.*
>
> *Lawd!! What' ya' gwine do wit a*
> *gal like dat.*[43]

Mamie contributed "Shortest Short Story," a witty prose poem on the plight of a servant:

> *Alma washing dishes in the kitchen of a*
> *well-to-do white family was down in Texas—*
> *perspiration running down her fat shiny face.*

Thinking about that man Sam, her husband,
probably smoking his pipe in the battered
chair on the battered front porch of their
equally battered residence...
Alma drying her hands on the dirty
apron to answer the telephone ringing in
the hall.
"Alma!"
"Yeah, Sam—you know better'n to call
up heah when you know I'se washin' dishes!"
"Well! You can drop eva' dam one o' dem
dishes an' come on home! We've struck oil!"
Alma streaking down the road to home
thinking about the maid she would get to
wash the new dishes she would buy tomorrow.[44]

In the spring of 1937, Kenneth proposed that they get engaged by the fall, but rumors of a secret marriage flew all the way to Arkansas and angered her parents, who wanted to see her diploma before any talk of wedding bells. Fearing their wrath, Mamie suggested a later engagement. Kenneth, however, dreaded leaving her unattached at Howard while beginning his doctoral studies at Columbia. He wanted a ring on her finger, pronto. Why choose Columbia? First, it was on the cusp of Harlem, where he could live at home, but more important, it was not all that far from Mamie in Washington, about two hundred miles. Because of his race, Columbia had denied Kenneth a scholarship and accepted him only on a conditional basis.

Drawing on savings from his Howard salary, he'd have to pay his own tuition.

Kenneth was scheduled to teach summer school at Howard, and in a vain attempt to be near him, Mamie sought her parents' permission to work a summer job on campus. They said no, and Katie Phipps traveled to Washington in June to bring her daughter home to Arkansas. But first, she brought Mamie to visit Miriam Clark in Harlem to assess the state of their children's romance. The two mothers agreed that the young couple were naive and not ready to wed.

Over the summer, Kenneth wrote Mamie's father to express his honorable intentions. "My dear Dr. Phipps," he began.[45] "I don't believe that it is necessary for me to try to convince you that Mamie and I are not married." Kenneth said that would be foolish. "Marriage at this time of our lives, I believe, would be very much at variance with common sense."

After a month's reflection, Dr. Phipps dictated a response to his secretary: "Our object with regard to Mamie is to have her complete her education and to be equipped to earn her own living if that should ever become necessary."[46] After her graduation, "we would then be in a position to examine in a liberal spirit any decision that she might make and give such advice as we would consider to be in her best interest." Dr. Phipps said Kenneth sounded like "a very level-headed young man" and Mrs. Phipps "was favorably impressed with your family connections in New York."

At home with Kenneth later that summer, his mother warned that if he hoped to marry Mamie, the wedding had to be in Hot

Springs. That sounded expensive to Kenneth, who'd set aside $180, a great sum, for an engagement ring. Thoughts of a ring thrilled Mamie in Hot Springs, for it would symbolize two things, she wrote Kenneth. "First, it means anticipation of marriage," including sex.[47] "Secondly it means for me that I promise to give myself to a man for life—I promise to give to that man all that I have to give all of the time—to give the most to him in order that he will be happy."

THREE

THE SECRET WEDDING

Them's the only two people I can say found love. The
rest of us play at it. That's 'cause love cost. Love got
a price to it. Everybody don't want to pay. They put
it on credit. Time it come due they got it on credit
somewhere else.

—AUGUST WILSON, *TWO TRAINS RUNNING*[1]

A t home in Harlem for the fall term of 1937, Kenneth piled his papers
and books from Howard in a corner of his bedroom, the same
room where Mamie had slept when she and her mother visited in June.
Kenneth's mother gaped at the pile and joked that Mamie should return
and haul all this junk away. A semblance of order began to emerge as
Kenneth moved an old bookcase and desk into his room, and his sister,
Beulah, helped arrange his things. He could be moody, and he worried
that he'd drive her and his mother crazy by living at home again.

To check out the Columbia campus before his fall classes, Kenneth visited the psychology department one day, and it gave him the jitters. Could he make it in the white world of the Ivy League? Could he pass September's qualifying exams for his PhD program and find time to give Mamie her engagement ring?

When she finally arrived in Washington, he raced down to Howard and slipped the ring onto her finger. A look of joy crossed her face as they sat on a park bench admiring the diamond's luster. Kenneth hurried with Mamie to Union Station the next day to return home and face his qualifying exams. Peering through the window of his idling train, he watched her walk away, then turn for a glimpse of him. Usually his spirits hit bottom when they parted, but not this time. He was engaged to be married at last, and as the train surged forward, he headed home to Harlem a happier man.

Kenneth was off to a good start at Columbia that fall, and it should have put a spring in his step. He'd done well in his exams, he spent hours in the psychology department's reading room each day, and his classes fascinated him. But when he was missing Mamie, it brought on the blues, and he'd fantasize about chucking it all to find a job and get married. Kenneth could be a Gloomy Gus. Although Columbia was on the cusp of Harlem, to Kenneth, it was another planet. The neoclassical buildings were grander than Howard's, the professors published their own textbooks, and he felt like an alien among the psychology students walking about in white lab coats. He saw just three Black people on campus in two weeks.

Still, Kenneth was in the right place at the right time to study social psychology, a field that matched his interests: social activism and human behavior. For more than a century, most writers who expounded on race were white supremacists, including Europeans who justified their colonial empires and Americans who supported slavery or segregation. German philosopher Georg Hegel was typical, writing in 1807, "The negro is an example of animal man in all his savagery and lawlessness."[2] In a similar vein in 1925, a report from the U.S. Army War College argued that Blacks were unfit for combat: "It is generally recognized that the pure blood American negro is inferior to our white population in mental capacity."[3]

Early in the last century, even PhDs clung to the notion that criminality and stupidity were racial traits. Using brass instruments, they measured heads in a vain attempt to categorize racial differences and prove the inferiority of minorities. Intelligence tests were all the rage, and white psychologists gave them to Black, Mexican, and Indigenous pupils from weak schools and compared the scores with those of white pupils at superior schools. Using such scores in 1916, Virginia educator George Oscar Ferguson argued, "And in view of all the evidence it does not seem possible to raise the scholastic attainment of the negro to an equality with that of the white."[4]

Humbug, proclaimed Columbia anthropologist Franz Boas: "All our best psychologists recognize clearly that there is no proof that the intelligence tests give an actual insight into the biologically determined function of the mind."[5] Boas had done research on Indigenous peoples in their habitat. Holding that race shaped neither intelligence nor personality, he produced a new generation of social scientists, including Margaret Mead, Ruth Benedict, and Otto Klineberg, who undermined the quackery behind white supremacy. Instead of blaming the poor for the social ills of the Depression, social psychologists probed for the root causes of inequality and formed the Society for the Psychological Study of Social Issues. Among the leaders were Klineberg and Gardner Murphy of Columbia, who would play key roles in the lives of Kenneth and Mamie.

Lonesome but with her new ring to comfort her, Mamie was a Howard senior about to turn twenty in October 1937. Professors and friends kept asking her about Kenneth, and it pained her. So she steeped herself in work as never before, taking six courses, four in psychology, and waiting tables for extra cash. She also worked as a psychology department assistant and counselor to freshmen. Mamie rejoined the *Hilltop* and *Stylus* staffs while staying active in her sorority. Pushing herself way too hard, Mamie was anxious and often ill that semester and sought relief in the bottle of Four Roses she hid in her closet. Fortunately, Harold, her brother, had enrolled in Howard's dental program, and they went to cafés and movies together. One day, she watched him peel the skin off a cadaver in a laboratory. "I stayed quite a while, as it fascinated me," she wrote Kenneth.[6] Harold never studied as hard as Mamie, and he often borrowed cash from her and spent it on drinks. His carefree ways worried his parents, and his mother wrote Mamie to make sure that he studied: "Kinder keep up with him if you can."[7]

Mamie finally notified her parents that she was engaged, and they responded with silence. To console her, Kenneth's mother wrote Mamie that her ring was lovely and "none too good for you."[8]

Miriam Clark also wrote to Katie Phipps to reassure her that all was well with the engagement. Katie responded coolly, "Hope that they know what they're doing."[9] Acting as Dr. Phipps's emissary, Mamie's Uncle Alfred stopped by her dormitory one night and urged her to see other men. "So that leaves us together—'to make good'—'to do or die,'" Kenneth said of the visit, and Mamie agreed.[10] The Phippses had tied their daughter even more tightly into his arms.

Though short of funds, Kenneth showed up at Mamie's dormitory with a present just before her twentieth birthday. They visited their favorite hangout, Gerry's, and held each other for hours that weekend without a word and began calling each other husband and wife. Once back in Harlem, Kenneth wrote, "Gee, Mamie, darling, if people could only see us—the way we evolved—if they could only understand the nature of our relationship the way we understand it."[11]

Mamie's spirits lifted when her father, apparently resigned to her engagement, broke his silence with a birthday telegram for her: "I wish for you good health much success and happiness."[12] The good health was not to be. She landed in the infirmary, exhausted from overwork. "As I told you on the phone, I was just run down to the point of not having the energy to even move," she wrote Kenneth.[13] "It was very much like a miniature breakdown (I think.)"

Kenneth too was struggling, but his studies under Dr. Sumner at Howard, along with intense, focused reading, were paying off at Columbia. Kenneth's favorite new professor was Dr. Klineberg, who taught a course on problems in racial psychology and approved Kenneth's term-paper topic, the Negro inferiority complex. But the inspiration for it had come from Dr. Sumner, who introduced Kenneth to the work of Alfred Adler, a Viennese psychologist whose theories about race would shape the careers of Kenneth and Mamie.

The great Sigmund Freud had chosen Adler to edit the *Psycho-Analytical Journal* before they became bitter rivals. Adler, who once joked that "I am the legitimate father of the inferiority complex," hypothesized that all of us harbor a feeling of inferiority in childhood.[14] Parents and older siblings, because of their greater size and power, give us this sense of inadequacy, the spark that motivates us to achieve in life, for good or ill. Some children aim to excel, but others compensate for their insecurity by bullying the weak and becoming delinquents. "Every neurosis can be understood as an attempt to free oneself from a feeling of inferiority in order to gain a feeling of superiority," Adler wrote.[15] Cruelty and authoritarianism can spring from this impulse. "Those who have traveled have found that people everywhere are approximately the same in that they are always inclined to find something by which to degrade others," Adler wrote.[16] "The Frenchman considers the German inferior, whereas the German, in turn, considers himself as belonging to a chosen nation." The persecution of Jewish persons and Blacks springs from their tormentors' deep sense of inferiority, Adler argued.

Intrigued by his theory, Kenneth reflected on how white America, the wretched refuse of Europe's teeming shores, had persecuted Blacks and other minorities throughout its history. Blond, blue-eyed Klineberg encouraged Kenneth to explore this line of thinking. Klineberg had explored the abuse of IQ testing with Indigenous and Mexican American test subjects. He'd also published *Race*

Differences, a classic text that pounced on pseudoscientific claims about minorities and argued that "there is nothing in the brain or blood of other races which justifies our ill-treatment of them."[17]

It's not surprising that Kenneth, the product of many good white teachers in Harlem schools, got along so well with Klineberg. But his white classmates at Columbia were another matter. Sensing they viewed him as inferior, Kenneth built a social wall between them and himself. He was pleasant enough with a lab partner but sidestepped every overture to fraternize. When white radicals pressed him to join the Psychologists League, Kenneth said no. They seemed too fawning in their attempts to recruit him.

In her last year as a Howard undergrad, Mamie was older, feistier, and fed up with curfews and the way professors treated female students. After her engagement, faculty men seemed too interested in her love life. Dr. Max Meenes, a short, balding white man, often asked about her weekends with Kenneth and suggested she was slacking off in his animal psychology course. Mamie had similar problems with renowned sociologist E. Franklin Frazier, who warned that she courted failure in social psychology. Frazier made crude comments in class and gave questionable assignments like this: "One page says, 'have you had experiences deeper than friendship with the opposite sex? If so describe in detail,'" Mamie wrote Kenneth.[18] She confronted both Meenes and Frazier—in Meenes's case, for two hours in a conference with Dr. Sumner present. She vowed to earn As in both men's courses, and granting her the A she finally earned,

Frazier joked that she was a tough customer and her A not high enough, given her "general hipness."[19]

Mamie also clashed with Alida Banks, the acting dean of women, whose iron rule in the women's dorms was notorious. Resenting Banks for vetoing her every request to visit the Clarks in Harlem, Mamie helped organize a group to document their grievances about Banks and meet with President Johnson. Mamie accused Banks of causing an exodus of staff and students from the women's dormitories—thirty-nine from her own building alone. Ultimately, Banks was rejected as Howard's next full-time dean of women. Mamie might have looked soft, sweet, and malleable, but underneath was a will of steel.

With the campus closed for the holidays, Mamie finally got to stay with Kenneth's family in Harlem, but her spirits slumped upon returning to Washington to face her first-term final exams. She was lonely and missed her serious talks with Kenneth. "Sometimes I wonder whether love isn't squeezing every vestige of knowledge, companionship and comfort out of a person who is perhaps doing the same thing to you," she wrote him.[20] She likened their relationship to a couple feasting on each other's brains. Sexually active now, Mamie had nightmares of pregnancy. In one dream, she gave birth to a sickly red-haired baby that she wrapped in a towel and checked continually to see if it was still alive. "Daddy was there," she wrote Kenneth, "and I remember having a real guilty feeling because of the baby being illegitimate."[21]

Mamie was torn. If she abstained from sex, her fears of pregnancy would vanish, but Kenneth might as well. And who was Mamie Phipps, she asked. She'd become a different person with Kenneth: smoking, rejecting religion, and quarreling with her parents. "My philosophy of life is rather in a sad state," she wrote Kenneth.[22] "It's been changed and rechanged so many times until I wonder whether there is anything left of it at all." She also worried about graduate school and her career. Did she want a PhD in psychology or a master's degree in social work to help juvenile delinquents?

After taking his exams, Kenneth got a letter from his father in Panama, who praised his son's academic success and advised him not to marry Mamie: "You will excuse me but, I am thinking that you should go on with your studies, and don't think of marriage just now."[23] Arthurton Clark advised Kenneth to think first about his mother. This, coming from a man who had failed to support his wife and children, seemed mighty rich to Kenneth. He vowed never to write or see his father again.

When his first-term grades arrived, Kenneth was pleased to learn he'd earned As in two of his five courses. Convinced he could handle anything that Columbia threw at him, he cut back to four courses for the spring term and sought a job to support Mamie in marriage. While visiting her one weekend at Howard, he stopped by Dr. Frazier's office in the sociology department to ask about a job as his interviewer on a research study in New York. Mamie had also pursued an interviewing job with Frazier, so when Kenneth suggested asking him for secretarial work, Mamie, close to graduating, was offended. "Your idea about speaking to Frazier is good," she wrote, bristling.[24] "However he had intimated that he would like to have me interview so I don't know about the possibilities of being a secretary." Atoning for his sexist faux pas, Kenneth wrote, "Please speak to Frazier, Miss Interviewer. And please excuse me for suggesting the secretary position."[25]

Life at Howard was merrier for Mamie in the spring term at Howard. Her best friend from Hot Springs, Adella Gardner, had enrolled, and Harold joined them for nights on the town. On visits every other weekend, Kenneth got to like Adella, who looked a lot like Mamie—to his Howard friends at least. To deflate the rumors that she and Kenneth had married and in particular to baffle Adella, Mamie fibbed that she and Kenneth had secretly married but then denied it. This sowed confusion so well that Mamie used the ruse with other friends to keep them all guessing.

During weekends together in Washington, Kenneth and Mamie visited Howard sociologist Hylan Lewis and his wife, Leighla, young friends with a baby girl. Hylan was Kenneth's pal and Mamie's criminology professor, and Leighla was an old friend of Kenneth's. Like Kenneth, Hylan was a serious scholar and lively conversationalist, and the two chattered endlessly about race, politics, and teaching. Hylan regarded Mamie as his best student ever and offered to help her find a research job. On warm spring weekends, the Lewises squeezed Kenneth and Mamie into the rumble seat in back of their 1935 Plymouth and headed off together for the beaches of Maryland. Tallying her son's many weekends in Washington, his mother figured his bachelor days were numbered. "Well, are you married yet?" she asked.[26]

Kenneth's visits were a tonic for Mamie. After one tryst in March, she wrote him, "I felt like a contented cow after you left and just walked around in green pastures building castles in the air."[27] With graduation day nearing, Mamie resolved to stay in Washington and work for the summer. Her brother, Harold, had found a summer job on campus, so how could her parents stop her? She also decided to spend another year at Howard for a master's degree in psychology if she could find a job and a fellowship.

Kenneth took his initial steps that spring toward a distinguished career as a public intellectual by speaking in New York at Howard's Charter Day gathering. His was a sensitive topic, "the inferiority complex of Negroes," the topic of his recent term paper.[28] He was afraid it would offend his audience but took the risk anyway. The gist of his speech, though lost in the shuffle of time, survives in his term paper and reveals his Adlerian views on racial politics and identity. Kenneth argued that the white migrants who settled America, despite their humble origins, treated the Indigenous and Black slaves they met in the New World as inferiors. As a result, Blacks developed a deep sense of inferiority. Kenneth held that in modern times, these problems were as much psychological as political or economic. He pointed out, for example, that half the advertisements in the African American press were for skin bleaches and hair products that aimed to make Blacks look more like whites: "If you want to lighten dark ugly skin fast, just try Fan Tan Bleach Cream."[29]

Kenneth wrote that poor Blacks often carried razors to assert their manhood and that dandies in green suits or other outlandish attire were salving damaged egos. He wrote that sex with whites enhanced the Black self-image, and many Harlem prostitutes catered solely to whites. Affluent Blacks, on the other hand, inflated their self-regard by stressing their white or Indigenous ancestry instead of African roots. Others made a show of white friends or kowtowed to white strangers. "What is perhaps the most insidious factor as a cause of this inferiority feeling of Negroes," Kenneth argued, "is the condition of segregation."[30] His speech went over well with the alumni, and he was asked to speak again at the City College of New York in March and before another group in April.

He and Mamie talked of eloping at Easter, but playing devil's advocate, Kenneth gave her three reasons not to marry him: he was obsessed with psychology, he lacked a good job, and she had yet to graduate. "I have looked at marriage from all possible angles," she responded.[31] "And I am not afraid to give my future to you—giving you all I have to offer—devoid of all emotions and castles in the air."

So Kenneth asked his friend Hylan Lewis to serve as best man and do the driving on the wedding day. Leighla, his wife, could serve as matron of honor. Suddenly, Mamie got cold feet. "Kenneth—I don't think we should get married Easter," she wrote, having found that newspapers published marriage licenses for every hamlet and hollow in the region.[32] Because of Howard's ban on undergraduate marriage, she could be expelled if news of her wedding got out. Mamie had another fear: neither of them knew much about birth control. She begged him for solutions.

Her letter staggered Kenneth, but he responded that they could venture farther afield to marry and tell the clerk not to publicize their license. Without spelling it out, he promised a quick fix for the birth-control problem: "It is really very simple."[33]

Days later, after walking with her friend Adella, Mamie changed her mind again. "This morning I am firmly convinced that we must get married," she wrote Kenneth.[34] She joked of buying up every newspaper in the region and cutting out their listings for marriage licenses.

On April 5, Mamie wrote that because of the annual May festival at Howard, their love life could face closer scrutiny. "We are voting on the May Queen tonight in the sorority," she wrote, "and I am not going as from all evidences it will be another mess of political antagonisms—and from what I've heard I'm supposed to be nominated and I would rather have no parts of it."[35] When the Alphas ended their meeting, Mamie emerged as the nominee. Later, she'd win the campus-wide election for May Queen, an honor reserved for the most popular, presumably virginal beauty on campus, but an honor that would spawn more gossip about her marital status.

While Kenneth fretted over the cost of wedding bands and a marriage license, Mamie, a stickler for style and etiquette, invested her month's allowance on a bridal trousseau. Every night, she lay worrying for hours about the wedding before finally dozing off. "Will Thursday never come!" she wrote Kenneth.[36] "Days just snail by." They both had colds and trouble sleeping, but the thought of eloping put Kenneth in a jolly mood. Beulah and his mother wondered why. Everything was perfect, he reassured them, just perfect. Hylan had sent him a note in code suggesting that the wedding arrangements were in order: the machinery was oiled and ready to roll.

———————

It was April 14, 1938, three days before Easter, and the cherry trees were abloom in Washington, normally a quiet Southern town of broad avenues and white temples to the gods of government. This was the hottest day of the year so far, in the mid-eighties, and lovers strolled in the parks amid the cherry blossoms. With spring training finished, the Washington Senators battled the Boston Bees at Griffith Stadium, the major league ballpark near Howard. Meanwhile, buses and trains were arriving with tens of thousands of tourists for the Easter weekend. The big news was President Roosevelt's fireside chat that evening. The Depression had deepened, hammering the stock market and erasing four million jobs. More families faced hunger and loss of their homes, but the president would offer hope of better days ahead: "we must sail—sail, not lie at anchor, sail, not drift."[37]

Kenneth and Mamie jumped into the open-air rumble seat in back of Hylan's Plymouth to leave town for their secret wedding in the country. Best man Hylan was at the wheel, and by his side was Leighla, the matron of honor, with baby Carole. The wedding party of five cruised south along the Jefferson Davis Highway, passing through Arlington, Alexandria, and Mount Vernon, dipping beneath train trestles and rising to cross the bridges of the Chesapeake watershed. White-clapboard farmhouses and churches whooshed past as the bride and groom sat in the rumble seat, their clothes flapping in the breeze. Kenneth wore a suit and tie and Mamie a new outfit from her trousseau. She was thin and girlish at age twenty with short curls brushed back. "She was very beautiful and very bright," Hylan recalled decades later.[38]

The newlyweds-to-be had a wicked case of spring fever, with prenuptial jitters to match, as they clung to each other in the rumble seat. They had tried once before to marry but failed. You had to be twenty-one to get a Virginia marriage license, and Mamie, a year shy of that, was turned away. "Don't fear," dapper, worldly Hylan told her.[39] "We can work this out." Before heading for the courthouse in Stafford, Virginia, Hylan coached Mamie to claim she was twenty-one. For the honeymoon, he'd suggested Fredericksburg, a historic river town of Colonial-era homes and Civil War battlefields—picturesque but segregated, of course. So Hylan recommended Brown's Hotel on the outskirts.

Arriving in Stafford, Hylan pulled up at the courthouse with tall, white columns out front, and Kenneth and Mamie hopped from their rumble seat, stepped between the columns, and walked indoors. Asked her age, Mamie said twenty-one, and the clerk signed the license. But where to marry? There was a Black preacher down the road, they learned. They found his farm all right but had to search for the preacher and finally found him in dirt-caked overalls, plowing his potato crop. Just hearing the word *marry* put a grin on Reverend J. M. Porter's face. He scurried indoors, scrubbed up, and put on a coat and tie. All six of them—including the preacher with his book and Leighla with her baby—gathered for a simple service in his rude little farmhouse. It looked like a shack to Mamie, and Leighla searched for tears in the bride's eyes. Fat chance of that. Mamie might have seemed a fragile flower, but underneath was a stem of steel. Finally pronounced man and wife, the newlyweds kissed and headed back to the Lewises' car.

Their next and final stop was Fredericksburg, where Kenneth sought a room at Brown's Hotel. With two dollars and change set aside, he asked to see the room first. So Mr. Brown showed him and Hylan upstairs. A smile creased Kenneth's face as he looked at Hylan and spanked the bridal bed with delight. Downstairs, the groom signed in, and with mission accomplished, the Lewises bid the honeymooners farewell.

Had Mamie's father known that she slept with her groom that night, he would have been apoplectic. Such marriages, Dr. Phipps believed, rarely lasted. But this young couple—without solid jobs or a home of their own—would one day reach heights in our nation that the doctor in Hot Springs could never imagine.

PART TWO
DYNAMIC COLLEAGUES

FOUR

THE SEED OF A LEGEND

Maybe the next generation will be able to take time out to rest, but we have too far to go and too much work to do.

—ATTORNEY CHARLES HOUSTON[1]

I n a white gown with a long, gauzy train, Mrs. Mamie Clark glided down a hillside staircase with a bouquet of flowers as cameras clicked and boys in short pants and men in fedoras gawked at her. She was not heading for a church to have it sanction her union with Kenneth. As May Queen at Howard, she was heading for the maypole on a day of song, frolic, and oration. Mamie looked nervous claiming her crown, and probably some in the crowd wisecracked that she was no virgin queen. Gossips had long blabbed that Mamie was secretly married. Finally, they were right, but her Howard diploma depended upon keeping the secret.

Her secret held as Mamie's parents arrived in Washington for her graduation. Still upset about her engagement, they had a frank talk with her, never suspecting she'd already married. They also talked about her summer job and private room on campus, confirming that Kenneth would stay in Harlem for the summer. Arriving at Howard to see his wife graduate, Kenneth met Mamie's father for the first time, and all agreed to meet again at his mother's home in Harlem—all except Mamie, that is. Feeling guilty about eloping, she claimed to be busy studying for a federal job exam. So the Phippses dined at Miriam Clark's table in Harlem. It must have been an awkward meal, given the Phippses had opposed Mamie's engagement and their hosts knew that she'd eloped. Mamie had asked Kenneth to chat with her parents about his job prospects and get on their good side. Mission accomplished, he later wrote her.

That summer at Howard marked a turning point in Mamie's life. Determined to support herself, she worked in the psychology department, sought other jobs, and bought cheap meals off campus. She was lonely in a dormitory filled with schoolteachers. Harold, her brother studying dentistry, lived nearby but seldom joined her for meals.

To cover her expenses, Mamie took a secretarial job at the Houston and Houston law firm on F Street, where she met the Black legal eagles leading the struggle against segregation and learned of their struggle against segregation. Founded by William Houston, the firm was run by his remarkable son, Charles, who at age forty-three was a tall, handsome man with immaculate suits, precise diction, and a commanding baritone voice. Charles Houston had a Harvard

Law degree and had used it as special counsel to the NAACP and as dean of the Howard Law School. He'd recruited a better faculty, upgraded the law library, and offered the nation's first course in civil rights law. Houston pressed his students to fight segregation in the courts. "He kept hammering at us all those years that, as lawyers, we had to be social engineers or else we were parasites," attorney Oliver Hill recalled.[2] Under Houston, Howard Law became the nation's training ground for civil rights attorneys. His star pupil was a lanky fellow in a rumpled suit who loved to tell off-color jokes: Thurgood Marshall, who was as earthy as Houston was polished. They toured the South together to document the deplorable state of segregated Black schools. "Doghouses," they called them. Houston described the filthy toilets he found at one school: "No pit, no lime; just ashes from the stoves to cover the waste."[3] At another school, there were "no tables, no desks, no stove." Houston aimed to bury dual, racially segregated school systems in the South and border states. "It all started with Charlie," Marshall once said.[4]

Knowing none of this on her first day at work, Mamie complained to Kenneth:

> *In the first place all these lawyers are nuts. In the second place they all use the same secretary. In the third place all of them have interests besides law (to be secretary for). In the fourth place three of them are fresh. In the fifth place I had to work from 8:30 a.m. until 7:30 p.m. with a half hour off for lunch and one of them had the nerve to ask me to come back from 8:30 to 10:30 p.m.!!! So I quit.[5]*

She still had her psychology department job, which included the tuition-free, graduate psychology course she was taking in summer school. When the Houston firm pressed Mamie to return to work, she agreed but only on an as-needed basis. She soon learned that the Houston firm was a hive of civil rights activity. Thurgood Marshall and William Hastie, Howard's new law dean, met there with Houston to upend segregation at all-white universities. Later, they'd focus on Black public schools. Mamie was impressed but irked that some of these same lawyers were more interested in her feminine charms than in her office skills. Kenneth, who'd seen the lawyers at Howard conferences, begged Mamie not to return to the firm to work. Mamie went back anyway. "Please don't be very angry with me for working at Mr. Houston's," she replied.[6] "Just as soon as the 15th [of July] comes I will stop." Kenneth wanted her to "tell those Houston people to go right to hell—by express—and no stops."[7] When Houston offered Mamie a full-time job, she declined, accepting instead a $300 Howard fellowship to earn a master's degree.

Dr. Meenes, who'd approved Mamie's grant, warned her that running off to marry would deprive someone else of financial aid. Marriage, however, would never keep striving, hard-working Mamie from her studies. Already she was conferring with Dr. Sumner about her master's thesis, which was not due for nearly a year.

———————

Kenneth was also balancing two jobs with his studies. Though facing a final set of doctoral exams in weeks, he worked days as a psychologist for the federal Works Progress Administration and some nights as an interviewer for Dr. Frazier's American youth study. A short, wiry sociologist with a triangular mustache, Frazier had offices at Howard and in Harlem, where Kenneth often chatted with him. Frazier was a radical integrationist and firebrand. While teaching at Morehouse College in 1927, he published an essay likening Southern racism to a form of insanity that he called the "Negro-complex."[8] This so enraged white Atlantans that Frazier had to quit his teaching job and flee the city.

Kenneth's job as Frazier's interviewer had its challenges. One night, he went to a rough Harlem hangout to meet a seventeen-year-old pimp. Kenneth waited for hours, but the pimp never showed. Kenneth's day job as a WPA psychologist in Harlem was less frustrating. He spent part of his time testing clients, managing the office, and counseling the unemployed and used the rest of his time arranging conferences and lecturing. The job paid twenty-five dollars a week, and Kenneth liked it, though the office was in turmoil. "The white psychologist who was, and still is, there is unbelievably incompetent," Kenneth wrote Mamie.[9] He ended up replacing the man.

Meanwhile, Mamie worried about the gossip mill at Howard. Fellow students told her they knew she was married, and two of her parents' friends confided to Mamie that a newspaper had listed her marriage license. "It seems that some sort of dragnet is closing in on us," she wrote Kenneth.[10] He encouraged her to ignore the rumors: "Keep cool, calm, and poised. Allow people to say and think whatever they want to."[11]

Although the newlyweds worked four jobs between them, they never had enough cash. With his mother out of work, Kenneth helped pay the bills at home and sent checks to Mamie as well. She was grateful. "I've just built up a determination not to write home for money," she wrote him.[12] One day, she dropped her glasses in the street and broke them. She was so upset she burst into tears. Worried about wasting money on phone calls and train fares to stay in touch, she advised Kenneth to make fewer calls and take more bus trips, which were cheaper. She closely monitored their bills and opened a bank account for their earnings. Kenneth gladly let her take charge. "You're the manager—let's see how you manage," he wrote, sending her thirty dollars to start and pledging to abide by her decisions.[13] Mamie set a goal for their savings: an apartment in Harlem.

Working around the clock, Kenneth had little time to write her, and whenever he did, it was late at night, and the strain showed in his letters. "Both of us seem to be all out of gear," Mamie wrote.[14] Despite the two hundred miles separating them, their marriage was sound. She still shooed away suitors, and he still addressed her as "darling." As a graduate student free to leave her dormitory on weekends, she often shared a bed with him in Harlem. Sometimes he visited her in Washington instead, but they avoided staying with Hylan and Leighla Lewis, who were having marital problems.

Mamie decided that summer to focus on preschool pupils for her master's thesis—a decision that would shape the trajectory of her life and Kenneth's. She hoped to discover when little children became conscious of themselves as individual beings. She discussed this with Kenneth, and he suggested articles she might read. It was still only the summer, a full academic year before her thesis was due, yet Mamie was impatient to get started: "I'm disgusted by the lack of progress being made by me on my thesis."[15]

Once summer school was over, Mamie's mother asked for a list of her expenses for the fall term. Fearing that her mother would learn she was secretly married, Mamie struggled with the right words to tell her and hesitated to respond. Her father, impatient with the delay, wrote to repeat his wife's request, and Mamie answered with a cryptic letter asking for $100 and a living room suite. She referred mysteriously to "the awful truth" and begged her father to "bear with me."[16] Baffled, Dr. Phipps responded:

Please answer these questions directly.

1. *Are you married. If so, when did it take place?*
2. *If not, when do you contemplate marriage?*
3. *When and where do you propose to use the living room suite you requested?*

Further comments on these matters will be reserved until I have unequivocal answers to the above questions.[17]

Once his check for school expenses arrived, Mamie finally revealed her elopement, justifying it as a way to save money on a wedding in Hot Springs. Her father did not reply—not even a card for her twenty-first birthday—and Mamie's spirits plunged. She found a warm and willing confidante in Kenneth's mother, who took Mamie into her arms.

Miriam Clark, an able negotiator from her days as a union shop steward, tried to heal the rift between the Phippses and their daughter. Miriam wrote that as a mother with a daughter, she understood the Phippses' feelings but that both families were to blame for assuming their children were different just because they were educated. "These things are not learned in books," Miriam wrote.[18] The newlyweds would finish their degrees, she predicted, and needed family support. "They are ours and we must stand by them." Miriam also wrote to Mamie for a favor: "One thing that I want you to do for me is to forget everything, even that you are married, and pin yourself down to your studies, so that you will get your degree in June."[19] Acknowledging that Mamie's parents doubted she'd finish school, Miriam continued, "Well if you love me as I love you, show them that you will." A week later, Mamie received a blistering note from her mother.

Now as for the marriage—You did just as you pleased about that. There is nothing that can ever heal the hurt and disappointment you chose to cause us. Little did we ever think that you would go off and marry in the cheap way that you did.[20]

The gibe about the cheap wedding stung Kenneth, who defended Mamie but apologized for the hard feelings he'd caused. "This letter, I know, cannot compensate in any way for the hurt which you may feel," he wrote Katie Phipps.[21] "I can say, however, that if I knew that your reaction would have been as unfavorable as it is, I would not have married in that way." Vowing that Mamie would finish her education, Kenneth wrote that he'd passed his doctoral exams, and before long, his dissertation would be finished. Responding to his long, diplomatic apology, Katie Phipps called it a masterpiece that he should submit as his dissertation.

Prone to anxiety attacks and seething over his daughter's marriage, Dr. Phipps spent days in bed to recover. It was nearly Thanksgiving before he wrote again to Mamie:

It is with mixed feelings that I write to you. On the one hand you are my daughter whom I dearly love; on the other, you have contracted a marriage that I cannot approve. And this in defiance of the advice offered to you on numerous occasions. In my judgment the reasons advanced for the hasty marriage carry no weight and offer no excuse for such contempt of parental advice. I have had the occasion to view a large number of such and they usually are never permanent or end in failure.[22]

To ward off money requests, Dr. Phipps warned that he was short on cash.

To save face in Hot Springs, Mamie's mother planned a formal wedding reception at home for the newlyweds during Christmas week. The young couple planned another reception for New Year's night at Miriam Clark's apartment in Harlem. Mamie worked feverishly to coordinate the two events while studying, working on her thesis, and starting yet another job: teaching psychology at Frelinghuysen, a tiny Black university in a two-story home near Howard. She taught

Monday nights for the grand sum of one dollar per class. Prone to stage fright, she must have been skittish about teaching at first, but that didn't last. Her students proved weak, and Frelinghuysen was so broke it fell behind in paying her one-dollar fee.

On December 22, the newlyweds met in New York for the three-day rail trip to Arkansas. Arriving in Hot Springs for the first time, Kenneth was appalled by the symbols of segregation he saw all about the town, including the train station's water fountains marked "White" and "Colored." Settling in at 302 Garden Street, he and Mamie made nice with her parents as Katie Phipps scurried about overseeing the holiday feast and wedding reception with tuxedos and gowns. Both events were a success, and Kenneth again proved a diplomat. It seemed that he and Mamie had just arrived when it was time to head back East for New Year's Eve. Their stack of wedding gifts was so high they had to leave it behind. They'd send for the gifts once they found an apartment.

After three more days on the rails, they arrived in Harlem for New Year's night at Kenneth's home. He put on his tuxedo again, and Mamie wore the blue crepe evening gown and cape that his mother had sewn for her. Among the Howard guests were Hylan and Leighla Lewis, the best man and matron of honor. Once the food and drink were gone and the hour turned late, the young people headed for the Savoy Ballroom, the perfect place to do the shag, the mooch, and the turkey trot to ring in the new year, 1939.

After a week of travels and revels, Mamie was back in her dormitory and out of sorts as she faced midyear exams. "Being back in this workhouse takes all the joy out of living," she wrote.[23] With Kenneth swamped and too busy to write her, Mamie was lonely and wondering if he still cared despite the ardor he showed in bed on weekends: "Perhaps you aren't interested in me anymore—I mean me as a mental person."[24]

Now that her marriage was revealed, professors regarded Mamie as a fallen star. Dr. Sumner seldom schmoozed with her or sought her help in the office and let it be known that another graduate student was now the department's best hope. Mamie's wedding felicitations from Dr. Frazier seemed half-hearted, and Dr. Meenes, who was supposed to direct her thesis, was more hindrance than help. Mamie struggled on, fretting that her topic, little children's consciousness of self, was too ambitious for a master's degree. Following Kenneth's advice, she explored research studies by Eugene and Ruth Horowitz, married psychologists in New York City who specialized in race and children. At Kenneth's urging, the Horowitzes agreed to meet and discuss their work with Mamie.

Eugene Horowitz had developed a "show me" or projective test for his dissertation at Columbia. Projective tests use inkblots, toys, drawings, or other objects to elicit hidden attitudes or feelings from test subjects. Horowitz showed drawings of Black and white boys to several hundred boys, most of them white. "Show me all those you want to be in your class at school," he told them, requiring the boys to rank the drawings according to their preference.[25] Many rejected the drawings of Black boys and favored those of white boys, which Horowitz, a white liberal, took as a sign of racial prejudice. After boys from a communist commune responded more equitably to the drawings, Horowitz concluded that society's bigotry filters down to the young. His study included one surprising result: several Black test takers preferred the drawings of white boys.

His wife, Ruth Horowitz, conducted a smaller study involving just twenty-four New York nursery-school children, including girls. Instead of focusing on prejudice, she explored their dawning awareness of racial identity, a topic more in line with Mamie's interest. Ruth Horowitz also used drawings of both Black and white boys for her study, but she added new options for her young test takers: drawings of a clown and animals—a hen, a dog, and a lion—random or irrelevant choices. To probe the children's sense of racial identity, she presented the drawings and said, "Show me which one is you."[26] Surprisingly, two-thirds of her Black test subjects preferred the drawings of a white child. She speculated that this was "wishful thinking," that they wished to be white.[27]

Mamie detected weaknesses in Ruth Horowitz's study from the start. For example, the sample of twenty-four pupils was far too small. Mamie decided that her thesis would test the validity of Ruth Horowitz's study; that is, she would see if the outcome was the same with a different set of test takers. She'd use the same drawings but test far more children, solely Black pupils. As a Black woman, Mamie was not allowed to work with white pupils in Washington.

As her project took shape, Kenneth became fascinated and offered suggestions. She'd helped him with his master's thesis; now he helped with hers. She ultimately decided that half of her Black test subjects would come from integrated schools in the North and the rest from segregated schools in the South—to see if segregation affected her results. More than just a master's thesis, her study was evolving into the seed of a future, legendary study that would make the Clarks famous. But Mamie's white thesis director, Dr. Meenes, was not keen on her topic. He preferred a study of eidetic imagery, photographic memory. So Mamie did an end run around Meenes by approaching Dr. Sumner, the department chair, who liked her project. Firmly but tactfully persistent, Mamie usually got what she wanted.

To begin her testing, she took taxis on cold winter mornings to one of six segregated nursery schools she found in Washington. Before testing the pupils, who ranged from about three to five years old, she played with them or joined in their storytelling sessions to get acquainted. Then she repaired to a separate room or remote corner and showed them drawings of the Black boys, white boys, the clown, and animals. She asked the Black pupils which of the drawings looked like them. Without drawings of girls, Mamie had to ask the girls which drawings looked like a brother, male cousin, or friend, just as Ruth Horowitz had done. Absorbed in collecting her data, Mamie often canceled visits to see Kenneth on weekends. Sometimes he visited her instead and later briefed the Horowitzes, Dr. Klineberg, and others on Mamie's test results. They seemed quite interested.

And so at last was Dr. Meenes—too interested for Mamie's taste. "Dr. Meenes decided that I might get a publication out of my thesis—and if I did not get it written by spring he would write it up in the summer," she wrote Kenneth in mid-February.[28] "Imagine! He's nuts though." Mamie estimated that she could develop three journal articles from her research if Kenneth would serve as her coauthor. She was determined to publish her final results as soon as possible, Meenes be damned.

Meanwhile, Kenneth was busy with his doctoral dissertation at Columbia. At first, he was fired up about exploring the IQ scores of Black students who'd migrated from Jamaica, where he had attended school for a year as a boy in the 1920s. Kenneth was inspired by an earlier study that his Columbia mentor, Dr. Klineberg, had done on Black migrant pupils from the American South who had moved to Harlem. Klineberg showed that their time in Harlem schools improved the Black pupils' IQ scores, challenging racist theories that Black children were inferior and uneducable. But conservatives in Kenneth's department, in line with the academic racism of the times, objected to the racial theme inherent in his proposal. Drs. Klineberg and Gardner Murphy—both white, liberal psychologists—sympathized with Kenneth but had to give ground. Kenneth's performance in his doctoral exams was so good they wanted the best for him, especially in light of his goal to one day integrate the faculty at a white college, a goal that Kenneth's mentors at Howard, including Dr. Sumner, had encouraged. So Kenneth chose a new topic: the effects of social attitudes on memory—to him just a dreary academic exercise.

Kenneth was not enthralled with the room he'd rented in Harlem either. He'd furnished it with a new bedroom set to accommodate Mamie on weekends. But the room was so cramped he began scouring Harlem for an apartment. On her weekend visits, Mamie enjoyed buying furniture, dishes, and a console radio on the installment plan for an apartment. Finally reconciled to her marriage, her father mailed a check to cover the furniture. Similarly, Kenneth's beloved Grandma Bea paid the balance on the radio. Once back in

Washington, Mamie splurged on silverware and books for a library. She wanted everything perfect for a proper apartment, even if it left her little cash for food and she had to go hungry. The conflict with her affluent parents over their "cheap" elopement had made the newlyweds more determined than ever to earn advanced degrees, find good jobs, and secure their place in the Black middle class.

In March, Kenneth found just what they needed: a two-bedroom, fifth-floor apartment at 20 St. Nicholas Place. Mamie was thrilled: "I'm so very excited I can't even see straight—to think that we have an apartment all our very own."[29] She pressed Kenneth to arrange furniture deliveries and take window measurements for curtains—tasks he had trouble accomplishing while struggling to finish his degree and working full time to support them. "As was expected, I cannot judge a thing from your measurements of the windows," she scolded.[30] "Do you know what you're doing?" This rubbed Kenneth the wrong way. To him, home was a place to hang your hat and have friends over—not a museum. "I am sorry—I am trying to do the things necessary—but I must confess that making all these arrangements by myself is really no picnic."[31]

Joining him in their apartment for Easter vacation, Mamie prepared dinners for friends and family. Their guests included the Horowitzes, Hylan and Leighla Lewis, and Mamie's brother, Harold. Mamie cooked up a storm. "In spite of the hecticness I had a really good time this Easter," she later wrote Kenneth from Howard.[32] "You were swell this time too and just let me run amuck with my own way."

For their wedding anniversary in April, Mamie sent him a letter reviewing their stressful first year together and praising his accomplishments. "Congratulations to you, funny!" she wrote, using a pet name for Kenneth.[33] "You've done so darn well in one year that I'm afraid to picture you in years to come—if this rapid striding keeps up." She predicted that all would go more smoothly once she got her master's degree in June and moved to Harlem. "As for sex life—I think that speaks for itself. You're all that I could ever want for. I look forward to this adjustment on a smooth plane."

All aglow from her letter, Kenneth responded, "You are the sweetest wife a man could ever hope for."[34] Despite a few rough patches, they'd shown a knack for teamwork in marriage, critiquing each other's term papers and quizzing each other before major exams. Mamie had tutored Kenneth to help him pass the French test required for his doctorate, and he'd given her crucial advice to tackle her ambitious master's thesis. He'd supplied her with silk stockings from a door-to-door salesman, and she'd reminded him to rinse out his socks.

Mamie also gave Kenneth the job tip that would keep them solvent and advance his career. She informed him that Gunnar Myrdal, the prominent Swedish economist, was hiring Black scholars from Howard for a major research study on American race relations that was based in New York. Mamie urged Kenneth to use his contacts at Howard, including Dr. Bunche, already at work on Myrdal's project. Up to his neck in his WPA job and studies at Columbia, Kenneth, an accomplished procrastinator, let the matter slide. Mamie, however, kept pressing him: "I hope you get on that study, as it seems more of a certainty than this WPA job."[35]

Meanwhile, her thesis was going well. Educators in Westchester County, just north of Manhattan, had agreed to testing dozens of Black pupils in their integrated schools. Mamie ended up with a total of 211 test takers and broke down her data by sex, age, region, and shade of the children's skin color. Her results showed that by three years old, most pupils had a consciousness of self as a distinct person. The vast majority, for example, picked a drawing of a boy and rejected the images of animals as best representing themselves. Not one four- or five-year-old chose an animal. Mamie discovered that the *light-skinned* tots preferred the drawing of a white boy, while the *dark-skinned* preferred a Black boy. This seemed logical, so Mamie set aside Horowitz's wishful-thinking theory that Black kids had chosen drawings of a white boy because they longed to be white. Still, as adherents of Adler's theory of the inferiority complex, she and Kenneth wondered if Horowitz might have been onto something. They'd have to design a new test of their own to get to the bottom of the matter.

In late April, as Mamie prepared to type her thesis, Dr. Meenes confronted her in the psychology office and asked her to turn over all her data to him. She immediately wrote Kenneth for help: "Dr. Meenes just came in here and told me that he would like to 'have' my thesis presented in a paper at a meeting of the American Psychological Association (this summer). You know what that means—that *he* will give the paper."[36] Mamie met with Dr. Sumner, who warned her that Meenes had taken other students' work in the past. Sumner urged her to publish her results as soon as possible. So Kenneth sprang in to action, consulting with Dr. Murphy, who was familiar with Mamie's thesis and knew Meenes. Murphy offered to publish Mamie's data in one of two journals over the summer and notify Meenes to that effect.

Mamie was ecstatic to learn this. "You are positively the nicest husband there ever was," she wrote Kenneth.[37] "I'm so glad that we have assurance of getting an article published." She vowed not to say another word to Meenes and resumed her work as if nothing had happened. She borrowed money from friends to buy typewriter ribbon and started cranking out her thesis. Over the next month, she passed the final exams for her courses as well as her comprehensive exams for the master's degree. She finished typing up her thesis and submitted it early. "The darn thing is so much longer than I anticipated," she wrote Kenneth.[38] Titled "An Investigation of the Development of Consciousness of Distinctive Self in Pre-School Children," her thesis ran sixty-seven pages in addition to charts and appendices. Mamie thanked Sumner, Meenes, Klineberg, and the Horowitzes in the acknowledgments section and included special thanks "To Mr. Kenneth Clark for his untiring help throughout the research."[39]

Relieved to hear that she finished her degree, Dr. Phipps wrote to thin, willowy Mamie in Harlem and predicted excellent final grades. "But I am wondering whether or not you need some rest from that sort of thing, for you are after all physically frail and such intensive mental concentration is not conducive to physical regeneration."[40] He said that Mamie's mother, due to visit her soon in New York, should do the housework while Mamie rested. Dr. Phipps could not come with his wife but longed to see Mamie and promised to send her a Smithfield ham. "I just simply cannot get it into my head that you, a mere kid of a few years ago, are managing a household of your own."

FIVE

NESTING IN HARLEM

It is easier to dally over black Bohemia or revel in
the hardy survivals of Negro art and culture than to
contemplate this dark Harlem of semi-starvation,
mass exploitation and seething unrest.

—ALAIN LOCKE[1]

The Harlem that Mamie adopted as home in the summer of 1939
was not the Harlem of Kenneth's childhood. Its complexion had
changed from mostly white to brown, and signs of the Depression
were everywhere. The homeless slept in doorways and alleys. Streets
and backyards were littered. In the homes on one block, "Rain pours
through the ceiling," a reporter wrote.[2] "Rats dart from great gaps
in the walls, windows are smashed, sickness flourishes especially
because the garbage is never collected from the dumbwaiters." The
optimism of the Harlem Renaissance had vanished, and its writers

could barely scratch out a living. Fewer whites arrived in limousines at elite Harlem hangouts like the Cotton Club. Robberies and gangland crime had frightened them. To Alain Locke, the distinguished Howard philosopher, the fashionable, bohemian Harlem of the 1920s had been a mirage.

The Harlem riot of 1935 marked the end of the good times. What began as a scuffle over shoplifting ended with looting and gunfire. Three Black people were killed and scores injured. Mayor Fiorello La Guardia chose Dr. Frazier, the Howard sociologist, to write a report on the riot after months of investigations. Flicking the scab off Harlem's social problems, Frazier summed up the riot's causes: "On March 19, 1935, several thousands of Harlem's citizens, after five years of the Depression, which had made them feel more keenly than ever the injustices of discrimination in employment, the aggressions of the police, and the racial segregation, rioted against these intolerable conditions."[3] Harlem had long been a powder keg, and at the heart of the problem was poverty born of job discrimination, Frazier wrote. Macy's in midtown hired Blacks only to do menial work; the Gimbels store refused to hire any at all. Other companies and trade unions routinely rejected Black applicants. Police in Harlem were seen as tormentors rather than protectors, and the schools there were shabby and ill equipped and steered Black students away from academic high schools. Their parents paid exorbitant rents for hovels in a segregated housing market while whites paid less for better homes on the open market. Crowded, filthy, and segregated, Harlem Hospital was staffed by Black nurses excluded from training in other hospitals. Frazier's report was so detailed and penetrating that city hall suppressed it.

Harlem, though decaying, still had enclaves of bourgeois respectability when Mamie moved to tidy St. Nicholas Place to be with Kenneth. She liked living close to taverns and restaurants and having Radio City, Broadway shows, and the 1939 World's Fair within commuting distance. Mamie loved having her own kitchen and a study to share with Kenneth. They were young and in love and played their jazz records loud while dancing with friends in the living room—to the chagrin of neighbors who complained. Kenneth loved Harlem. He liked that neighbors boycotted the stores that refused to hire them and that activists protested home evictions. Harlem had its street corner orators, its lively Black newspapers, political clubs, and such pressure groups as the National Negro Congress and the Universal Negro Improvement Association. Harlem's rich Black culture resonated with him.

But Mamie had no job, not even the prospect of one. Rarely were the city's Black women hired as professionals. So she busied herself writing three journal articles based on her thesis. Kenneth helped, but he was preoccupied with his job and dissertation. Mamie hustled to get her data into print, and all three articles, especially the first two, revealed her writing style: cautious, tentative, closely adhering to the facts. Scholars would study them for decades. The first appeared that fall in the *Journal of Social Psychology*, the second in the *Journal of Experimental Education* in December, and the third after the new year, 1940, again in *Social Psychology*. Bearing both of the Clarks' names, the articles contended that children's awareness of race increases most between ages three and four. A mysterious wrinkle in Mamie's data still gnawed at the Clarks: many of the darker-skinned children tested had identified with the drawing of the white boy. Was this a sign of wishful thinking, a Black inferiority complex?

To explore this and other issues, the Clarks planned a more sensitive experiment. This time, most of the test subjects would be a little older, up to age eight, and indicate their racial preferences by choosing dolls instead of drawings—white and brown baby dolls. Both Mamie and Kenneth applied for grants to cover expenses and keep food on the table. The Rosenwald Fund awarded them $1,500 each. Learning that Mamie was expecting a baby, her father offered his moral support. "I do sincerely hope and pray that you will pass through the ordeal of giving birth to a child safely," he wrote.[4] "You must muster all your strength and courage and you will be all right." Mamie picked a new apartment on the third floor at 20 St. Nicholas Place, had it painted, moved in with Kenneth, and began decorating her nesting place.

Kenneth climbed the stairs at Columbia's Low Memorial Library and found the man he was looking for in a cubicle beneath the rafters. Swedish economist Gunnar Myrdal was fair-haired, fortyish, and bent over his books, working on a landmark study of racism in America. Introducing himself as a Columbia doctoral student, Kenneth told Myrdal that he should hire him as a researcher. The Swede trained a skeptical eye on the brash young man and asked for samples of his writing. Kenneth presented them, bid Myrdal good day, and left with high hopes. With a baby on the way, Kenneth needed the job and held a pair of aces: references from Drs. Klineberg and Bunche, both on Myrdal's research team.

Hired as a research assistant to Klineberg and senior staffer Arnold Rose, Kenneth found he could work at home or in the library—no clock to punch. The job required tracking down documents and articles, summarizing them, and supplying other data for Myrdal and Rose to distill in chapters on topics such as racial traits and Black schools. Kenneth loved the work and was elated that his monthly pay of $175 was nearly double his WPA wage. He now had a role in a monumental study of American racism that would help usher in the civil rights era.

Discussing race over lunch together, Kenneth and Myrdal hit it off. Despite their differences in age, ethnicity, and experience, both were serious scholars fascinated by politics and race. Both were unapologetic moralists drawn to the life of a public intellectual, and both had wives for colleagues. Myrdal's wife, Alva, was a scholar in her own right, and both would win Nobel prizes: his for economics, hers for peace. A dynamic personality and able orator, Gunnar Myrdal held government posts in Sweden and taught at universities in America, which he called his second home. Even so, he skewered its social scientists for claiming objectivity and hiding behind statistics instead of working to improve society. But Myrdal was no radical. He was skeptical of Dr. Frazier's left-wing theories on racism and Bunche's militant criticism of the NAACP. That was why the Carnegie Corporation had tapped the Swede for its study. When it came to race, every social scientist in America seemed to have a political agenda. Carnegie wanted fresh, foreign eyes on American racism.

At the outset, Myrdal and Bunche headed south in a car for a firsthand look at segregation in Dixie. Bunche knew it could be dangerous, but Myrdal was naive and took chances, sneaking Bunche, who was light-skinned, into all-white cafés and hotels. More than once, they had to hurry to Bunche's car and flee white pursuers. The South functioned as a police state in the service of segregation, and Myrdal was appalled. "I didn't realize what a terrible problem you have put me into," he wrote Carnegie president Frederick Keppel.[5] "I mean we are horrified." Myrdal offered to resign, but Keppel urged him to soldier on and installed him and his staff on the forty-sixth floor of Manhattan's gleaming Chrysler Building.

Kenneth enjoyed Myrdal's staff meetings, which were like a Howard homecoming with Drs. Bunche, Frazier, Harris, and others taking part. The "Howard boys," Myrdal called them.[6] Early on, Myrdal formulated the thesis of his study, arguing that U.S. citizens subscribed to an "American Creed," a set of political ideals drilled into them from childhood. The creed declared the equality of all people and their right to freedom and justice. But Myrdal had seen firsthand the gap between these shining ideals and grim reality, *An American Dilemma*, the title of his study. An optimist, Myrdal predicted that whites would resolve the dilemma by heeding their ideals and supporting civil rights. Kenneth scoffed at this and told Myrdal that racism was as American as the Constitution, which had winked at slavery. True to his Adlerian principles, Kenneth argued that whites were blinded by a psychological need to feel superior to Blacks.

Like Dr. Bunche, Kenneth didn't have to tour the South with Myrdal to feel the sting of racism. As a Black man, Kenneth could feel it anywhere at any time—even the headquarters of *Time* magazine, where he stopped one day to gather data for Myrdal. Kenneth took an elevator to the thirty-third floor, where a *Time* receptionist handed him the set of documents he needed. As he stood scanning them, pen in hand, a white man walked by and did a double take, surprised to see a young Black man in a suit and eyeglasses poring over paperwork. The white man scoffed, hurled a racial gibe at Kenneth, and shut the door behind him.

With his graduate courses finished, Kenneth went full bore at his dissertation on human memory and how prejudice distorts it. Though his department had barred race as a topic, he ventured as close as he dared, asking his test subjects to read a story about another kind of prejudice and to write it down from memory. If their recollections were studded with biases, as he suspected, this would illuminate the selective nature of memory and raise questions about its reliability in criminal court cases—no small matter for Black defendants. Building on the work of British psychologist Frederick Bartlett, Kenneth developed a series of memory tests for 271 students at George Washington High, his alma mater, and 83 more students at Columbia. Each would read a paragraph-long story, twice and carefully but at a normal rate, and minutes later write it down from memory. He asked some of them to rewrite the story weekly for a month—again, solely from memory. He'd study the influence of age, sex, time, and attitude on their recollections, especially their attitudes—that is, their prejudices.

Kenneth asked the students to read a paragraph about a man

and a woman meeting for the first time. The woman was "quite a handful," drank like a man, and carried a heavy sack that a man could barely manage for five miles.[7] This tale of female dominance was designed to detect what we now call gender bias, which is what Kenneth found in the male versions of the tale. Many male students seemed to identify with the threatened male figure in the story and wrote the tale down in the first person. The female students did not. The male versions of the tale emphasized the loss of male prestige, but the female accounts did not. The young women tended to literally depict the female character as "quite a handful," but the men used sexually charged phrases such as "a large handful" and "what a bundle." This was just one of four experiments for Kenneth's dissertation, and the testing kept him busy into the spring when the good news about winning the Rosenwald grants arrived. The cash would come in handy, since Kenneth's job with Myrdal was temporary and Mamie was expecting their baby in July.

Nearing completion of his doctorate, Kenneth had no teaching job to look forward to in the fall—a source of bitterness. At Columbia, the doctoral candidates with the best job prospects were generally white, Protestant, and affluent, though not always the top scholars. Kenneth was convinced that Jewish students were at the top but seldom recruited by elite colleges. His own opportunities were even more limited. Black colleges had approached Kenneth about teaching jobs, but he was not interested. Following the goal for him set by his Howard mentors, he aimed to be a trailblazer, crossing the color line to teach at a white college. Kenneth dreamed of landing where he was raised, in New York, perhaps City College in Harlem.

That spring, he finished his dissertation in time for graduation. Titled "Some Factors Influencing the Remembering of Prose Material," it included his thanks to Drs. Klineberg and Murphy and added, "To my wife, whose untiring help made the completion of this research possible, I again express the depth of my gratitude."[8] The full extent of Mamie's contribution is unclear, but early drafts show that she helped tabulate his test results, and given past practice, she likely edited and typed his manuscript. Kenneth had earned his degree in just three years despite a series of time-consuming jobs. Mamie helped make it happen.

Kenneth's work so impressed Dr. Henry Garrett, his psychometrics professor, that he nominated Kenneth to Sigma Xi, the scientific research society. This must have surprised Garrett's colleagues, who knew that he was a segregationist from Virginia. Nonetheless, Garrett, who regarded Kenneth as more diligent than brilliant, introduced him at the Sigma Xi banquet and chatted amiably at the table, breaking one of the South's great taboos. Kenneth was astonished. Their future dealings on race and education, however, would not go so well.

A month after he earned his PhD, Kenneth's graduation present arrived. Around noon on July 12 at Edgecombe Sanitarium in Harlem, Mamie gave birth to a seven-pound baby girl, Kate Miriam—Kate for Mamie's mother and Miriam for Kenneth's. Mamie could hear the baby crying while it was still in her body. Kenneth was busy elsewhere at the time, and as soon as he could, he rushed to the hospital and found his baby girl sucking the fingers of her right hand. He pulled the fingers from her mouth, but she put them back in.

When he pulled them away again and held them, the baby wailed in protest. Already little Kate had a mind of her own.

———————

Rising early each morning, Mamie nursed and burped little Kate and lay her in the crib to sleep until waking and bathing her at 9:00 a.m. Once the baby was dry, Mamie nursed her again before another nap. There were more feedings before dinner with Kenneth, still another at 9:00 p.m., and the final one after midnight. Near dawn the next day, the routine resumed, including such duties as washing diapers, wringing them out, and hanging them in the kitchen to dry. Mamie loved being a mother, and Kate made it easier than it might have been: she seldom awoke her parents at night. Mamie monitored Kate's development, and the approach was more than maternal. Planning to study psychology at Columbia in the fall, Mamie wrote down that Kate had lost four ounces at first before starting to gain. "Baby responded to sounds and voices during first week," Mamie recorded in her baby book.[9] "Responded to deliberate auditory stimulations during second week. Followed sound with head during fifth week."

With the help of Rose, the young woman from Hot Springs she hired, Mamie balanced the needs of her baby with the doctoral courses and tests she faced at Columbia in September. Kenneth, in the meantime, managed the family business: a new round of projective tests on racial identity that he'd developed with Mamie. He found the tools of his trade one day in a Harlem Woolworth store: four androgynous baby dolls in diapers, all of them alike except that two were brown with black hair and two were white blonds—just what Kenneth needed.

He was in the right place, Harlem, to buy the dolls of color he needed for his work. Black parents elsewhere were hard pressed to buy quality dolls for their children. The history of Black dolls and racial identity is closely tied to the Clarks' legendary research.

During slavery and for decades afterward, Black parents made their children's dolls with wood, rags, bottles, gourds, or discarded white dolls repainted brown. But as far back as the 1820s, stores sold Black dolls of papier-mâché that were made in Germany, then the world's toymaker. Intended for white girls, these dolls were made in the image of female slaves or servants dressed as if for kitchen work. "They were painted the darkest of black possible with no hint of any shading or variety of coloring offered," wrote author Myla Perkins.[10]

Germany's Black dolls evolved through the 1800s, featuring wigs of mohair, eyes of black glass, and ceramic heads that withstood moisture. Some had stereotypically Black features, including broad noses, thick lips, and curly painted hair. In the 1840s, abolitionist women of both races in Massachusetts made Black dolls with cloth and sold them at bazaars to raise money for William Lloyd Garrison's antislavery newspaper, the *Liberator*. After the Civil War, the design of Black dolls improved, but the image they projected did not. *Harper's* magazine described a line of new dolls in 1877 as "negresses in gaudy head kerchief and sleeves rolled up as if for washing day."[11] The Butler Brothers catalog in 1895 featured a one-cent, inch-and-a-half "Glazed Nigger Baby."[12] Well into the 1900s, factories cranked out stereotypical darky dolls, mammy dolls, dancing coons, and pickaninnies for white buyers. Affluent white parents bought Black servant dolls for their daughters to play house or stage tea parties. "This is done to keep it before the white child that your place is that of servant," Nannie H. Burroughs told a convention of Black women in 1908.[13]

In 1909, R. H. Boyd, a businessman and former slave, founded the National Negro Doll Company in Nashville. "These toys are not made of that disgraceful and humiliating type that we have been accustomed to seeing," Boyd advertised.[14] During World War I, Evelyn Berry and Victoria Ross, both African Americans, manufactured dolls on West 135th Street in Harlem, including a uniformed Black soldier. "Teach your children pride of race and appreciation of race," they proclaimed.[15] "These are not the old time, black face, red lip Aunt Jemima colored dolls but dolls well made and truly representative of the race in hair and features."

By the late 1920s, Black entrepreneurs made dolls that walked, talked, wept, and rolled their eyes. Walter B. Abbott, a New York business manager for the *Chicago Defender*, invented a brown paint formula for dolls and founded Nutshell Varieties Company to market them. With headquarters in Harlem, Abbott was still selling his Sun Tan baby dolls, the "World's Prettiest," in 1940 when the Clarks were at work on their doll test.[16] But the heyday of the Black doll maker was over, and white firms largely abandoned the Black doll market. It's unclear which company made the four baby dolls that Kenneth plucked from a shelf at Woolworth's, but it might have been Sun Rubber Company of Barberton, Ohio. "Their dolls were dressed only in diapers," doll expert Perkins recalled.[17] All the dolls came from the same molds and had curly molded hair.

It's also unclear whether Kenneth or Mamie first thought of using dolls in their experiment. Perhaps it was Mamie, who had played with Black ragdolls as a little girl, but it might have been Kenneth's idea as well, for he had watched his little sister playing with a Black doll at home. Kenneth once said that using dolls in their experiment was a joint decision with Mamie. It was an inspired choice, for dolls have a hold on the human imagination, and the Clarks' doll test would stir hearts—and controversy—for generations to come.

By November 1940, Kenneth had finished testing Black pupils with his brown and white dolls in Springfield, Massachusetts. Most kids had preferred the white dolls to the brown ones, but it would be wrong to assume that all the rest picked brown dolls. Human behavior is seldom that neat. Some of the older kids showed they had minds of their own by refusing to narrow their choices to just one doll. One child, for instance, picked both brown dolls as nice. The choices of several two-year-olds seemed random, and Kenneth concluded they were too young for the test. The selections of many other kids seemed whimsical. Constance T., for example, who was light-skinned and age six, chose a Black doll as having a nice color but selected a white one as best. Several children who preferred a white doll refused to single out a brown doll as bad. "Just because colored no [reason] why they have to look bad at all," said Grace M.[18] But the fact remains that most of the Massachusetts children had selected white dolls as best.

Kenneth's testing in Springfield also included a coloring test designed by Mamie, and for many of the kids, the results paralleled their choices on the doll test. One of Kenneth's first test takers, for instance—dark-skinned, eight-year-old KJ—had consistently preferred a white doll to a brown one. And when Kenneth asked him to color the drawings of a boy labeled "you," KJ seemed embarrassed and conflicted about his skin color. He chose a blue crayon for the boy's shorts, the same color as his suit, but then he colored the boy's legs white. And when it came to coloring the face, KJ switched to an orange crayon, which Kenneth regarded as bizarre. He asked the boy why, and KJ responded, "I'm black," adding that he liked to color faces orange.[19] Reconsidering, he then switched to a brown crayon to color over both the white legs and the orange face and to finish the hair and limbs with brown as well. He hadn't balked at accurately coloring the other objects on his test sheet—a leaf, a mouse, an apple, and a girl—but dark-skinned KJ was torn over coloring the skin of the little boy labeled "you."

Kenneth had left Springfield with two indelible memories of his testing. First, he couldn't forget the children who looked so ill at ease, squirming or even crying when asked to choose between brown and white dolls or asked which one most looked like them. Kenneth felt guilty about bringing pain to these children. He'd wanted to study their attitudes toward race, not victimize them. The other memory that stayed with him was how many of the children had preferred a white doll—most of them. After testing 119 children, Kenneth left Springfield with more questions than answers. The testing in segregated Hot Springs lay before him.

Shortly before Christmas, the Clarks boarded a train to spend the holidays with Mamie's parents in Arkansas. Because of their baby, the winter weather, and Kenneth's plan to test children there through January, the family brought loads of luggage, including his dolls. After arriving in Hot Springs, the Clarks toasted, feasted, and exchanged Christmas presents with the Phippses, who cooed over little Kate. On a mild, Southern winter day, Mamie and her mother went for a walk along a lake on the town's outskirts, and on another day, the whole family gathered outdoors beside the Garden Street house for photos. Kenneth and Mamie posed in the driveway, he in a suit, winter coat, and fedora, and she in high heels, a fur coat, and fancy hat as Dr. Phipps stood off to the side with chubby-cheeked Kate in his arms.

After New Year's Day, while Mamie's train idled at the depot near her parents' home, Kenneth kissed her and their baby goodbye. Mamie had to study for final exams at Columbia while he stayed behind to test pupils. Given the hullabaloo over their elopement two years before, living alone with the Phippses had to be awkward for Kenneth. He addressed his grandly formal father-in-law as "Dr. Phipps" and felt the need to meet his high expectations.

Arriving days later at the train station in New York, Mamie sent Kenneth a telegram to reassure him: "ARRIVED SAFELY KATE IS FINE EVERYTHING—MAMIE."[20] At home, she wrote him again about the train ride and her arrival: "Kate behaved beautifully—flirted with all the men on the train."[21] Rose, her helper, had kept their apartment shipshape. "It will be lonesome here until you come," Mamie wrote. "Hurry and finish the work."

On Monday, January 6, 1941, Kenneth met his first test subjects in a room at segregated Douglas School in Hot Springs. Rosella B., a brown-skinned girl of five, was among those he tested. Shown all four dolls and asked which ones were "Negro," she looked puzzled. The term was lost on her. Rosella picked a white doll as the best one and the same doll as having a nice color. Why? "'Cause made like that," she said.[22] She laughed nervously while singling out a brown doll as bad, even though it was closest to her own skin color. Are you Black? Kenneth asked her. No, she said. "White peoples is white. They is better than colored peoples."

Freddie B., age five and dark-skinned, was more evenhanded in his doll choices. He selected a brown doll as both the one he wanted to play with and the nice doll. He also picked a brown doll as bad but then changed his mind and turned to a white doll instead. He described a white doll as having a nice color because "it looks pretty."[23] Asked if he was Black, Freddie said yes. "Grandma is Black." Would he like to be white or Black? "Would like to be white," he responded. Why? "Like to be white—that's all."

Nathaniel R., nearly five years old, said that his skin looked more like a white doll's, despite the fact that his skin was dark. He chose a white doll as best and a brown one as bad. "Looks bad all over 'cause he's brown," he said.[24] The white doll was nice, he said, "'Cause he white."

Eager to return to his family in New York, Kenneth kept his test notes to a minimum and finished testing in Hot Springs. One trend emerged early on: more so than the children in Springfield, the Southern kids were unfamiliar with the word *Negro*. Otherwise, his Southern and Northern data seemed comparable so far. Most of the Hot Springs pupils preferred white dolls. This did not change after

Kenneth headed seventy miles south to Pine Bluff, a quiet college town where he tested more pupils at the Missouri Street School and the teacher-training school at historically Black Arkansas State College. He tested brown-skinned, six-year-old Delores M. there. She preferred white dolls and singled out a brown doll as bad. Though she never played with white kids, she liked them better, she said. Asked if she wished she were white, Delores nodded. "Yes, sir, I'd like to be white—don't like to be black."[25] Once he finished in Pine Bluff, Kenneth ventured north to Little Rock, the state capital, where he tested other Black children with similar, dispiriting results.

After a month in Arkansas, Kenneth bid his in-laws goodbye and headed homeward in a Jim Crow rail car through the Deep South. With hopes of meeting W. E. B. Du Bois, the renowned Black scholar and cofounder of the NAACP, Kenneth stopped in Georgia to visit him at Atlanta University. Dr. Du Bois was a heroic figure, a scholar-activist, and author of *The Philadelphia Negro* and white-hot essays in the NAACP's *Crisis* magazine that attacked racism and segregation. But Kenneth lacked an appointment to see Du Bois. Kenneth was like that—popping in unannounced for quick chats with friends. But Du Bois was not a friend and could be rude with starstruck young scholars. Fortunately, Du Bois agreed to meet him, and they talked about Kenneth's research with dolls. Du Bois seemed interested and said the struggle for justice depended upon trained minds: "And we have to see that more of our young people discipline their intelligence to continue this struggle on the intellectual level that it's going to require."[26] Kenneth would long remember the meeting, for their careers would end up on parallel tracks: both professors, activists, public intellectuals, and authors of classic texts.

Mamie had passed all her first-term exams at Columbia and was well on her way to earning a PhD in psychology. She'd borne a heavy load, five graduate courses—extraordinary so soon after the birth of her first child. Though she liked her courses and professors, graduate school required an adjustment. Mamie's education had always been segregated, and competing with privileged white students on an Ivy League campus was a new experience. Walking among the white lab coats in her department must have seemed even stranger to Mamie than it had seemed to Kenneth. Fortunately, some of her colleagues were women, and she worked with them in labs and on projects as needed. But like Kenneth before her, she avoided social ties that could lead to social slights because of her race. Mamie focused on her studies instead, just as Kenneth had.

Since her department offered few courses in child psychology, Mamie chose to use her math skills in the emerging field of psychological testing. That landed her in the year-long psychometrics course with Dr. Henry Garrett, who'd once nominated Kenneth for Sigma Xi. Picking Garrett as her mentor was not a casual choice, for Mamie knew that he was a Southerner who regarded Blacks as inferior. The relationship became a topic of humor at home as Kenneth joked that stuffy old Doc Garrett and iron-willed Mamie made an unlikely duo.

With Kenneth back home from Arkansas, Mamie looked over his test data with an eye toward preparing the final report required by the Rosenwald Fund. Hoping the fund would extend her grant another year or two to cover her tuition at Columbia, she made the report a priority. If it weren't for Mamie, the project might well have stalled, because Kenneth, so good at dreaming up new projects, was terrible at meeting deadlines to finish them. She was the practical, punctual one, the manager who dogged the details of any task at hand. To Mamie, the Rosenwald deadline was sacrosanct. "We were paid to get these [tabulations] out," she once said, "and we had to get them out, and we had to get them out on time."[27]

Mamie bought a notebook and scoured Kenneth's test sheets to record the responses of all 253 children tested. Using a pencil, she filled page after page with data, adding up the children's choices of white doll, brown doll, both, or neither. She broke down the data by age, sex, skin tone, and region, North or South. She calculated the percentages in each instance and the statistical significance of key findings. She noted that the difference between the boys' responses and the girls' was slight. She wrote all this down in her immaculate handwriting and did the same with the children's responses on the coloring test. She quoted their most unsettling, color-conscious remarks that Kenneth had jotted down in pencil. Mamie probably spent more time tabulating his results than he'd spent gathering them. Clarity began to emerge from the jumble of data, and she wrote an outline for the final report. Kenneth, the more facile expository writer, joined in the writing, and they edited each other's work. They also labored over the tables and charts together. Mamie typed the final document, and a surviving fragment of their report—excluding tables, charts, and sources—runs about sixty pages.

Here's what the Clarks found. The vast majority of the children tested, two-thirds, selected a white doll as best, the one they wanted to play with—a total of 66.8 percent of the 253 pupils. Similarly, nearly 60 percent picked a white doll as the nice one with a nice color, and nearly 59 percent of the pupils singled out a brown doll as bad. The results were stunning, and the Clarks believed they revealed an inferiority complex among Black children, that is, psychological damage caused by a segregated society dominated by whites. But the Clarks were not ready to proclaim this in print to the world. They wanted more data to confirm their beliefs. So in restrained, scholarly prose, they wrote that their results raised questions about the mental hygiene and education of Black pupils at a tender age: "The importance of these results for an understanding of the origin and development of racial concepts and attitudes in Negro children cannot be minimized."[28] Given the strictly segregated schools in Southern and border states, Mamie lamented that the pupils there would never know what it was like to get better grades than a white classmate: "They'll always think they're inferior."[29] She wondered if her own schooling in Hot Springs had scarred her.

The Clarks' new findings paralleled those in Mamie's master's thesis and confirmed that children start to become aware of skin color or race at three years old. Once again, the light-skinned pupils were the ones most likely to identify with a white doll. The Clarks found one puzzling regional difference in their results that would stir controversy. The Southern children from segregated schools were more likely than the integrated, Northern pupils to pick a brown doll as most like themselves. To the Clarks, this regional difference of 8 percentage points seemed slight and not statistically reliable. Even so, if segregation was psychologically harmful, why did the Southern pupils reveal a more healthy identification with dolls of their own race? The Clarks had no pat answer but noted that their Northern sample included many more light-skinned children—those more likely to identify with a white doll.

In the spring, after submitting their report, Mamie learned that her Rosenwald grant was renewed to cover her tuition at Columbia. She was thrilled. She'd done well in her first term, despite taking five courses, working on the test data, and handling her duties at home. However, she got only a C in psychometrics from Dr. Garrett, who would oversee her dissertation. Mamie would have to do better in the second half of Garrett's year-long course.

The Clarks considered publishing their extraordinary findings, but they were so busy they set them aside for years—strange, given the doll test would one day bring them such fame. Mamie was busy with her graduate work and caring for Kate, while Kenneth had to focus on earning a living for the family. He taught summer school part time at City College and searched for a permanent position in the fall. The doll test still troubled the Clarks, especially Kenneth, who felt guilty about the kids who had wept during his testing. He felt like Satan himself for drawing their tears. Far from rushing to claim credit for the doll test, he fantasized about shredding the data.

Kenneth showed his test results to colleagues, and several urged him to publish the data. Dr. Klineberg told him that psychologists should do more than just gather facts; they should *do* something about them. "Kenneth, what are you going to do to help these children?"[30]

SIX

STARTING IN THE BASEMENT

The policy of the public authorities of never taking an initiative, and always waiting to be urged to do their duty, is obviously fatal in a neighborhood where there is little initiative among the citizens.

—JANE ADDAMS OF HULL HOUSE[1]

M amie was hanging diapers to dry in the kitchen when the doorbell rang. It was Reverend Adam Clayton Powell Jr., the Harlem pastor and politician on the make, with a photographer in tow. Asking for Kenneth, Powell bragged that he'd pulled strings to get her husband his summer teaching job at City College. Did she know that? No, Mamie said, she did not. As Kate cried in her crib and diapers dripped on the floor, Powell asked to wait and take Kenneth's picture. "You can come back, but please don't wait," Mamie told him.[2] Powell persisted, and Mamie stood her ground. Finally, he left.

Activists had often pressed City College to hire its first Black professor to the permanent faculty, and while teaching there part time in the summer of 1941, Kenneth hoped to be that person. Senior faculty had observed his teaching and given him the thumbs-up. Still, he got no contract, and he needed one badly to support his family.

While teaching one day, Kenneth noticed a Black man in a suit and tie at his classroom door. R. O'Hara Lanier, the dean at Hampton Institute, had come to offer him a teaching job at the Black college in Virginia. At Howard, Kenneth's mentors had often urged him to avoid Black colleges and break the color barrier at a white college instead, but now he had to accept Lanier's offer. So Mamie stayed behind with little Kate while he tested the waters in Virginia, the start of nearly two years in a segregated career desert. Unlike Howard, Hampton was led by a white man, Malcolm MacLean, who stressed vocational training over academics and adjusting to segregation instead of fighting it. Kenneth, however, taught the way he'd been taught at Howard: to cut against the grain of segregation. Billie Allen, one of his Hampton students, recalled his central message in class: "You better understand what's going on in this country, what your position is in this country."[3]

On a weekend visit to Hampton, Mamie joined Kenneth for dinner at the Holly Tree Inn on campus. Little Kate toddled about as Kenneth pursued her with a spoonful of food. Anne Brooks, one of Kenneth's students, asked why he didn't use psychology to trick the baby into eating? "Miss Brooks," he replied, "psychology only works on other people, never on members of your own family."[4]

President MacLean wasn't joking the night he invited Kenneth over for cocktails. Hampton shouldn't frustrate Black students, MacLean warned him. It should help them adjust and leave time for their jobs. MacLean told Kenneth to think it over, that he could have a good home and salary, if he fit in. Instead, Kenneth visited Drs. Sumner and Bunche in Washington, and both men urged him to resign. This was at the outset of America's involvement in World War II, and Bunche found Kenneth a new research job with the U.S. Office of War Information (OWI).

Mamie welcomed the change, and Kenneth counted on the OWI job to stay out of uniform. He loathed war and knew that Black troops were segregated, bullied by Southern officers, and often stuck doing menial work like kitchen or latrine patrol. He was not alone in such views. Black newspapers railed against the abuse of Black GIs, and activist Bayard Rustin, imprisoned as a war objector, remarked, "I have heard many say they might as well die right here fighting for their rights as die abroad for other people's."[5]

Kenneth's OWI job, based in New York, required him to travel in the South and supervise an integrated team of researchers who interviewed people of both races about civilian morale in wartime. He saw his mission as explaining to white officials how racism at home undermined the war abroad. In his paper titled "Morale among Negroes," Kenneth lambasted racial stereotypes in film, radio, and the Little Black Sambo tale for children. Kenneth criticized "the pathological quality of Negro-white relationships throughout a large part of America, particularly the South."[6] But his reports fell on deaf ears.

Kenneth's integrated team of interviewers, which included women, raised the hackles of white Southerners. The group couldn't eat together in diners or share a hotel. Kenneth had to inform local officials before they arrived. Even so, cops harassed the team, and one Black member was beaten. Barred from meeting at a white hotel in Memphis, Kenneth asked his white staffers to report instead to his Black motel. After a cabdriver tipped off the cops, they surrounded the building. Kenneth phoned the FBI and OWI for help, but to no avail. "Dammit, I'm not going to be able to fulfill my responsibility if you people don't get these damn idiots off my back," he told his bosses.[7]

Kenneth resigned again, and again Mamie backed his decision. When he sought a job at New York's Hunter College for women, he was told that it was wrong for a Black man to teach white girls. His luck finally turned at City College, where Dr. Gardner Murphy, a former Columbia mentor, now led the psychology department. Murphy offered Kenneth a job teaching night classes as a humble instructor. It was no dream job, but Kenneth was thrilled.

He was still feeling the glow when a photographer stopped by his City College office one day to snap his picture for a story in the *People's Voice* newspaper edited by Reverend Adam Clayton Powell Jr., who sat on the city council. The article claimed that Powell helped get Kenneth his new job. So in the end, Powell gained the publicity that Mamie once denied him. It was not the last time he'd outmaneuver the Clarks.

———

Mamie found an apartment at 555 Edgecombe Avenue, one of the poshest apartment buildings on Sugar Hill. The doorman faced the street and a bluff overlooking the Polo Grounds where the Giants played major league baseball. Residents took rooftop seats to view the games. Theirs was a fourteen-story gem of a building with a lobby of marble and stained glass—home to Harlem's elite in sports, the professions, and the arts: boxer Joe Louis, actor Canada Lee, composer Billy Strayhorn. "Bob Hope, Ed Sullivan would come all the time," musician Alex Lombard recalled.[8] "It was to play golf with Joe Lewis." Thurgood Marshall, Walter White, and Roy Wilkins of the NAACP lived nearby, and some said that if a bomb exploded on Edgecombe Avenue, it would wipe out the nation's Black leadership.

The Clarks liked the neighborhood. Kids roller-skated, hopscotched, and jumped rope on the sidewalk as mothers pushed baby strollers. Mamie was pregnant again and working on her dissertation. She took little joy in the statistical study of pupil test scores in six areas of mental ability, including memory, verbal, and numerical skills. She studied how they developed at three stages: ages eleven, thirteen, and fifteen. Her text was to be short on words, long on statistics, and would include data from hundreds of city students of all races.

Writing to schools to help her find test subjects, Professor Robert Woodworth praised Mamie: "I recommend her as a serious investigator who may be depended upon to use tact in handling the children and to come through with a good piece of work."[9] Dr. Garrett, her segregationist mentor, told Mamie, "You are, of course, going back home to teach," suggesting her future was in Arkansas at a Black public school.[10] Mamie ignored the slight. "She told me he was horrible," daughter Kate later recalled.[11]

Mamie learned that the brightest pupils in her study excelled in all areas of mental ability, not just one or two skills. But before she could write up her results, she gave birth to Hilton, a nearly seven-pound boy with gray-green eyes and fair hair. Though busy with her dissertation, Mamie breastfed the baby just as she had Kate. But instead of scrubbing his diapers and hanging them in the kitchen, this time, she hired a diaper service.

Kenneth loved teaching at City College in Harlem. His colleagues were fun to be with and lamented his problems at OWI. Theirs was a Gothic campus with gargoyles and five cathedral-like buildings of rough-hewn stone erected after the turn of the century. Students in coats and ties hustled each day to morning classes from a nearby subway station, and Kenneth, briefcase in hand, was often among them.

City College was a tuition-free commuter school for men, and in the fall of 1943, with the nation at war, about a third of the freshmen were under eighteen. Teaching them introductory psychology suited Kenneth. They were bright, motivated, and mostly poor and Jewish, the sons of immigrants and often the first in their families to attend college. They gathered at noon for brown-bag lunches in the cafeteria, where many debated over the truest shade of leftist ideology. Among them were communists, Trotskyists, and social democrats. Some professors found them uncouth and quarrelsome, but Kenneth rather liked them. They hurled tough questions at him as he smoked and chalked up the blackboard. Hoping to shatter their naivete, he challenged them to look squarely at the tribalism and prejudice in the world. Some found him a sad, bitter man and figured it must be hell to be Black in America.

Harlem was hell indeed the night a riot erupted after a tussle between a white cop and a Black woman at a hotel. When a Black soldier intervened, the cop shot him in the shoulder. As false rumors of the GI's death spread, people filled the streets, smashing windows, setting fires, and looting stores. Six people were killed and nearly two hundred injured. James Baldwin witnessed the riot and later wrote, "To smash something is the ghetto's chronic need."[12]

Kenneth gathered an interracial group of students to study the psychological roots of the riot. They interviewed residents and shopkeepers and published their findings in the *Journal of Social Psychology*. Of the sixty-four people they questioned, 60 percent condemned the riot, 30 percent condoned it. "Hope it happens again," one man said.[13]

To avoid being drafted, Kenneth took on another campus project: risky wartime research on oxygen deprivation for high-flying pilots. One day, he sat for more than ten hours with a colleague, G. Milton Smith, and handful of students in a locked chamber with a dwindling supply of oxygen. He helped measure the students' ability to see, hear, and handle the stress but never noticed the mercury spilled on the floor. As expected, the men experienced elation and irritability, but after eight hours they began choking and vomiting and all had to be evacuated for emergency treatment. It took Kenneth days to recover from mercury poisoning, and as he once said, "Milt Smith and I almost died."[14]

Otherwise, life on the home front was much the same for the

Clarks as for millions of New Yorkers during the war. Mamie used the ration books they needed to buy sugar, meat, shoes, and other items. Reading newspapers and listening to the radio, the Clarks were horrified by the reports of carnage on the battlefields abroad. "How are we going to come through this?" Kenneth asked.[15] "We'll bungle through," Mamie said.

Her dissertation, chock-full of statistics, was finally approved in the spring of 1944. Despite eloping and giving birth to two children, Mamie had earned an Ivy League doctorate in four years. Her thirty-page thesis was titled "Changes in Primary Mental Abilities with Age," and she sent printed copies to the male professors at Howard who once doubted her: Meenes, Frazier, and Sumner. But given the segregated job market, especially for professional women, what could Mamie do with her PhD?

The wartime job market was booming, but Dr. Mamie Clark got the runaround. Twice, the Civil Service office judged her qualified for a job in psychological testing at the Madison Avenue offices of the U.S. War Department. And twice, she arrived there only to be told there was no such job. So Mamie phoned the Adjutant General's Office, spoke to Major D. E. Baier, and followed with a letter: "I personally do not desire to be a center of controversy or disturbance but I sincerely feel that the issue, if it be one of racial discrimination, is more fundamental than my personal wishes."[16]

Mamie went to Major Baier's office with Kenneth as a witness and argued her case. Denying any racial bias, the major said the job she sought was "disestablished." So Mamie filed a complaint with the federal Fair Employment Practice Committee, which ruled that her case "cannot be considered other than an act of discrimination."[17] But the military stood behind Major Baier. Mamie, however, was not finished with him yet.

After other rejections, she heard that the American Public Health Association, led by a white woman with a PhD, needed a research psychologist. Expecting another rejection, Mamie applied but was delighted to get a job offer at last.

But at home, she had a lot on her plate. Cutting teeth and suffering from asthma, little Hilton cried nightly in his parents' bedroom, and his wails drove them to distraction. "He had a huge mouth, cavernous," babysitter and family friend Billie Allen said of his weeping.[18] Despite the stresses of childrearing and jobs, the Clarks managed a lively social life. Their parties were like spirited seminars with drinks and hors d'oeuvres. Kenneth invited Harlem activists, artists, and professionals he knew, including a white liberal or two from downtown, to debate the issues of the day, especially race, in the living room. "All the people who later became famous to everybody came to the Clarks' at one time or another," recalled white activist Russia Luca Hughes.[19] "I remember one night Langston Hughes was there sitting on the floor, and every time anybody said something a little extreme, angry, or overenthusiastic, he burst into laughter."

Mamie was not smiling at her new job analyzing data about nurses. First, she was overqualified, and worse, the only Black staffer. White colleagues snubbed her. Mamie soldiered on, but one night, she said, "Kenneth, I've come to the conclusion that I can't work for anyone else."[20] All right, he said, and they began planning a clinic she'd run for Harlem children at risk of delinquency. Meanwhile, Mamie took a part-time job with the U.S. Armed Forces Institute nearby at Columbia, ending her tussle with the War Department. She quit her health association job and took a second part-time job, this one in testing at a Bronx shelter for Black children ages six to sixteen.

The Riverdale Children's Association had a storied past. Founded as the Colored Orphan Asylum in 1836 by Quakers, it was an orphanage for Black children on Manhattan's Fifth Avenue during the Civil War. In the notorious 1863 riots against a new military draft, white mobs lynched Blacks across the city and burned down the orphanage. The children escaped and took refuge in a police station. By 1944, when Mamie arrived, the orphanage had moved and become the Riverdale Children's Association. Though it was the sole refuge for the city's Protestant Black kids, it was bankrupt and facing closure. A Quaker ran the shelter with a mostly Black staff, and Mamie's job was to test every child's basic skills before they left for new schools.

She enjoyed working with the children and the integrated staff. Her reports went to Dr. Stella Chess, a Jewish psychiatrist who shared their office and reviewed Mamie's data. They had much in common: both were mothers who loved psychology and working with children, and both had faced trouble launching careers. Many hospitals had rejected Chess as a young intern, stating, in effect, "I am sorry but we have filled our quota of women" or "I am sorry, we have filled our quota of Jewish persons."[21]

Many emotionally disturbed kids lived in the Riverdale shelter, some of them delinquents, others runaways, but nearly all abused, abandoned, or neglected. Mamie had no idea that so many Black children were discarded. Their psychological problems ran the gamut. One traumatized child had stopped speaking, and others suffered the stigma of illiteracy—bright kids in many cases. So Mamie proposed a reading program and got it. She'd found her life's work, and hoping to open her own clinic, she studied the Riverdale model closely. She concluded that it treated far too many pupils with too few resources. Dr. Chess, for example, offered therapy just ten hours a week, hardly enough for scores of children. Their problems festered till they turned sixteen and returned to the community.

Mamie dreamed of treating pupils like these in her own clinic in Harlem. Founded to prevent mental illness and delinquency, child guidance clinics emerged nationwide in the 1920s and treated kids with behavioral problems linked to corrosive social ills. Mamie's dream of founding a clinic was in the tradition of female reformers like Dorothea Dix, who opened mental hospitals, and Jane Addams, whose Hull House helped bring child guidance services to Chicago. There was little of the sort for Black kids in New York—only for white children. Young Blacks were typically sent to jail or reform school. Working together, the Clarks would answer Dr. Klineberg's question after he saw their doll test data: *What would they do for these children?*

———

Kenneth was wearing himself out writing articles, giving speeches, conducting research, and working with professional and activist groups. He even took a second full-time job with a new Jewish agency, the Commission on Community Interrelations (CCI). Kenneth's ties to the Jewish community were considerable. Activist friends and most of his academic colleagues were Jewish. With the Nazis exterminating Jewish persons abroad, progressive Blacks and Jewish persons formed alliances to combat bigotry at home.

The CCI aimed to snuff out ethnic conflicts before they spread, and one of Kenneth's first projects involved a brawl between Jewish persons and gentiles at a Coney Island synagogue. He interviewed Italians, Blacks, and Jewish persons about the conflict but faced discrimination of his own at the CCI. A white colleague had shoved Kenneth's desk out into the hallway, and Kenneth complained he was being treated like an office boy or a token hire. He forged valuable friendships at the agency, but working there was a struggle.

Divisions between Blacks and Jewish persons ran deep, as Kenneth argued in an article he was asked to write for the Jewish journal *Commentary*. Both groups shared the blame, he wrote, citing his own survey results showing that Jewish persons and Blacks harbored negative stereotypes about each other. He described two insecure minorities vying for survival: "Each suffers from the psychological threats of humiliation; each has been the victim of organized bigotry."[22] Kenneth called for federal policies to unify ethnic groups nationwide. "Loyalty to mankind may have to be given priority over all other loyalties."

Months later, an American plane dropped a single bomb on Hiroshima, which collapsed in rubble as a mushroom cloud blotted out the sun. Tens of thousands of Japanese people perished, along with thousands more days later in a similar attack on Nagasaki. The war was finally over, but the holocaust in Japan left Kenneth more appalled than relieved.

———————

Still employed at Riverdale, Mamie spent her free time writing to hospitals, churches, charities, and city agencies about sponsoring a child guidance clinic in Harlem. The answer was invariably no or the job was already being done, which was false. The Clarks concluded that they'd have to open a clinic on their own. Mamie asked Kenneth to approach her father for help, and Dr. Phipps asked how much money and for what. As the Clarks were figuring that out, they gathered friends and colleagues in their apartment, and over food and drinks, they laid out their plans. They discussed fundraising, choosing a staff, and a board of directors to oversee the operation.

Mamie envisioned a clinic for troubled kids three to eighteen years old. First, she'd evaluate them with IQ, achievement, and personality tests, then doctors would check their vision, hearing, and general health for conditions that hinder learning. Psychiatrists would offer therapy while other staffers conferred with parents and teachers and linked the families with social services. Mamie rented the tiny office her father agreed to furnish, and three psychiatrists, three social workers, and a psychologist—all friends—offered to work part-time for free. Two City College interns would also help. Drawing on his teaching salary, Kenneth paid the rent and wages for a secretary. "Mamie was very strong in pushing this and developing it," recalled board member Dr. John Moseley. "But they both worked like hell getting it started."[23]

Mamie named their clinic the Northside Testing and Consultation Center—"Northside"—for its 150th Street site at the northern edge of Harlem. The office was in the Dunbar Apartments a few blocks from the Clarks' home. Named for the Black poet Paul Laurence Dunbar, the five-hundred-unit complex included homes and offices in brick buildings of six stories. W. E. B. Du Bois and Paul Robeson had lived there. Mamie assembled volunteers to renovate the office, and among them was Mark Luca, a white artist and war objector. "Mark and Mamie hit it off terrifically," Luca's wife, Russia, recalled.[24] "Mamie was not an aggressive woman, and yet you felt a tremendous force, a tremendous power she had. I always felt that without Mamie, Kenneth would never have made it."

Chiefly a waiting room with five cubicles and a spare room for the children, Northside Center was a tidy oasis for the needy. Paintings covered the brightly painted walls, and the furniture was fit for a modern living room. At the front desk was a receptionist with a pleasant West Indies accent, and Mamie kept a fistful of sharpened pencils on her desk in a cubicle. The spare room included tiny tables and chairs for the kids as well as toy blocks and brown and white baby dolls like the ones used in the Clarks' doll test. The staff would long remember the space as "the basement," but it was only a few feet below street level. As in offices nearly everywhere at the time, the staff smoked on the job, filling the clinic with a blue haze.

Mamie held two open houses and wrote agencies, schools, and doctors to draw clients. Kenneth reached out to reporters, explaining that the clinic would deal with children's bed-wetting, truancy, stealing, and misbehavior in school—all with roots in Harlem's social ills. The Clarks promoted their clinic on a radio show, and newspapers covered the opening. *Headlines and Pictures*, a Black magazine, noted, "The only word to describe the Center, with its perfect decorations, playroom for children, and all kinds of technical equipment is 'unique'—certainly in Negro communities."[25]

Northside Center's staff and clientele were integrated. Friends, several of them white, paid to have their own children tested or treated. Since browbeating Black clients was common in city agencies, Mamie insisted that each child and parent be treated with dignity. Soon, a small but steady flow of children arrived for help. A few were not troubled at all; these were teenagers taking vocational tests. The Clarks hoped that their low fees based on parents' income would keep the clinic running. Most of the kids, however, were poor and accused of truancy, theft, bullying, or disrupting classrooms.

KENNETH HOLDS TWO DOLLS
AS A BOY PICKS THE WHITE
DOLL AT NORTHSIDE CENTER

Some neighbors feared that Northside's children were crazy, and to counter the stigma, the Clarks formed an outreach committee that included Thurgood Marshall of the NAACP. One day, a Black mother from Queens told Mamie that her daughter was labeled feebleminded and stuck in a class for children with intellectual disabilities and she'd be lucky to learn how to wash dishes or read a newspaper. Mamie gave the girl an IQ test, and the results registered "dull normal,"[26] not intellectually disabled. Mamie concluded that with remedial help, the girl could lead a normal life. Before long, ten more parents from Queens reported the same problem, and Mamie told the *Amsterdam News* that most did not belong in these classes. Harlem children started showing up with the same complaint. "It was almost a deluge," Mamie said, and she pressed the schools to place most in regular classes.[27] The Harlem community began to trust her.

Northside was evolving into a center for child advocacy and civic activism, and curious Harlemites began to visit. Cathy Lombard, a college student troubled by a recent job interview with a prejudiced employer, asked Mamie how to handle him. "She was a beautiful woman with a tiny, little voice," Lombard recalled of Mamie.[28] "You got a feeling that she was very soft, very gentle, but at the same time she really knew how to cut if you went the wrong way." Mamie's advice to Lombard: "Sometimes we have to overlook white people. Just ignore it." Lombard left Northside feeling better and vowed to work there one day after graduating.

———

Kenneth's appeal as a speaker and writer was spreading beyond the five boroughs. Each speech was a chance to spread his gospel of integration and promote Northside. He spoke to Quakers in Philadelphia, to the faculty at Fisk University in Tennessee, and testified on the abuse of Black troops before a committee in Washington. Kenneth got the jitters before every speech, and Mamie, who arranged his schedule and kept track of his expenses, was usually there to support him. Meanwhile *Commentary* and the *Negro Digest* in Chicago sought more articles from Kenneth.

Ebony magazine published a five-page article on the Clarks and Northside Center that raised their profile as never before. Gordon Parks, a Harlem friend and rising star in photography, had spent weeks taking pictures of Northside, its children, and the Clarks—classic photos that have since hung on museum walls. Parks staged the shots to show how Northside and the Clarks' doll test worked. The story was headlined "Problem Kids," and a photo showed a Black boy named Peter choosing a white doll over a brown one.[29] The *Ebony* article said that Peter suffered from an inferiority complex because of his color: "The Clarks know they cannot change the larger Jim Crow environment which twists young personalities. But they have shown that applied psychology can modify school and home environments, can unburden sick emotions and guide children to new interests."[30]

After the success of the *Ebony* article, the Clarks published the results of their doll test in an anthology titled *Readings in Social Psychology* and the *Journal of Negro Education* at Howard. In the latter case, Mamie did much of the writing.

In the meantime, Kenneth was so steeped in his teaching and work with progressive groups that he was stressed out and quarreled often with Mamie. "My father had dark moods," daughter Kate recalled, speculating that he might have been manic-depressive.[31] Seven years after earning his doctorate, he still held the low rank of instructor and felt that his career had stalled. He was torn: should he be a scholar-activist in the mold of W. E. B. Du Bois, a public intellectual fighting for social justice, or a detached scholar with a career on the fast track? His crisis of confidence came at a time of ferment in the Black struggle. Nazi racial policies had cast a new light on segregation in America and handed the Soviet Union a new weapon in the Cold War. Black veterans and other activists insisted on change. "It was the army experience that made a militant of me," NAACP lawyer Robert Carter recalled.[32] "It instilled in me a fierce determination—a zealousness—to fight racism with all my intellectual and physical strength."

Kenneth, however, had yet to find his niche in either academe or the crusade for equal rights, and Mamie, worried about his dark moods, urged him to see a psychiatrist. Kenneth argued it was a waste of money and time, but Mamie prevailed, and he showed up one day at the offices of Dr. Aaron Karush on East Seventy-Third Street.

Northside barely survived its first year, raising the stress level for the Clarks. On the plus side, sixty-four kids were treated, and dozens took lessons in remedial reading. Too many, however, came for one appointment and never returned, and it was impossible to get the volunteer staff to attend all the meetings and keep good records. Further, the Clarks faced a staggering $31,000 deficit—ten times Kenneth's teaching salary. The volunteer staff loaned the Clarks money, but the clinic's days were numbered.

Help arrived in the form of Marian Ascoli, a philanthropist

in her forties and daughter of the Sears tycoon who'd funded the doll test—Julius Rosenwald. Like her father, Ascoli was concerned about the plight of Black children, and after hearing of Northside's troubles, she asked a friend to size up the Clarks and their clinic. So Dr. Viola Bernard, a psychiatrist, invited them to her Fifth Avenue apartment. Because the doormen required Blacks to take the service entrance, Dr. Bernard met the Clarks in the lobby to spare them embarrassment. She was impressed that they had doctorates, founded an interracial clinic, and developed the doll test. But clearly they were novices at funding and managing an agency. The all-volunteer staff was another handicap. After additional meetings, Dr. Bernard told Ascoli that the Clarks and their clinic were unique and deserved help. Ascoli was excited and adopted Northside as her project.

Rapid change followed an infusion of cash from Ascoli. The clinic reincorporated under a new name, Northside Child Development Center, with an expanded, interracial board. The Black directors remained, but Jewish board members now controlled the clinic's future. Ascoli paid off the Clarks' loans, assumed the board presidency, and held meetings in her elegant Gramercy Park apartment. She found an attorney to gain the license and tax-exempt status the clinic needed to qualify for lucrative city contracts, and soon Northside was in the black with three-quarters of the staff, including the Clarks, paid a salary. Dr. Stella Chess, who had worked with Mamie at Riverdale Children's Association, was hired as the chief psychiatrist, though only part-time. And Victor Carter, one of Kenneth's Harlem school chums, became the supervisor of caseworkers. Mamie was named the full-time executive director and Kenneth her associate at half pay.

Still, Mamie remained the heart and soul of the clinic. She continued to meet with parents, soothe staff egos, arrange schedules, balance accounts, and keep the operation running six days a week. She typed her own reports and tested children as needed. Looking to the future, Ascoli sought new office space to serve more children. Morale soared, and employees felt they were part of a family working for the children of Harlem. "We all really felt that Northside was just such a contribution and the Clarks were both very special people," secretary Mildred Stevens recalled.[33]

With Northside on an even keel, the stress of daily life eased a bit for the Clarks. Undergoing psychoanalysis, Kenneth tried to budget his time better and not be so gruff and gloomy at home. He quit his research job for the CCI, and City College finally promoted him to assistant professor and gave him a raise.

At home, Kate and Hilton played ball in the apartment hallway and rushed to their father's arms when he returned from work each day. Kate rocked, cuddled, and read to her dolls, often a baby doll like those used for the doll test. "I was more attracted to the Black doll," she recalled.[34] To relax at home, Mamie did crossword puzzles and played the piano, preferring the classical pieces she'd learned as a girl—Mozart, Chopin—instead of the jazz tunes that she and Kenneth liked dancing to in the parlor.

Among the Black friends the Clarks entertained at home were

the Ellisons—Fanny and her husband, Ralph—who lived nearby in Washington Heights. He was writing one of the great novels of the century, *Invisible Man*, about Black identity. The Clarks also entertained the Alstons: Dr. Myra, a surgeon, and Charles, nicknamed "Spinky," a rising star in the art world who opened his studio to Northside children and donated artworks to the clinic. Other close friends were Wenonah and Dr. Arthur Logan, ardent supporters of civil rights and Northside, and Louise Moseley, a model, and Dr. John Moseley, the radiologist who watched baseball games on television with Kenneth and Hilton. Hylan Lewis, the best man at the Clarks' wedding but now divorced from Leighla, remained an inseparable friend.

On weekends, Kenneth cracked jokes, told stories, and discussed the day's issues over cocktails with friends. He was the happy-go-lucky guy who invited friends for dinner without clearing it with Mamie. He'd grab her in front of guests, pinch her, and nuzzle her neck. "Haven't I got a lovely wife?" he'd say.[35] Mamie would blush, squirm in his arms, and say, "Oh, Kenneth," in her soft, singsongy voice. Dr. Moseley recalled, "He was always praising her, saying how wonderful she was, how beautiful she was."

On weekdays, a hired cook made the family meals, but Mamie was the chef on weekends, with roast of lamb or chicken among her favorites. "Her cooking was nothing special," family friend Billie Allen recalled.[36] "I don't think she cared." Kenneth drank steadily with friends and got jollier as the night proceeded, but Mamie abstained till the dishes were done, and then she made up for lost time. The more she drank, the quieter she got.

The Clarks often took their children on urban excursions. A favored haunt was the Cloisters Museum in Fort Tryon Park with art treasures going back to the twelfth century. The family often visited the Lionel Train store, where Hilton admired the model trains swishing up hills, through tunnels, and over bridges. The Clarks often ate near Broadway at the Le Petit Paris where Kate and Mamie ordered the fried scallops.

Closer to home, they'd walk down their street and around the corner to the St. Nicholas Avenue building where Kenneth's mother and her two sisters, Ruth and Iris, lived in separate apartments. The sisters from Panama were earthy, working-class gals who toiled in the garment district, brought food to cook at Miriam Clark's home, and gossiped about the men in their lives—in Spanish so their beaus present were none the wiser. Quiet, reserved Mamie seldom joined in the hilarity. Kate recalled an awkward distance between her mother and the exuberant Clark sisters. "My grandmother probably thought my mother was a little bit precious."[37]

To the horror of Kenneth's mother, he and Mamie were agnostics who never sent their kids to church. Miriam gave the children Bibles and brought them to church on Sundays whenever they'd stayed overnight. Mamie enjoyed listening Sundays to the Mormon Tabernacle Choir on the radio, but Kenneth did not. "No, there was not much of a spiritual side to him at all," son Hilton recalled.[38] Kenneth served politics with the family meals and loved holding forth. Mamie did not, though their political views jibed. Both registered as members of the progressive American Labor Party and backed the most liberal candidates they could find on the ballot. "Kenneth used to surprise me sometimes," Dr. Moseley recalled.[39] "He could be militant and radical, but he could also be conservative."

The Clarks chose private, integrated schooling for their children and avoided Harlem's public schools, which were segregated and in shambles. "You wouldn't think of sending your kids to the schools in Harlem," Moseley recalled.[40] Hilton attended a preschool near Northside, and Kate went to the integrated New Lincoln School, a bastion of progressive education. Kenneth was a founder and served on its board. Most New Lincoln parents were white, liberal, and prosperous, and some pupils arrived in limousines. On their way to work in the morning, the Clarks dropped off Kate, and Kenneth sometimes returned afterward, popping into the classroom to watch quietly. "All of a sudden, I'd realize he was in a corner and observing the class. I didn't mind," teacher Russia Luca Hughes recalled.[41] "He liked children."

Kenneth was essentially a pacifist, and unlike many fathers of the time, he never taught his son how to box. The Clarks disliked corporal punishment, but Kenneth strayed from the principle, sometimes with a belt. "He would usually do it when he was angry," Hilton recalled.[42] Kate added, "It hurt. I would cry a lot."[43] Once the school year ended, the Clarks drove to Arkansas, where the children stayed with the Phippses for weeks at a time. The kids loved Hot Springs, visiting their granddaddy at the Pythian Hotel, where they marveled at the ancient switchboard and the deep tubs upstairs in the bathhouse. They found other kids to play with and sensed the resentment for the Phippses' high social status—nothing new to their mother. Whenever they saw movies at a segregated theater downtown, Kate and Hilton had to sit in the Black balcony, just as

Mamie had done years before, and Hilton recalled, "I enjoyed being with the colored folks and where they were."[44]

Together again in New York, the family hopped into the car and headed for Lake Placid for summer fun in the Adirondack Mountains. They stayed with friends in a Black inn on McKinley Street, where Mrs. Durant, the proprietor, served family-style meals. The Clarks couldn't dine at the high-toned Lake Placid Club, which banned Blacks and Jewish persons. Obsessed with work, Kenneth always grumped about all the packing and the long drive for the trip, but once he arrived, he enjoyed the fresh mountain air. "My mother was dedicated to seeing that we had activities and that we were having fun," Kate recalled.[45] "And meanwhile my father's grumbling and carrying on."

In the fall of 1948, Kenneth decided to end his therapy sessions. "I believe that I altered appreciably my anxiety and frustration threshold," he wrote Dr. Karush.[46] "I am finding a great deal of pleasure in my relations with my wife and children." Kenneth had much to be thankful for: a wonderful wife, two healthy children, a pleasant home, and a job he loved. And yet something in his work life was missing.

SEVEN
THE NAACP COMES KNOCKING

Other things being equal, the [racially] mixed school
is the more natural, broader basis for the education of all youth. It gives wider contacts; it inspires
greater self-confidence; and suppresses the inferiority
complex.

—W. E. B. DU BOIS[1]

In the fall of 1949, a white reporter went looking for the Clarks'
new offices near Spanish Harlem and Central Park. Finding their
eight-story building on West 110th Street, he took the elevator to the
sixth floor and stepped into Northside Center with its big windows
overlooking the treetops of Central Park. He was Wambly Bald of
the liberal *New York Post*. Showing him around, the Clarks pointed
out thirteen rooms in bright colors and said they used to work in a
tiny basement office with no space for a private talk with parents.

Now they had an office of their own with a soundproof partition they rolled between their desks for privacy. In the waiting area were easy chairs and a receptionist who greeted guests by name. The new Northside was a sunny haven for troubled children in Harlem.

Mamie recalled the center's earliest days. "It was a real struggle until we got help from foundations and private contributions," she said, singling out philanthropist Marion Ascoli for praise.[2] Bald found willowy, buttery-voiced Mamie most fetching and got a kick out of Kenneth's comical banter. Kenneth said Mamie worked too hard and smoked too much. "He smokes as much as I do," she jabbed back. "About a pack and a half, at least."

Any other bad habits? the reporter asked.

"No," Mamie deadpanned. "That's why I married him." But Kenneth was often away nights speaking to civic groups, she added. "And we have so little home life as it is."

After visiting the Clarks at home, Bald considered how different they were: Kenneth so jocular, Mamie so guarded with strangers. "She is quite friendly to the few persons of her selection, and reserved and polite to the rest."

It was a new day for the Clarks and their clinic. When it first opened three years before with a volunteer staff, it served just sixty-four children a year. Now, with salaried professionals and extra space, Northside served three hundred kids and their parents. Near the prosperous Upper East Side and some of Harlem's grittiest streets, the clinic's location was ideal for attracting an integrated clientele. Yet Clara Rabinowitz, a white therapist, once told Mamie that Northside should be a Black clinic. "This is an interracial clinic," Mamie said firmly.[3] In the coming year, Blacks would account for 63 percent of Northside's children; whites, 22 percent; Puerto Ricans, 13 percent; and Chinese, 2 percent. Ascoli's largesse had made it all possible; still, Northside faced a deficit, and the paychecks for its staff often arrived late.

No one got rich at Northside. Seven part-time psychiatrists received little more than an honorarium for their work. "It was not a paying job," recalled Rutherford Stevens, a Black psychiatrist.[4] Staffers could find more money elsewhere but not the friends or sense of accomplishment they gained at Northside. "It was 'our' place," Rabinowitz said.[5] Still, it haunted the staff that so many kids had to be turned away or kept on a long waiting list. The Clarks wanted to keep Northside small and efficient, but they also hoped that other clinics would emerge and theirs could serve as a model.

To help pay the bills, Mamie held fundraisers like the annual Queen of Clubs Ball. "They would have these showgirls sell tickets to the ball," daughter Kate recalled, "and the one who sold the most tickets would become the Queen of Clubs."[6] Ruby Richards, girlfriend of boxing champ Joe Louis, the Clarks' neighbor, became the first queen. There were raffles, art auctions, and Broadway theater benefits as well. Foundation grants kept the lights on as the budget neared $100,000. A new contract with the city Youth Board was a major leap forward. But Northside was not about balance sheets; it was about kids, Mamie reminded her staff. "And no matter how fancy the talk got or how many tangents we went off on, she always got everybody back to whether the children were being served and what was the best way to serve them," board member Joanne Stern recalled.[7]

One Northside client was Jane, seven years old and Black. She was anxious, forgetful, and confused about her identity. Jane had lived in three different foster homes, and each time, she was given different surnames and told to call the other kids sister or brother. Her behavior ranged from hostile to buffoonish. Another client was Edward, age eight, who didn't read or play with others. From a sharecropping family terrorized in the South, he so feared his white teacher he seldom asked to use the toilet and sometimes wet himself. A number of the children were delinquents, twelve-year-old Arnold among them. Arrested for burglary, theft of a car and a pistol, he belonged to a Black gang. Kenneth wrote about these children in a *Psychiatric Quarterly* article he published with Northside psychiatrists Stella Chess and Alexander Thomas, a married white couple. The article said that a therapist might conclude that all three kids had psychopathic personalities, but that Northside's integrated staff was less likely to make such an error: "It has become the custom never to make a diagnosis unless some member of the staff is present who is familiar with the [child's] particular cultural background."[8]

Northside, however, was not all serenity and harmony. The Clarks had their differences with board president Ascoli but negotiated them tactfully. Ascoli faulted Kenneth, a part-timer swamped with outside obligations, for being absent too often—a fair criticism. But when Ascoli called for merging Northside with a larger agency, the Clarks bridled. They'd worked too hard to hand over the clinic and its children to a bureaucracy. Kenneth said Northside needed time to evolve, that it was shooting its roots deep into Harlem, and that two new clinics—one on Long Island and another in New

Jersey—were modeled on Northside. Ascoli backed off but asked for a new definition of Northside's goals.

Meanwhile, morale surged at Northside. Mamie put gifts for the kids under the Christmas tree, and staff parties were held at Ascoli's home and Dr. Chess's in Riverdale. Never one to bark out orders, Mamie used persistent, friendly persuasion to get what she wanted. Beginning a negative evaluation with caseworker Cathy Lombard, Mamie said in a soft voice, "Cathy, I'm sorry we have to get together like this, but your records are in terrible shape, awful. What are we going to do about it? Because I know you can do better."[9] Lombard said the criticism was fair.

Not one to just sit in the office and supervise, Mamie took on tasks from typing to tutoring when others were too busy. She saw to it that bills were paid, quarrels were resolved, and parents and board members were content. She was often the first one in the clinic each morning and the last to leave at night. Harlem's social ills arrived daily at her desk and took a toll on Mamie, who was prone to bouts of anxiety. "She ground her teeth a lot during the day at the dinner table or any time she was sitting," Kate recalled.[10] "You could hear it. It was an awful sound." Mamie kept tranquilizers in her medicine cabinet.

Kenneth arrived at Northside in the afternoon after his City College classes. He padded about in his soft-soled shoes with paperwork in hand, chain-smoking and joking with caseworkers or snatching a morsel from their lunches. Northside was no casual commitment. Kenneth seldom missed a board meeting, and while Mamie took center stage, he spoke up when sharp elbows were needed. "She didn't like to make waves," Dr. Chess said of Mamie.[11] "Kenneth was great at making waves." Northside's new offices were home base for their activism in Harlem. Kenneth drew on his extensive contacts to bring talent, publicity, and funds to Northside. He recruited friends, colleagues, and students as volunteers, and mental health professionals joined other experts in touring the offices. Only the staff tested or treated the kids; no one, not even the Clarks, used them in experiments.

Just months after Northside settled in its new offices, the building's chief occupant, a community center, moved out. With office space scarce and costly, the Clarks feared that Northside might have to move again or close. Fortunately, the New Lincoln School acquired the building and welcomed the clinic to remain. Kenneth, who served on the private school's board, played a key role in the deal, which included a fringe benefit: both Kate and Hilton could go to school now in the same building where their parents worked. For a time anyway.

With Northside secure in its new home, Mamie was looking to buy a house. The refrigerator in the apartment was on the blink again, and she had a devil of a time getting the superintendent to replace it. She was tired of 555 Edgecombe, where residents complained of falling plaster, heatless days, and a lack of hot water. Kenneth did not want to leave Harlem, but Mamie wanted a house with a garden, yard, and leafy neighborhood for her children like the one she had in Hot Springs. Whenever her parents visited, they looked askance at her cramped apartment. Daughter Kate recalled, "I think she bought into the idea that my father was not quite up to the standard for her parents."[12]

Mamie also wanted good schools for her children. The experimental New Lincoln School was a bit loosey-goosey for her taste. The pupils were slow to gain reading skills, and the high school program was tiny. Furthermore, gangs, drug abuse, and urban decay were spreading through Harlem, and many Blacks with the resources, including Kenneth's mother and sister, were fleeing. Miriam Clark had remarried and moved with her husband into a single-family house in Queens that her married daughter, Beulah, had bought with her husband.

In the fall of 1950, Mamie contacted a shrewd Harlem real estate agent who helped her break through the segregated housing market. White agents and banks routinely rejected Black couples, and restrictive covenants, though illegal, still kept Blacks and Jewish persons out of suburban neighborhoods. But if you had cash and contacts, there were ways to escape the ghetto. Mamie's Black agent owned a house in a suburb fifteen miles north of the city where just the right home was for sale. Mamie liked the sound of it and persuaded Kenneth to look at it with her.

Arriving in Hastings-on-Hudson, they found a village of seventy-five hundred amid green hills that dipped down to the Hudson River. On the opposite shore loomed the gray cliffs of the New Jersey Palisades. Near Hastings's waterfront was a small depot for trains that shuttled commuters into the city each morning, and nearby were the Anaconda Wire and Cable factory and the wood-frame homes of its workers, many of them Irish and Italian Catholics. "We had the white ethnics, and we also had the uppity-ups on the hill," son Hilton Clark recalled.[13]

A minute's drive south along the river, away from the tiny business district, was a fork in the road. Turning left led to Pinecrest Drive, a steep road on a wooded hill with the tidy houses of professionals. The Clarks spotted a big, two-story house at 17 Pinecrest with a huge oak tree in the yard and a front porch overlooking the river and Palisades. On the first floor was a parlor with a stone fireplace, and upstairs were four bedrooms, two of them sharing a terrace that looked out on the Hudson River. To Mamie, it was perfect.

Moving was far from Kenneth's mind. He was swamped with work after accepting a research job with the Midcentury White House Conference on Children and Youth. Not just another consulting gig, the conference was authorized by President Truman to examine the mental health of the nation's children. Drs. Alain Locke of Howard and Otto Klineberg of Columbia, both advisers to the conference, had nominated Kenneth to write a meticulously researched report about the effects of prejudice on children. Kenneth, in turn, tapped Mamie to organize a team of expert advisers for the project and prepare additional reports at Northside. The Clarks' lives were taking a sharp turn that would nudge the course of history.

Facing a four-month deadline, Kenneth hunkered down and threw everything he had into the White House project. He rejected requests for speeches and articles and took a summer's leave from

Northside Center. Scouring libraries and asking colleagues for tips, he uncovered a trove of material about the effects of bigotry on minority youngsters, including Jewish persons, Hispanics, and Indigenous people. He drew on his and Mamie's doll test data and similar findings in doll studies done by white researchers Marian Radke, Helen Trager, and Mary Ellen Goodman. Most of the data focused on self-esteem and awareness of racial differences, and Kenneth was surprised to learn that the majority of experts believed, as he did, that prejudice marred the human personality. Mamie suggested changes in his early drafts before others could pounce on his missteps. "My mother was a practitioner, but she was very intellectual," daughter Kate recalled.[14] "In fact, she stimulated my father."

Early in September, before returning to City College, Kenneth mailed the first chunk of his manuscript to Ruth Kotinsky of the fact-finding staff in Washington. "Blood, Sweat and Tears, gallons of each mixed well with profanity have resulted in your being able to get this in its present very rough form," he wrote, promising the rest in two weeks.[15] But the revisions that his advisory committee wanted required more time, and the American Jewish Committee (AJC), Kenneth's sponsor, paid him extra to work through the fall. One sticking point was his statement that prejudice was as American as the Declaration of Independence. This would stir needless controversy, Klineberg and Locke warned him, and Kenneth conceded the point. His final draft, titled "The Effects of Prejudice and Discrimination on Personality Development," was on time and ran 203 pages. The AJC, his sponsor, lauded the paper as brilliant.

In the first week of December, six thousand experts packed the

National Guard Armory for the Midcentury White House Conference on Children and Youth. The AJC and other groups had booths in the crowded, noisy lobby. After President Truman's address, the experts in Kenneth's section got their first glimpse of his findings, which would generate controversy for decades. He revealed that most researchers on prejudice and children focused on Blacks and Jewish persons but other minority kids as well, including Italian American, Asian American, Indigenous, and migrant children. He reported that many suffered the harmful effects of bigotry, which varied from child to child:

> *Minority-group children are characteristically hypersensitive and anxious about their minority status, hostile toward the members of the dominant group, and other minority groups. They exhibit a generalized pattern of personality difficulties that seems to be associated with the humiliation to which they are subjected. Not that all of them are obviously emotionally maladjusted. The majority pulls through somehow or other, but with what burden of resentment and bitterness few know.*[16]

Citing a survey of five hundred social scientists, Kenneth stated that nearly all believed segregation harmed minorities caught in a vise between the nation's democratic ideals and its bigoted practices. "Feelings of inferiority and of not being wanted are induced by segregation," he wrote.[17] "Submissiveness, martyrdom, feelings of persecution, withdrawal tendencies, self-ambivalence, and aggression are likely to develop." Kenneth's conclusions about the damage to minority children, accepted with equanimity at the conference, would draw heavy fire from many Blacks a decade later. At the conference, his most outspoken critic was child psychologist Bruno Bettelheim, a Holocaust survivor who argued that there was no solid evidence that segregation damaged the personality.

Kenneth's critics often overlook two key points in his White House paper: one, that *most* Black children are not permanently scarred by the badge of inferiority assigned them by society, and two, that white children are also damaged by prejudice. Segregation corroded the moral values, dulled the sensitivities, and aroused the guilty feelings of these children.

Kenneth the activist went well beyond presenting a scholarly paper. He organized a group of twenty experts at the conference to call for a series of hard-hitting reforms, including an end to segregation, especially in schools, and a boycott on all conferences in Washington until it desegregated its public facilities. With a large Southern contingent in the hall, his proposals made little headway. Still, he left town with a spring in his step. "I must confess," he wrote to a journalist, "that even my hopes have been raised somewhat by events of the past few weeks."[18]

With Kenneth down in Washington, Mamie signed the papers at the closing for their house in Hastings. In a stressful period for both, she'd been his adviser, editor, and emotional anchor. She'd kept home and family intact, as well as Northside, in his absence.

Back in New York before the holidays, Kenneth had his hands full teaching, working again at Northside, and gathering his belongings for the big move to Hastings. At age ten, daughter Kate was frantic and refusing to leave her Harlem friends. "I was angry," she recalled.[19] "When I saw the house, I thought it was dark, gruesome." Black newcomers were often harassed or besieged by white vandals in the suburbs, and the Clarks were anxious. One wintry night, there was a knock on their door, and it opened to a group of white neighbors bursting into song. Seeing smiles on the Christmas carolers' faces set the whole family at ease.

Unlike many in Hastings, the Clarks seldom took the train into Manhattan. Kenneth loved to drive, and each morning, he piloted his big, humpbacked '48 Mercury down the parkway and into Harlem. He and Mamie talked, smoked, and listened to the news on the radio as the hills of Westchester County slipped by. Once they reached Northside Center, Kenneth pulled up to the curb, kissed Mamie goodbye, and drove on to City College.

Back at the clinic one afternoon, Kenneth got a phone call from Robert Carter, a lawyer with the NAACP's Legal Defense and Education Fund. As chief deputy to attorney Thurgood Marshall, Carter asked to meet Kenneth. A tall, thin, brown-skinned man with a widow's peak in his close-cropped hair, Carter was raised in West Orange, New Jersey, where he and other Black students were allowed in the school pool only on Fridays. Then it was drained, scrubbed, and refilled for the white students' uncontaminated use on Monday. Meeting Kenneth at Northside, Carter said the NAACP needed a social science consultant for an all-out attack on school segregation in the courts. Carter said Dr.

Klineberg had recommended Kenneth to present evidence that segregation inflicted damage on Black students—psychological damage, not physical harm. Could Kenneth help? Handing over his White House paper, Kenneth told Carter to judge for himself.

Days later, Carter called back. "This couldn't have been better if it had been done for us," he said of Kenneth's paper.[20] Carter invited him to the NAACP offices to meet with Thurgood Marshall and his staff.

Kenneth must have felt like a fish out of water at the NAACP's headquarters in midtown Manhattan. He'd long regarded the organization as hopelessly conservative. Marshall and his lawyers told Kenneth they needed a social scientist's help in preparing legal briefs, testifying in court, and locating other experts to testify. All this without pay, and could he start yesterday? The lawyers also wanted to know if Kenneth's research proved that school segregation, in and of itself, harmed the minds of Black pupils. No, Kenneth said, the data suggested that discrimination in general was harmful, but not segregated schooling alone—a key issue in the court skirmishes ahead. When he learned that the first in a series of trials was going to federal court in South Carolina in just a few weeks, he was thrilled. At thirty-six, this was his chance to strike a major blow for racial justice. So Kenneth agreed to help, not realizing it meant years of unpaid toil, and with no guarantee of victory.

But Marshall and his lawyers made it clear that they'd already fought and won battles in the U.S. Supreme Court against segregated public universities and law schools. Their new target was states that either allowed or required children to attend all-Black schools. This time, Marshall would attack the very idea of segregated education, not just unequal school facilities, by targeting the Supreme Court's pivotal 1896 ruling in *Plessy v. Ferguson*, which declared separate-but-equal schools legal.

Plessy involved Homer Plessy, a Black man who sued after being forced to give up his seat in a white rail car in Louisiana. Ruling against him, the justices rejected the idea that segregation "stamps the colored race with a badge of inferiority."[21] Writing for the major-ity, Justice Henry Brown argued that if segregation made Blacks feel inferior, it was "solely because the colored race chooses to put that construction upon it."[22] That is, the sense of inferiority was only in their minds. But to the NAACP lawyers, this was the whole point: state-sanctioned school segregation burned into Black students' minds a sense they were unworthy of white schools, that they were born inferior. The lawyers needed Kenneth's help to document this damage. The NAACP's goal was to gain the integrated schooling that Blacks needed to rise in society so that other bastions of segregation would fall as well: segregated neighborhoods, hospitals, and public facilities like cafés, hotels, and stores—even the job market.

Attending the lawyers' meetings at night in the NAACP's cluttered, smoke-filled offices, Kenneth mastered their lingo and learned about the upcoming case in South Carolina, where Black parents from rural Clarendon County had sued the state because their kids had to walk miles to inferior schools each morning while white students rode buses to better schools. Kenneth also learned that the NAACP expected to lose the case in a Charleston trial but possibly win on appeal before the U.S. Supreme Court.

Kenneth asked social scientists he knew for help and watched the NAACP lawyers debate legal strategy as they prepared for the Charleston trial. Theirs was a rough-and-tumble style like nothing he'd ever seen at a faculty meeting. Professors prided themselves on a genteel exchange of ideas, but the lawyers got down and dirty. Some, especially William Coleman, ridiculed social science as no science at all. "Jesus Christ, those damned dolls! I thought it was a joke!" Coleman once said of the Clarks' doll test.[23] Kenneth took the criticism personally. "They really abused Kenneth on this," Carter recalled.[24] "So I had to protect Kenneth a lot from these people and hold his hand and so forth for a while until he got more or less used to the guys."

Carter, who had a keen interest in psychology, liked Kenneth and tried to convince him that all the roughhousing was just the lawyers' way of testing ideas before they drew fire in court. But another nonlawyer in the room, NAACP staff member June Shagaloff, sensed that professional snobbery was at the heart of the conflict. "Kenneth was an outsider," Shagaloff recalled.[25] "The lawyers didn't like the social sciences."

With time running out, Carter moved to silence the skeptics, arguing that data from medical science and the social sciences had been used in court cases for decades. "You've got anything else?"[26] Carter asked his colleagues. Serving as judge and jury over the debate, Thurgood Marshall sided with Carter and adopted the social science strategy.

Carter and Marshall had planned to fly to Charleston for the trial, but Kenneth feared airplanes and insisted on taking a train.

To stick close to their star witness, Carter and Marshall reluctantly agreed to board the same train with him in Manhattan. Meanwhile, Mamie worried about Kenneth's safety in the rural South. He had little experience in Dixie, but she knew it all too well. After packing for the trip, Kenneth left home one morning in May with his suitcase and four dolls—two brown, two white. Kate, who often played with the dolls, watched as her father walked out the door with them.

Kenneth boarded the train that afternoon with the two NAACP lawyers, and in the dining car, he watched as Black waiters treated Marshall like a prince. No stranger to rail travel, Marshall was famous for defending Blacks in the nation's segregated courtrooms. Some had been unfairly accused of rape, barred from voting, or forced to ride Jim Crow railcars. When the train stopped that night in Richmond, Virginia, Spottswood Robinson, another NAACP lawyer, hopped aboard and bunked with Carter in a Pullman sleeper. Meanwhile, Kenneth shared a compartment with Marshall. After taking off their suits and ties, the two men climbed into their berths and chatted a while. Marshall was his jocular self at first, reminiscing about his escapades in Southern courtrooms. He'd been cussed and chased by armed white men and dodged a lynching more than once. Known for his gallows humor, Marshall liked to joke about his trips below the Mason-Dixon line, which he called "the Smith-and-Wesson line."[27] At forty-three with a bulging waistline and bags under his eyes, Marshall said he was weary. "Yeah, I'm really tired of trying to save the white man's soul."[28] Turning to the task ahead, he reminded Kenneth about testing schoolchildren in rural Clarendon County. Marshall needed evidence that they'd been harmed by segregation.

Kenneth asked which of the NAACP lawyers would go with him into the countryside. None, Marshall said. Surprised, Kenneth wondered if Marshall was joking.

As the two men nodded off to sleep, their train swayed and clacked down the track, hurtling through the darkness deep into Dixie.

EIGHT

JIM CROW ON TRIAL

The only way to bring public opinion to action is for those whose race is suffering to cry aloud, and keep on crying aloud until something is done.

—IDA B. WELLS[1]

On the morning of May 24, 1951, Kenneth's train pulled into the station in Charleston, South Carolina. His bunkmate, Thurgood Marshall, stepped down onto the rail platform to join his fellow NAACP attorneys Robert Carter and Spottswood Robinson, a tall, skinny man from Virginia. Once Kenneth caught up with the lawyers, he panicked. "My dolls! My dolls!" he said.[2] "Where are my dolls?" He scurried off, and when he finally returned with his dolls, the lawyers gave him a good razzing.

Arriving at a rental home in a Black neighborhood, the lawyers set aside the garage and game room to prepare for the trial in federal court. Reporters from across the nation were coming to cover the case, *Briggs v. Elliott*, and the fate of school segregation in the state, perhaps the nation, weighed in the balance. Kenneth again asked Marshall if a lawyer would go with him to rural Clarendon County to test school-children. No, Marshall said, but someone who knew the terrain, which was dangerous, would drive him there. "Oh, come on now, you must be kidding," Kenneth said.[3] Marshall said he wasn't and handed Kenneth fifty dollars. In case of trouble, cash might work better than words.

When Eugene Montgomery, an NAACP organizer in his twenties, pulled up in a car, Kenneth put his dolls in the back and sat for the two-hour drive north along country roads. Montgomery told Kenneth about Clarendon County, population fifteen hundred, a dirt-poor community of mostly Black farmers who'd raised a ruckus by requesting a school bus for their children. Their kids walked up to nine miles a day to and from school. After white officials rejected the request, the Black parents bought an old bus and asked the school board for gas money. Again, the whites said no, and the parents contacted the NAACP, which sued to end segregated schools state-wide. The parents involved in the suit lost jobs, bank credit, and a market for their crops. Reverend J. A. DeLaine, the minister who led them, was fired from his teaching job, shot at, and arrested for returning fire on his white attackers. Reverend DeLaine's wife also lost her teaching job, and after terrorists stoned their church and burned down their house, the DeLaines fled the county.

Arriving in Summerton, Kenneth found a flyspeck of a town more flat than hilly with dingy storefronts and a cotton ginnery. Montgomery pulled up at the school district offices for Kenneth to meet Superintendent H. B. Betchman, who had a reputation as a nasty white supremacist. Under a federal court order, Betchman had to allow Kenneth to test Black pupils, but he didn't have to like it. Sounding more like a Klansman than a school official, Betchman said there was no way the Blacks could compete with white students and that he'd warned Montgomery once before to stay out of town. He didn't want to see the young man get hurt.

Still shaken by Betchman's threat when Montgomery pulled up at the Scott's Branch School, Kenneth saw a drab white schoolhouse with a scraggly lawn and bushes out front. The Black school faced a dirt road in a tiny Black neighborhood, and across the road lay the charred ruins of Reverend DeLaine's house. Kenneth learned that the school had just ten barren classrooms and two outhouses for hundreds of children in elementary and high school classes. The classrooms were heated by old coal stoves that Black parents paid to heat. There was no janitor, gym, auditorium, or lunchroom, although the white high school had all of these along with central heat, flush toilets, and water fountains.

Kenneth found a room and began testing sixteen Scott's Branch pupils ages six through nine. Showing them four baby dolls—two brown, two white—Kenneth told the first child, "Show me the doll that you like best or that you'd like to play with."[4] He offered the child crayons to color several drawings, including those of a girl and a boy. "Color him the color that you are." Once finished with the first pupil, Kenneth heard a stir in the hallway as two big Black men in overalls arrived with the next child, about age six, between them. Asked if they were his bodyguards, the men nodded to Kenneth, and he resumed his testing until the next stir in the hallway. This time, it was Superintendent Betchman to check on Kenneth, who was glad that two big men still guarded the door.

Once his testing was done for the day, Kenneth packed up his dolls and rode with Montgomery to a home across the county line where it was safer. The next morning, Friday, Kenneth returned to the Scott's Branch School and interviewed ten youngsters twelve to seventeen years old. He asked each one about race and segregated schools. After the interviews, Kenneth learned that Marshall wanted him safe in Charleston for the weekend. Kenneth was glad to go.

In Charleston, he picked up a brochure to learn about the mansions that white planters had built near the harbor with their profits from slave labor in the 1800s. Their homes allowed them to conduct business, enjoy a social life, and find suitable white spouses in town for their offspring. When South Carolina became the first state to leave the Union in 1861, the secession ordinance was signed in Charleston. And the first rounds of the Civil War were fired here as well in an attack on Fort Sumter. But the city's storied days were over. War, tropical storms, an earthquake, and the Depression had tarnished this pearl of a city. By the 1950s, its mansions were down at the heels. But sightseeing was not a priority; instead, Kenneth sat for hours with the lawyers and other witnesses as Marshall challenged his colleagues, rehearsing their courtroom maneuvers. The lawyers smoked, drank beer, and ate sandwiches while joking and arguing about how best to state their case. To Kenneth, they seemed happy warriors confident of victory. "He was bright, likeable, committed," white NAACP attorney Jack Greenberg said of Kenneth.[5] "Someone you'd really like."

Monday, May 28, was Memorial Day, but in South Carolina, which ignored the Yankee holiday, it was just another workday. The headline in the Charleston *News and Courier* proclaimed the day's top story: "South Carolina School System Goes on Trial Today."[6] Governor James Byrnes had vowed to close all public schools rather than integrate them. Arriving at the federal courthouse, Kenneth saw hundreds of Black people standing in line in the eighty-degree heat, inching forward along the sidewalk, up the courthouse steps, into the lobby, up another staircase, and through the double doors of dark pine that led to Judge J. Waties Waring's courtroom. One of three federal judges presiding over the case without a jury, Judge Waring was a Charleston native who lived a few minutes' walk from his courtroom. He had a thick crop of silver hair parted in the middle and was a pariah in town. He'd divorced his first wife, a Charleston native, to marry a liberal firebrand from up North who loathed segregation and made no secret of it. White folks griped that Waring had hired a Black bailiff, integrated his courtroom's seating, and favored Black plaintiffs. Attorneys Marshall and Carter knew that Waring was in their corner but not the other two judges: John J. Parker and George Bell Timmerman.

With every seat in the courtroom taken, most of them by Blacks, there was drama at the outset. Addressing the bench, defense attorney Robert Figg, arguably the state's best lawyer, conceded that Clarendon County's Black schools were inferior. There were reasons for this other than race, he claimed, and a new state sales tax would bring all Black schools up to par and spare the need for a trial. Startled, Thurgood Marshall rose and said this was irrelevant. His goal was to show how substandard the schools were—a violation of his clients' constitutional rights—and how school segregation itself was inequitable. The NAACP team was allowed to proceed.

Attorney Robert Carter began with witnesses from Kenneth's alma mater, Howard University. The professors of education showed how unequal Clarendon County's schools were. The system spent $179 per white pupil but only $43 for each Black child. Black pupils outnumbered whites nearly three to one, yet the Black schools were valued at less than $200,000 and the few white schools at nearly $700,000. The numbers, however, were not the core issue; the harm to students' minds was. So Carter had Kenneth, his star witness, take the stand.

Kenneth testified that he and Mamie had developed a test using brown and white dolls to gauge a Black child's sensitivity to race. The results over the years, along with research by others, had led him to conclude that segregation and prejudice marred the personality development of Black children. "The essence of this detrimental effect," Kenneth said, "is a confusion in the child's concept of his own self-esteem—basic feelings of inferiority, conflict, confusion in his self-image, resentment, hostility towards himself, hostility toward whites, intensification of sometimes a desire to resolve his basic conflict by sometimes escaping or withdrawing."[7] White students were victims too, Kenneth argued. They faced guilt feelings and moral confusion in a society that preached democracy but practiced racial segregation.

To document the harm to Black students, Kenneth testified that nearly two-thirds of the six- to nine-year-olds he'd tested at the Scott's Branch School preferred a white doll to one of their own race. And about two-thirds singled out a brown doll as the "bad" one. "This is consistent with previous results which we have obtained testing over three hundred children," Kenneth said, "and we interpret it to mean that the Negro child accepts as early as 6, 7, or 8 the negative stereotypes about his own group."[8]

For example, I had a young girl, a dark brown child of seven, who was so dark brown that she was almost black. When she was asked to color herself, she was one of the few children who picked a flesh color, pink, to color herself. When asked to color a little boy, the color she liked little boys to be, she looked all around the twenty-four crayons and picked up a white crayon and looked up at me with a shy smile and began to color. She said, "Well, this doesn't show." So, she pressed a little harder.[9]

In his cross-examination, Figg touched on a weak point in Kenneth's testimony, asking if the doll test proved that the Scott's Branch School harmed Black pupils. Kenneth waffled. "I was forced to the conclusion that they have definite disturbances and problems in their own self-esteems," he answered, "that they had feelings of inferiority that related to race."[10]

"Because they had attended the Scott's Branch School?" Figg repeated.

"No, because they perceived themselves in an inferior status— generally inferior."

Figg also got Kenneth to acknowledge that he'd tested each child alone in a room without witnesses, that he'd tested no whites and interviewed teenagers without giving them a standardized test. Figg could have pounced on other issues of test validity, such as the tiny sample of students or Kenneth's subjective interpretation of the test results. But Figg never raised these issues, nor did he produce a single social science witness.

The trial continued with testimony from white social scientists recommended by Kenneth. Among them was Helen Trager of Vassar, who'd followed the Clarks' doll test with one of her own. Trager described her study of 250 Philadelphia pupils of both races, ages five to eight. These kids, while playing with brown and white dolls made of plywood, were asked to dress them in either neat or shabby clothes, put them in neat or shabby dollhouses, and assign them well-paid or menial jobs. The white children assigned the worst clothing, housing, and jobs to the brown dolls, she said. Pupils of both races "perceived Negro as meaning that you are not liked by people, that you won't be asked to play, that you won't be allowed to do things that other children can do."[11]

A month after the trial in Charleston, the three-judge panel ruled against the NAACP and its Black plaintiffs. Writing for the majority, Judge Parker noted that seventeen states had required school segregation for most of the century: "It is a late day to say that such segregation is violative of fundamental constitutional rights."[12] Parker took a shot at the NAACP's social science strategy: "The members of the judiciary have no more right to read their ideas of sociology into the Constitution than their ideas of economics." In a blistering dissent, Judge Waring argued that the social scientists "showed beyond a doubt that the evils of segregation and color prejudice come from early training."[13] All pupils are harmed. "I am of the opinion," Waring continued, "that all of the legal guideposts, expert testimony, common sense, and reason point unerringly to the conclusion that the system of segregation in education adopted and practiced in the State of South Carolina must go and must go now."

Two days after the ruling in Charleston, NAACP attorney Carter headed for Kansas, a border state, for the *Brown v. Board of Education of Topeka* trial in federal court. He arrived in Topeka, the capital, to prepare the case with Jack Greenberg, a white, twenty-six-year-old colleague. Only 3.8 percent of Kansans were Black, but the state allowed Jim Crow schools, and the NAACP wanted them desegregated. With more than one hundred thousand residents, Topeka was only 8 percent Black, yet the hotels, restaurants, and movie theaters remained segregated. News about Black citizens in the *Topeka Daily Capital* was as rare as a statesman in the legislature.

Under state law, large school districts like Topeka's could segregate their elementary schools, and most did. Topeka's white pupils walked to neighborhood grade schools each morning and returned home for lunch. Barred from those schools, Black children had to walk many blocks before hopping onto a school bus that shuttled them to distant Black schools without lunchrooms. At Topeka High School, segregation was intramural, with separate clubs, sports, and student government for the Black students.

Oliver Brown had taken all this in stride until it endangered Linda, his oldest daughter. Brown was a Black welder, war veteran, and assistant pastor living near a dangerous railroad switching yard. Linda had to cross that rail yard every morning on her way to a bus that brought her to a Black school. Brown tried to enroll Linda in a white school close by, but he was turned away. So he asked NAACP lawyers for help, and his surname topped the list of parents who joined in a federal lawsuit.

Busy with other cases, Thurgood Marshall let Carter and Greenberg handle the Topeka trial with two local lawyers. To cut travel costs, Greenberg had to rely on expert witnesses from the region. That meant Kenneth could not testify, but he named social scientists who could. As in Charleston, three federal judges sat for the opening arguments in Topeka without a jury, and most people in the courtroom were Black. Early in the trial, Brown described his daughter's precarious morning walk through the rail yard without a crossing guard. He testified that she had to wait in the rain, sleet, or snow for her bus to arrive and then wait again for her Black school to open its doors: "Well, there is nothing she can do except stand out and clap her hands to keep them warm or jump up and down."[14]

To counter the myth that Blacks were inherently dull and needed separate schools, Horace B. English, an Ohio expert in human intelligence, testified there was no innate difference in IQ between Blacks and whites. Pupils of both races ranked at the top, middle, and bottom of the IQ spectrum. "The best IQ on record is that of a Negro girl who has no white blood as far as that can be told at all," English testified, "but right after this child are four white children."[15]

Of the half-dozen experts who took the stand, white psychologist Louisa Holt of the University of Kansas was the most eloquent.

She had a child in a Topeka school and testified that segregation was harmful because it gave legal sanction to the idea of Black inferiority: "A sense of inferiority must always affect one's motivation for learning since it affects the feeling one has of one's self as a person, as a personality."[16] Black pupils, she said, often revealed apathy and a fatalistic acceptance of their lot—the younger the child, the deeper and more lasting the trauma.

As in Charleston, the defense attorneys in Topeka had no social science witnesses and did little to counter the expert testimony from the other side. A month after the trial, Judge Walter Huxman delivered a ruling favorable to the NAACP:

> *Segregation of white and colored children in public schools has a detrimental effect upon the colored children... A sense of inferiority affects the motivation of a child to learn. Segregation with the sanction of law, therefore, has a tendency to retard the educational and mental development of negro children and to deprive them of some of the benefits they would receive in a racially integrated school system.*[17]

Nonetheless, the court in Topeka lacked the authority to strike down school segregation statewide and had to leave that task to the U.S. Supreme Court.

With summer school over and the fall term at City College yet to begin, Kenneth traveled to another border state, Delaware, targeted by the NAACP. He arrived in Wilmington, the state's biggest city, to interview dozens of teenagers from Howard High, the only academic high school for Blacks in the state. Just a whistle stop from Philadelphia, Wilmington was a city of 110,000, the state's financial center, and a tax haven for corporations in a state segregated by law. Not only its schools but even the orphanages and nursing homes were segregated. Theaters, hotels, and Catholic schools, however, were beginning to admit Blacks.

From the outside, Howard High looked like any other two-story high school with brick walls and concrete columns out front, but it was tucked into a Black neighborhood of shabby row houses. The rigorous courses that white schools offered were seldom taught at Howard High, and students complained that it was crowded, with classes packed into the woodshop and cafeteria. The teenagers had to eat standing up at a counter that wrapped around the cafeteria. Many came from Claymont, New Castle, and other towns that barred Blacks from their white high schools. They had to live with relatives in Wilmington or pay to ride a bus sixty miles a day to attend Howard High. Whenever Black parents tried to register their kids at a white school near home, they were turned away. "It's not right," Ethel B., fifteen, told Kenneth in an interview with him.[18] "We're all God's people." Richard D., also fifteen, said that Black students were ashamed of their second-rate schools, and as for whites, "No doubt about it, they are the superior race in the country."[19] To Kenneth, comments like these showed that segregation scarred Black students. Having little contact with whites, they knew little of white faults and complained that their Black classmates were loud and unruly, as if white students never were. Similarly, these teenagers had a low opinion of Black adults. "They fuss on the street and drink all the time," Clyde C. told Kenneth.[20] "You don't see white people doin' that."

Before leaving town, Kenneth gave the doll test to a small group of grade-school pupils, and the results were similar to those from his prior testing. Little Glen R., brown-skinned and nearly seven, chose a white doll as the best one. "'Cause he white," he said, smiling.[21] He also picked a white doll as the one with a nice color. "'Cause he white," he repeated.

Once finished with the testing, Kenneth returned to New York. But on October 22, he was back in Wilmington for the Delaware trial combining two cases: one involving Howard High students and the other a group of grade-school pupils. The trial opened in state Chancery Court—again without a jury—but this time with only one judge, Chancellor Collins Seitz, the state's top-ranked jurist. At thirty-seven, Seitz was new in the job and had recently ruled in favor of desegregating the all-white University of Delaware. This was a big victory for lawyers Jack Greenberg and Louis Redding, a Harvard Law graduate and the first Black admitted to the bar in Delaware. Their prospects for another victory in Seitz's courtroom looked good.

With Kenneth's help, Greenberg had lined up fourteen expert witnesses, including educators who testified that Delaware's Black schools, compared with its white schools, were poorly funded and ill equipped. Among the other experts who testified was Fredric Wertham, a white psychiatrist with a Viennese accent who ran a part-time clinic of his own in Harlem. Wertham said that white students from Delaware revealed a false sense of superiority in their interviews with him, and the Black students he questioned regarded their deficient Black schools as a form of punishment. No matter how good their facilities might be, Wertham argued, segregated schools marred the development of children: "In other words, if I may express it graphically, if the state of Delaware would employ Professor Einstein to teach physics in marble halls to these children, I would still say everything I have said goes."[22]

Called to the stand, Kenneth described his interviews with Howard High students: "I think we have clear-cut evidence of rather deep damage to the self-esteem of these youngsters, a feeling of inferiority, a feeling of inadequacy—evidence which was further supported by the kind of things which the youngsters said: 'I suppose we do act kind of bad. We don't act like white people.'"[23] Three out of four grade-school pupils who took the doll test had chosen a brown doll when asked which doll was bad. Kenneth said of segregation, "It sets up in them self doubt where the evidence suggests that from a very early age—5 or 6 or 7—Negro children begin to learn to expect from the society some of the society's rejection of them, so that they begin to reject themselves and feel that certain kinds of things are not for them because they are brown."

In his ruling, Chancellor Seitz held that Black schools were unequal and that state-imposed segregation harmed the health and education of Black students. He ordered that the Black plaintiffs in the two cases at hand be admitted at once to white schools. "To do otherwise is to say to such a plaintiff: 'Yes, your Constitutional rights are being invaded, but be patient, we will see whether in time they are still being violated.'"[24] Nonetheless, Seitz lacked the power of the U.S. Supreme Court to strike down school segregation statewide. Even so, his ruling, in combination with Topeka's, showed that Kenneth's social science principles were in the mainstream of informed opinion and might prevail in the U.S. Supreme Court.

Fed up with the shabby state of her Black school in Farmville, Virginia, sixteen-year-old Barbara Johns stood on the stage and called for a student strike. Students chanted, "Two bits—four bits—six bits a dollar—all for this strike stand up and holler."[25] Barbara yanked off a shoe, slammed it on a bench, and ordered her schoolmates to walk out. They emptied the auditorium and picketed the school grounds. Their strike touched off a battle royal over school segregation that would draw both of the Clarks to Virginia.

Barbara John's school, Moton High, was a small brick building in a weedy field along a highway. Named for Robert Russa Moton, successor to Booker T. Washington at Tuskegee Institute, the school had eight rooms for 180 students. After the enrollment soared to 450, carpenters slapped together three outbuildings covered in tar paper to serve as new classrooms. "The shacks," students called them, with leaky roofs and old stoves for heat. When hot coals landed on the floor, the closest student had to scoop them up and toss them back into the fire. The shacks had no toilets or drinking water, and the main building had no gym, cafeteria, lockers, or science lab. Moton High was so crowded that classes were taught in a school bus.

All-white Farmville High, on the other hand, was a tidy,

two-story, Colonial-style building with more rigorous courses and better-paid teachers—plus an infirmary, gym, machine shop, and locker rooms. When Barbara heard about the machine shop, she was furious. She plotted with other students to force white officials to build a new school. "Even though we were only high school students, we planned this thing to a gnat's eyebrow," recalled student leader John Stokes.[26]

When NAACP lawyers Spottswood Robinson and Oliver Hill arrived to help, they had no illusions. Near the geographic center of the state, Farmville lay in Virginia's ultraconservative Southside region, where slaves had been flogged to raise tobacco. Farmville was a market town, an agricultural center, the seat of Prince Edward County, which was 60 percent white and 40 percent Black. Most residents were farmers who lacked plumbing, electricity, or phone service, and white officials were unswerving segregationists. To resolve the school crisis, lawyers Robinson and Hill tried to get the strikers back into classes, but they said no. When the lawyers warned that the NAACP would never push for a new segregated school, the students agreed to integrate. Moved by their zeal and parental support, Robinson and Hill filed a federal lawsuit, *Davis v. County School Board of Prince Edward County*. The school board fired Moton High's principal and a teacher, and as racial tensions boiled, Black farmers lost a market for their crops, and banks denied them loans. Some who faced threats armed themselves, and Barbara Johns fled to safety and a new life with relatives in Alabama.

Unlike in the other states sued by the NAACP, Virginia officials fought back by providing research and legal aid to defend their Jim

Crow schools. Forewarned about Kenneth and the doll test, the state's attorneys recruited a prominent segregationist as their star witness: Dr. Henry Garrett, the psychologist and Virginia native who'd taught Kenneth and Mamie at Columbia. "They were out to cut our throats—and we, theirs," NAACP attorney Carter recalled.[27] Feeling the pressure, he and Kenneth belatedly called upon Mamie to fly down to counter Garrett's testimony in court.

On February 25, 1952, more than two hundred people, many of them Black, packed a federal courtroom in Richmond, capital of the old Confederacy, to witness the all-out battle. The trial opened as three federal judges, without a jury, took their seats. At the NAACP counsels' table were Black attorneys Carter, Robinson, and Hill as well as Kenneth to advise them during cross-examinations. At the opposite table were three white attorneys: Archibald Robertson, one of the state's leading lawyers; his law partner T. Justin Moore; and state Attorney General James Lindsay Almond Jr. As in all the earlier trials, witnesses for the NAACP described the shabby facilities at the Black schools in question, but this time, the white defense attorneys doubled down and denied they were significantly different from the white schools.

Taking the stand again as Carter's star witness, Kenneth gave his most eloquent testimony to date. "Segregation is like a mist," he told the court, "like a wall, which society erects, of stone and steel—psychological stone and steel—constantly telling them they are inferior and constantly telling them that they cannot escape prejudice."[28] Black students have to waste energy coping with a racial stigma, he said—energy better spent on their studies. Describing interviews he'd conducted with Moton High students, Kenneth said they all held a negative view of their school—its freezing classrooms, leaky roofs, and the like. None of them found any fault with all-white Farmville High—a distortion of reality likely due to segregation, Kenneth suggested, because Black students had no contact with white schools.

Cross-examining him, attorney Moore pandered to segregationists by questioning Kenneth's heritage. "You appear to be of a rather light color—what percentage, as near as you can tell us, are you white and what percentage some other?" Moore asked.[29]

"I haven't the slightest idea," Kenneth replied, bristling. "What do you mean by 'percentage'?"

"I mean are you half-white, or half-colored, and half Panamanian, or what?"

Switching the subject, Moore suggested that Kenneth might have coached the Moton High students before interviewing them. Kenneth denied this, and Moore asked him to simulate an interview. Kenneth complied by reenacting his questions for a typical student, and Moore responded by making a fool's face and pretending to be a dull Black student struggling for the answers. The snickers of whites rippled across the courtroom.

On the trial's final day, sixty-year-old Dr. Henry Garrett, Moore's star witness, took the stand, a coup for the defense team, because Garrett was a Virginian who'd served as both the president of the prestigious American Psychological Association and psychology department chair at Columbia. To undermine the doll test, Moore asked Garrett if psychological testing had reached the stage where it could assess the impact of segregation upon the human personality. "I think it is very doubtful," Garrett said, because psychology was a new science.[30] Did segregated schools harm students? This need not be the case, Garrett answered: "Boys and girls are taught in separate schools, Catholic children in parochial schools, Jewish children in Hebrew schools."[31] To avoid conflict, Garrett said, Virginia's adolescents were better taught in segregated high schools.

So Carter asked Garrett if the Clarks, his former students, had gotten along well at Columbia. "Very well indeed," Garrett had to acknowledge.[32] Carter challenged Garrett on his dim view of the doll test by asking about the value of projective tests in general. Garrett argued that they were hard to administer. "It requires a skilled person," and the results "are always subjective and subject to considerable doubt."[33] Pressed by Carter, Garrett had to admit that experts of Kenneth's caliber were competent to give such tests. And since Garrett had minimized the value of Kenneth's tests and interviews, Carter read passages from a textbook Garrett had written that spoke glowingly of these methods. Under relentless cross-examination, Garrett had to concede that projective tests like the Clarks' could help assess the impact of segregation on students.

Carter struck a rich vein when he asked Garrett whether segregation was detrimental to the individual. "It is a large question," Garrett began.[34] "In general, wherever a person is cut off from the main body of society or a group, if he is put in a position that stigmatizes him and makes him feel inferior, I would say yes, it is detrimental and deleterious to him." Asked if he knew of segregated schooling anywhere that left no stigma, Garrett offered a remarkable reply:

*I think, in the high schools of Virginia, if the Negro child
had equal facilities, his own teachers, his own friends and
a good feeling, he would be more likely to develop pride in
himself as a Negro, potentialities, his sense of duty, his sense
of art, his sense of histrionics… I think it would be poetic
justice. They would develop their sense of dramatic art, and
music, which they seem to have a talent for—athletics—and
they would say, "We prefer to remain as a Negro group."*[35]

Listening closely, Kenneth was stunned by Dr. Garrett's racist testimony.

Mamie took the stand to counter Garrett's views. After she stated her name in a soft, low voice, Judge Armistead M. Dobie interrupted, "Will you talk a little bit louder, please?"[36] Mamie was nervous and promised to try. She described her training, her job at Northside, and the studies of Black pupils she'd done with Kenneth. State Attorney General Almond interrupted and told Judge Dobie that the NAACP lawyers should not rake over the same ground already covered in the trial. It was Friday, and after five days in court, the white attorneys wanted the trial over. Judge Dobie promised it wouldn't last much longer.

Forced to hurry and pledging not to cover the same ground, Carter asked Mamie if there was truth to Garrett's view that university students are able to thrive at integrated schools but teenagers are not. "In my opinion, I would say there is absolutely no basis for saying that it is more difficult to adjust at the high school level," Mamie said.[37] "I think it has been demonstrated that when segregation laws are broken down at the graduate level, integration can take place," and this would be true as well for public schools. "I think that process," she added, "is a gradual one. It just does not happen on the last day of high school, it happens over a period of years."

Mamie was compelled to finish after only a few minutes of testimony, but at thirty-four, she was a bright, beautiful, living refutation of Garrett's outmoded racial theories. To hurry the trial along, defense attorney Moore declined to cross-examine her. There was brief testimony from just one more witness, and the Richmond trial was over. During a break in the proceedings, Kenneth had encountered Garrett outside the courtroom. Garrett seemed embarrassed and said that he was only trying to gain equal school facilities for Black students. "That was the last time we saw him," Mamie later said.[38] Garrett would soon retire to teach in Virginia and publish segregationist tracts.

Only days after the trial, as expected, the three Virginia judges ruled in favor of the state's segregated schools and warned that integration "would severely lessen the interest of the people of the state in the public schools, lessen the financial support, and so injure both races."[39] Nevertheless, the judges ordered the county school board to improve its Black schools.

In response, the NAACP attorneys asked the U.S. Supreme Court to review the decision in Virginia along with the rulings from South Carolina, Kansas, and Delaware. Meanwhile, the Clarks were back at work in Harlem, pushing for school integration, but not in the South. This time, they were looking closer to home.

NINE

A TASTE OF VICTORY

We are well aware of the crippled minds that are produced by a segregated school system.

—MALCOLM X[1]

With the last of the segregation trials behind him in the winter of 1952, Kenneth hoped to finish a book about prejudice and focus on teaching. But he also had speeches to deliver, letters to answer, and radio broadcasts with Mamie to promote Northside Center. He was still on the board of more groups than one mere mortal could serve, including the National Urban League and New York Civil Liberties Union, while consulting for the NAACP. All this took a toll on Kenneth, and Mamie was worried, as he told a colleague: "Mamie and I are pretty seriously concerned about this pace but the same question keeps popping up, What can we do about it? For every request that we accept, we make ten refusals. The guilt feeling resulting from refusing seems almost as bad as the strain of accepting."[2]

Kenneth fantasized about a sabbatical leave to travel abroad, but in truth, he'd never been so content with his work. A breakthrough in the struggle for school integration seemed imminent. Mamie, on the other hand, was far better at limiting her commitments, but she faced challenges as well. Running Northside Center had always been stressful, but now she faced a 45 percent cut in a key federal grant. With her clinic in debt, she scrambled to keep the doors open.

In stressful times, their Hastings home was a haven. Mamie planted rose bushes in the yard, and Kenneth helped keep them watered. On weekends, they had drinks on the porch overlooking the Hudson and the Palisades. Neither got much exercise, but Kenneth walked the aqueduct path behind the house now and then to visit Jacques Lipchitz, his famous sculptor friend who liked talking politics and showing off his African art collection. On Saturdays, Mamie played the piano and enjoyed opera on the radio. Though the Clarks had little time for their new Hallicrafters television set, the family watched comedians Imogene Coca and Sid Caesar on *Your Show of Shows* on Saturday nights. "I remember my mother laughing, laughing, laughing," daughter Kate recalled.[3]

Weekends brought Sunday drives in the country or dinners with Black friends, including novelist Ralph Ellison and his wife, Fanny, and artists Jacob and Gwen Lawrence. On summer days, the guests moved outdoors to the barbecue pit, where philosopher Alain Locke and sociologists E. Franklin Frazier and Hylan Lewis

KENNETH WITH HILTON
AND KATE, CIRCA 1952

joined the Clarks for hot dog roasts. Locke confessed once that he'd been wrong to urge Kenneth not to marry so young; he and Mamie had been good for each other. Once a year, the Northside staff gathered at the barbecue pit with Mamie serving as hostess and Kenneth, in a chef's toque and apron, handing out beers and flipping meat slathered in his own sauce. Indoors for dinner parties, Mamie usually sat in silence while he regaled the guests with stories, jokes, and his views on race. One night, he smiled and prodded her to speak up: "Mamie, say something. Express yourself. You know something."[4] He reached over and pinched her nipple. "Oh, Kenneth," she said, blushing. His roguish displays of ardor were far from rare. "You know, she liked it," daughter Kate recalled.[5] "You could tell."

To their children, Hastings was no haven. At age twelve, Kate missed her friends at the progressive New Lincoln School, where a diverse group of students sat on the floor and learned at their own pace. She loathed her white suburban school, where students sat in rows, read from textbooks, and learned the state capitals. As she parried the slurs of schoolmates, her parents said the bullies were ignorant and insecure and she should feel sorry for them. Kate sensed the disdain of some white teachers, especially a math instructor: "She actually told me she didn't like me and would do all she could to fail me."[6] The daughter of liberals in a Republican town, Kate stood out with her "Free the Rosenbergs" lapel button.

She was openly bitter, but Hilton did a slow burn: "The first thing I can remember: the kids used to like to feel my hair, They used to make fun of my lips."[7] His mother reassured him that his hair was fine, like Daddy's. When the children complained about school, the Clarks did little or nothing. "I think they wanted their kids to get the best education they could," recalled their friend Dr. John Moseley, "and if they had to put up with some slights here and there, that's just the price they had to pay."[8]

Most people in conservative Hastings were clueless about Blacks or the needy. The annual VFW Minstrel Show offered singing, dancing, and jokes about skits in blackface. The *Hastings News* touted the affairs of the Rotary Club, the Republican Party, and the Daughters of the American Revolution. At a time of scarce housing for war veterans and their families, affluent homeowners groused about plans for a 120-unit rental apartment complex. Village leaders rejected every proposal for a public swimming pool.

Loathing her life in Hastings, Kate was often at odds with her mother. Kate resented having to take the train into Harlem each week for piano lessons. And when she got her first menstrual period and phoned for help, she was irked that her mother hurried home, solved the problem, and rushed back to Northside. "She wasn't that verbal a person," Kate recalled.[9] "The reason it's hard to describe my mother is that she was self-contained, very self-contained. Some people would say she was aloof."

In her midthirties and immersed in the duties of parenthood and career, Mamie was the antithesis of her mischievous, effervescent girlhood in Hot Springs. Like her father, she ended a hard day's work by reading at night in her bedroom, where she summoned her daughter for the occasional scolding. And like Dr. Phipps, Mamie issued a stare of utter disapproval when one of her children misbehaved, and it stung more than a slap. Mamie was not one to smother her kids with kisses. Kenneth was the hugger and smoocher, the storyteller, teaser, and inviter of friends. Mamie's friends were usually the wives of his bosom buddies. Not surprisingly, Kate was daddy's girl, although he grumbled when she practiced on the piano. Still, Kate knew that her parents loved her. Mamie was the family fun maker, gift giver, and organizer of trips and vacations. After Kate made it through a piano recital at thirteen, her mother rewarded her with a student-exchange trip to Europe.

Rarely did the Clarks join in Hastings civic affairs; they were too involved in Harlem's. Still, Mamie attended the open houses at their children's school, and Kenneth scrutinized their report cards. Every morning, the Clarks put the town in their rearview mirror and sped down the parkway toward Harlem, where their work and social lives were moored. They met with friends and spent many a working evening there. They kept their old doctors, dentists, bankers, and hairdressers in the city.

With Northside Center as the Clarks' home base, scholars, journalists, and clinicians came by to observe or help. Some arrived from abroad—Sweden, Germany, even India—and noticed the brown and the white baby dolls that therapists used with the children. A headline in *Glamour* magazine lauded the Clarks as "Mr. and Mrs. Inc."[10] Citing Mamie's work at Northside, comedian Bob Hope gave her the Woman of the Week Award on his WNBC radio show, and the Schaefer Brewing Company honored the Clarks as humanitarians at a Lexington Hotel dinner. As her clinic's executive director, Mamie spoke first that night, then Kenneth. "That's the first time I ever got the last word," he joked.[11] He liked posing as the long-suffering, henpecked husband.

The Clarks' reputation did not depend on the white press. The Black press found them fascinating, especially Mamie, "who is the unusual combination of brains and beauty," the *New York Amsterdam News* reported.[12] Lauding Northside as "a respected giant landmark in the community of Harlem," reporter James L. Hicks added:

> *With the natural curiosity that most people attach to a doctorate in psychology, the Clarks have been especially the object of curiosity in Harlem because they both hold such a degree and are married to each other... Despite this curiosity, however, they have managed to weave their way into the hearts and minds of Harlem to the extent that Harlem people have trusted them with their most precious possession—their children.*

In a full-page spread with photos, the *Chicago Defender* described Mamie as cool and Kenneth as emotive. "Differing and diverse, they make a good team, and their unique agency is a testament to it."[13]

As America's interest in psychology deepened, reporters were drawn to the Clarks and their clinic. The *New York Times Magazine* chronicled the case studies of several Northside children, including seven-year-old Victor, a thin, undersized Puerto Rican boy. The day he met his Spanish-speaking therapist, Victor climbed up on a table and smashed everything on it. Another client was Jimmy, an abused eleven-year-old with a speech defect and twitching head and shoulders. The magazine lamented that the Clarks' clinic was so small despite the great need of the city's children. "Northside is reaching some," the magazine reported.[14] "But there are too few Northsides."

Located near Spanish Harlem, it served a rapidly changing clientele of four hundred kids and parents, nearly one in five of them speaking Spanish. To better serve them, Mamie recruited a Spanish-speaking team of two psychiatrists, a psychologist, and a psychiatric caseworker. To bridge the culture gap, Kenneth gathered a team of graduate students from the New York School of Social Work to interview Puerto Rican parents and help prepare a handbook on serving their families.

Mamie was Northside's mainspring. Her tact, caring, and attention to detail kept the clinic ticking. When a caseworker had problems with a client, she intervened to patch up the relationship. When a group of needy kids required a change of scenery in summer, she found camp scholarships for them. If a family was left homeless, she got them housing. Large families and others with illegitimate children were routinely denied public housing. "It's a matter which we haven't been able to win at all," she told a reporter, "even though a different home situation is sometimes the best therapy of all."[15]

Staff members called her "Dr. Mamie" and mimicked her soft, buttery voice, usually in good fun, though she had her critics. By most accounts, she was a strong but low-key boss—no autocrat. "She had a very firm hand on how she wanted things done and what she wanted done," secretary Mildred Thompson Stevens recalled.[16] "But she was not bossy. She really talked to us like humans." Mamie worked long hours but often left early on Fridays, and staffers let down their hair. One Friday afternoon, they were chatting, smoking, and playing music as a male psychologist mounted a row of file cabinets and belted out a song while crawling from one cabinet to the other. "In comes Mamie, and she never said a word and went into her office and started to do her work," caseworker Cathy Lombard recalled.[17] "Everybody got quiet and everyone started back to work, so she asked, 'What happened to the music?' Nobody answered."

After Kenneth, Mamie's right-hand man was Victor Carter, the coordinator of psychiatric casework and a close friend of Kenneth's since childhood. A gay, boy-faced West Indian, Victor was as chatty and ebullient as Mamie was reserved. He was popular with the staff and took charge whenever she was away, even though Dr. Stella Chess was at the top of the pecking order. Victor was practically a member of the Clark family, a regular at their holiday feasts who danced like a dervish at Northside shindigs. Parents at the clinic loved him. He understood their impatience with psychobabble and sermons on how to raise their children.

At City College, Kenneth's absences from class to appear in court for the NAACP caused him problems, even though colleagues covered his lectures. One day, a college dean called him into the office for a scolding. Kenneth listened politely but shrugged it off, grateful for faculty tenure.

Once the schools closed that summer, the Clarks hopped into their car and headed for Hot Springs. Mamie had a warm spot for the town and wanted her kids to enjoy time with their grandparents. "It was more like home in Arkansas than in Hastings," Hilton recalled.[18] "Down there, it was Black. We just had the problems that kids have, absent the problems of racism." At seventy, Dr. Phipps was semiretired and no longer managed the Pythian Hotel. He'd moved his medical practice next door into the tiny Phipps Building. After everyone got reacquainted, Kenneth—seldom one to relax—drove down to Oklahoma City for the annual NAACP convention and met with Thurgood Marshall.

Soon he and Mamie headed back to New York, she to resume her work at Northside and he to teach summer school. In the meantime, Marshall reopened the issue still smoldering in his inner circle: whether to continue with the social science strategy to combat school segregation before the U.S. Supreme Court. Attorney William Coleman warned that the doll test wouldn't pass muster with the court. And a recent *Yale Law Journal* article argued that the Clarks' doll test

MAMIE AND KENNETH, 1953

results for Southern, segregated pupils were nearly the same as for the Northern, integrated pupils. If segregation was so bad, how could this be? Further, even the youngest kids Kenneth tested, the preschoolers, were already familiar with racial differences: "This rules out the possibility that the schools play an initiating role in creating psychological conflicts."[19]

To bolster the social science strategy, attorney Robert Carter asked Kenneth to prepare a crucial document, a concise summary of the available data critical of school segregation. Kenneth turned to two white colleagues, Isidor Chein and Stuart Cook, who helped him boil down his White House paper and the testimony of the NAACP's expert witnesses. The three scholars labored over several drafts that summer, and Mamie studied each one and offered her advice. The result was an incisive, jargon-free report of about a dozen pages, "The Effects of Segregation and the Consequences of Desegregation: A Social Science Statement." Marshall was so impressed he submitted it as a separate brief to the Supreme Court along with the NAACP's legal brief.

Next, Kenneth worked with sociologist Alfred McClung Lee on a list of about fifty scholars who might endorse the social science brief. Persuading scholars to agree on anything this controversial was like training houseflies to fly in formation—plus, it was summer, with many away on vacation. Kenneth wrote to each one and asked for a response within a week. He phoned them all and got thirty-five signatures from prominent social scientists such as Gordon Allport and Jerome Bruner. The Clarks and sociologist Charles S. Johnson were among the few Blacks to sign. Marshall submitted the endorsed social science brief to the U.S. Supreme Court, which combined his four school segregation cases with another from Washington, DC, to review together. The battle was joined.

It was foggy and cold before dawn on December 9, 1952, when a line formed at the Supreme Court building in Washington. By the time the fog lifted, hundreds had joined the line, most of them Black. They stood three abreast in the corridor leading to the courtroom, eager for a seat and a glimpse at history. A few women had stood so long they kicked off their shoes. Others chatted about Christmas shopping, but the main topic was race and education. Nine white men in black robes were to determine the future of school segregation sanctioned in seventeen states and the District of Columbia. Under this rigidly segregated system, little or no high school instruction was available to most Black teenagers. At issue were the lives and learning of the vast majority of Black children in America.

Most people in line that day never made it into the courtroom, but with passes from the NAACP, Kenneth and Mamie took seats among the lucky ones. As the nine justices entered and sat at a long mahogany bench to face the public, the marshal intoned, "Oyez, oyez, oyez" and rapped his gavel.[20] "God save the United States and this honorable court." Having examined the legal briefs and trial transcripts from the lower courts, the justices were familiar with the school segregation cases. NAACP attorney Robert Carter approached the lectern to discuss *Brown v. Board of Education of Topeka*. In an easy, conversational tone, Carter said that school segregation must end because it denied Blacks an equal education and violated their rights under the Fourteenth Amendment, which guaranteed the equal protection of all people under the law. Separate schools relegated Blacks to an inferior caste and created feelings of insecurity that lowered their hopes and retarded their mental development, Carter said. "It is our position that any legislative or governmental classification must fall with an even hand on all persons similarly situated."[21]

After Carter finished, Thurgood Marshall approached the lectern to discuss *Briggs v. Elliott* in South Carolina. Marshall said that Dr. Kenneth Clark had examined Black pupils there and found they'd been harmed, yet the lower court in Charleston disregarded it. "I do not know what clearer testimony we could produce," Marshall said.[22] Dr. Clark had shown that "the humiliation that these children have been going through is the type of injury to the minds that will be permanent as long as they are in segregated schools, not theoretical injury but actual injury."[23]

Taking the lectern to defend Dixie was white-haired John W. Davis, head of the segregationist legal team. Davis had run for president against Calvin Coolidge in 1924 and lost. Davis had argued hundreds of cases before the Supreme Court—more than any other lawyer. Conservative to the bone, he wore a black club coat and striped pants, traditional dress before the high court in decades long since past. Davis told the justices that South Carolina had allocated up to $73 million in bonds to improve its schools, and he scorned the doll test. "Dr. Clark professed to speak as an expert and an informed investigator on this topic," Davis said, but Clark had shown dolls to only sixteen pupils, claimed this was an objective test, and said the children were confused.[24] "That is a sad result, and we are invited to accept it as a scientific conclusion. But I am reminded of the scriptural saying, 'Oh that mine adversary had written a book.'"[25] Since the children tested in the South were more likely to prefer a Black doll than those in the North, "what becomes of the blasting influence of segregation to which Dr. Clark so eloquently testifies?" Davis called for leaving the issue to local parents and school boards and preserving the widespread practice of ninety years.

Over a period of three workdays, the justices also heard arguments in the Delaware, Virginia, and Washington school cases. The Clarks were not present for these. They had to get back to their children and jobs in New York. They were hopeful of victory but, like the NAACP lawyers, far from certain the justices were on their side. After all, four of the nine men were Southerners, including conservative Fred Vinson of Kentucky, the chief justice.

More than a year later, the Supreme Court had yet to rule on the school segregation cases. First, the justices remained divided on the issue and had delayed their proceedings to examine additional information from the attorneys on both sides. Further, Chief Justice Fred Vinson had died of a heart attack at age sixty-three. His death led Justice Felix Frankfurter, a liberal on racial issues, to remark, "This is the first indication I have ever had that there is a God."[26] A Republican politician from California, Earl Warren, was now the chief justice.

In the meantime, Ella Baker, president of the NAACP branch in

Harlem, had told Kenneth one day that the South was not alone in segregating its schools and that something had to be done about this in New York City. He knew she was right and that segregation in the city's classrooms was no accident. It was the result of prejudice and policy in both business and government at every level. And the same was true for the city's segregated housing and job markets. Kenneth concluded that if racially separate classrooms were bad for children in Dixie, they were just as bad for a million schoolchildren in New York City.

Working with Baker, a gifted organizer, he and Mamie held meetings in their Hastings home and at Northside Center to reach out to parents, educators, and leaders of both races. They formed a coalition called the Intergroup Committee on New York Public Schools to pressure city officials to desegregate. As chair, Kenneth recruited college students to study the schools in minority neighborhoods. Armed with questionnaires, they interviewed principals and documented the state of their school buildings and the prevalence of substitute teachers. Other activists raised funds, gathered data, and helped shape a public relations campaign. Kenneth served as their chief spokesperson and Baker as the paid administrator. Mamie worked on subcommittees that oversaw the budget and developed proposals for school reform.

During Black History Week in February, Kenneth laid out his ideas on city school segregation in a speech at the Hotel Theresa in Harlem. City powerbrokers were in the audience, including Mayor Robert F. Wagner and Hulan Jack, the first Black borough president of Manhattan. Kenneth told them that school segregation in the city went all the way back to 1704, when a religious school for slaves opened. He noted that Governor Theodore Roosevelt signed a bill in 1900 that finally repealed a state law that allowed segregated schools. But by the late 1930s, segregated neighborhoods had led to segregated classrooms, and Harlem's schools declined, Kenneth argued. The attendance zones for academic high schools were gerrymandered to exclude Black students. Meanwhile, middle-class Black parents headed for the suburbs or sent their children to private schools. "This pattern clearly facilitates a process of deterioration of our public school system in New York City."[27]

Kenneth called for an objective study to compare the city's predominantly white and Black schools. He asked for data on school equipment, academic standards, classroom size, guidance programs, as well as classes for gifted pupils and others labeled as intellectually disabled. No Black man had ever spelled out in such clear, comprehensive detail the case for integration and higher standards in city schools—and right in front of the mayor. Though his tone was moderate, Kenneth's words struck the Brooklyn headquarters of the board of education like a lightning bolt. William Jansen, the city's thin-skinned school superintendent, denied that high school zones were drawn to bar Blacks. "I know of no such attempt during the time that I've been Superintendent of Schools and I know of no such condition prior to my time," Jansen wrote Kenneth.[28] Jansen demanded proof that Kenneth's charges were accurate. Arthur Levitt, a politically savvy school board member, was more diplomatic: "The problems so eloquently highlighted by Dr. Clark have troubled me ever since I became a member of the Board of Education."[29] Levitt supported Kenneth's call for an investigation and put the issue on the board's agenda. Mayor Wagner asked Kenneth to join his educational subcommittee.

On April 24, after weeks of planning, the Clarks and Baker held a high-profile conference on city school segregation. Titled "Children Apart," the conference in Harlem drew two hundred parents, educators, and activists from dozens of organizations, including Black, Jewish, and Puerto Rican groups. Reporters attended and got copies of every speech. As the main speaker, Kenneth said that both Black and Puerto Rican students paid the price of segregated schools. Their reading and math skills lagged behind others' by two years, he said. Harlem schools offered 103 classes for pupils classed as "retarded" but only six classes for the gifted. Students in classes for the intellectually disabled were assigned on the basis of group IQ tests—a violation of the law, Kenneth said. Minority students were counseled to attend vocational schools with dropout rates near 50 percent. Kenneth acknowledged that the problems were complex and the board of education had tried to face them, but the situation called for an investigation. The conference concluded with the participants voting unanimously for a rigorous study of the school system.

The press coverage of the conference was extensive. "Some City Schools Held Segregated," declared a *New York Times* headline.[30] The *Herald Tribune* reported that with so much concern about segregation in the South, New Yorkers had overlooked it in their own schools. The communist *Daily Worker* lamented that another week had passed without a Supreme Court ruling, "but school segregation is an issue in New York no less than it is in South Carolina."[31]

The Black-owned *New York Age Defender* ran a picture of Kenneth with other speakers and the banner headline, "School Bias Probe Demanded."[32] The *Amsterdam News* devoted a full page to the story, and the *Pittsburgh Courier* observed, "The entire country should be as interested in this investigation as is the great metropolis [of New York] because similar conditions exist elsewhere in scores of urban centers."[33] Kenneth had put Northern school segregation on the news agenda in the media capital of the nation. The white-hot debate that followed would rage across the land for decades to come.

Outraged, Superintendent Jansen again demanded that Kenneth prove the accuracy of his allegations. Kenneth responded by inviting Jansen to meet with the Intergroup Committee, but the superintendent declined: "There is no point to my sitting down to discuss problems with you as long as charges are made, which as far as I know have no basis in fact."[34] Jansen was not used to Black men speaking out and generating so much publicity. He wanted it stopped, now. But it would never stop, because the Clarks' crusade against segregated city schools had come at precisely the right time.

On Monday afternoon, May 17, 1954, a secretary interrupted Kenneth during class for a phone call. When he picked up the phone, Thurgood Marshall's excited voice came over the line from Washington: "Kenneth, we did it, we did it."[35] Kenneth's heart pounded like a trip-hammer as Marshall told him that the Supreme Court had ruled unanimously that segregated, dual school systems were unconstitutional. Marshall promised a major celebration in

New York and noted that the court had cited Kenneth's research in its decision. When Kenneth finally read the document, the words seemed to echo what he'd been saying for years about Black students: "To separate them from others of similar age and qualifications solely because of their race generates a feeling of inferiority as to their status in the community that may affect their hearts and minds in a way unlikely ever to be undone."[36]

The ruling added, "We conclude that in the field of public education the doctrine of 'separate but equal' has no place." Rejecting the court's 1896 decision in *Plessy*, the new ruling continued, "Whatever may have been the extent of psychological knowledge at the time of *Plessy v. Ferguson*, this [1954] finding is amply supported by modern authority." The now-famous footnote 11 followed, placing Kenneth's name first with a handful of other experts whose research was in accord with the court's decision. The footnote cited his White House Conference report on children and prejudice.

No one expected all nine justices to strike down state-sanctioned school segregation. It was the Supreme Court ruling of the century, a threat to segregation in all walks of American life. Marshall predicted that racial integration would come in five years. For the Clarks, it was one of the happiest days of their lives. As the family discussed the ruling, Hilton, age ten, told his father, "Well, Dad, I'm really proud of you."[37]

As news of the Supreme Court victory spread, Kenneth was inundated by letters and phone calls. Harvard psychologist Gordon Allport praised his handling of the social science evidence, and Buell Gallagher, president of City College, wrote, "I cannot let the moment of rejoicing pass without entering in the record my profound appreciation of your part in setting straight the course of American history."[38] The Clarks were ecstatic, as Kenneth confessed to Otto Klineberg: "The first three days we were in the clouds and refused to be brought down to earth by a consideration of the really serious problems which we must now all face."[39] Celebrating with his team at a New York restaurant, Thurgood Marshall toasted Kenneth and leveled his gaze at the lawyers who once jeered the doll test. "Now, apologize," Marshall told them, and all had a good laugh.[40]

News of the high-court ruling, known today simply as *Brown v. Board of Education*, stunned many African Americans. Dr. Ralph Bunche was so excited he left thirty-five dollars in cash on a counter at a bank. Novelist Ralph Ellison, another friend of Kenneth's, wept at the news. When it was announced on the radio, the staff at Northside Center gathered the children to celebrate. Ethel Payne, who covered the decision for the *Chicago Defender*, reported, "I'm so excited, like I'm drunk. I'm turning around like those spinning tops."[41]

PART THREE

THE STRUGGLE FOR INTEGRATION

TEN

MASSIVE RESISTANCE

We will walk until we are free, until we can walk to
any school and take our children to any school in the
United States.

—DAISY BATES[1]

Kenneth was sitting in a car heading for the tense little town of
Milford, Delaware, one morning with Alfred McClung Lee, a
white sociologist from New York. At the wheel was Wagner Jackson,
the NAACP leader for the tiny border state, and on the back of his
car was a sticker clearly marked N-A-A-C-P. Jackson noticed that he
was being tailed, that whenever he sped up or slowed down, so did
the white driver behind him, and that made Kenneth very nervous. So
Jackson hit the brakes, wrenched the wheel, raced down a side road,
and, to Kenneth's relief, eluded the white driver.

It was September 1954, soon after Delaware's schools had

opened for the fall and just four months after the landmark *Brown v. Board of Education* ruling had thrilled the Clarks. But it was clear to them now that white America, especially in the South, was not going to integrate without a fight. As Kenneth emerged from Jackson's car in downtown Milford that day, he sensed tension in the air. "This is a powder keg and the slightest match could set off an explosion," chubby, round-faced Mayor Ed Evans told him.[2]

Soon after the court's ruling in *Brown*, there had been signs of progress. School districts in border states like Delaware began to comply, particularly those in the capital cities of Wilmington and Topeka, Kansas—both defendants in the NAACP's school desegregation cases. But this was merely token compliance, as each district desegregated just one or two grades at a time or a few school buildings. In the solid South, however, there was no compliance at all, just the hope that the *Brown* decision would wither in the heat of prejudice. Because the court had set no date for compliance, the South could lie low.

The nation's press largely welcomed the *Brown* decision, but Southern newspapers roundly denounced it, a sign of the bitter resistance to come. In Mississippi, the *Jackson Daily News* ran a black-bordered editorial on the front page with the headline "Blood on the White Marble Steps."[3] Editor Fred Sullens exhorted his readers to resist: "This is a fight for white supremacy."

Milford, Delaware, was a small farming town with a textile plant, poultry factory, canneries, and just six thousand residents, 20 percent of them Black. Like most rural towns in the segregated South and some border states, Milford had no high school for Black students. The nearest was fifteen miles away, and to comply with *Brown*, the school board admitted just eleven Black tenth graders to the Lakeside School and allowed the boys to try out for the football team. Soon white parents complained about a dance at the desegregated school, and the followers of Bryant Bowles, the rabble-rousing leader of the National Association for the Advancement of White People, circulated petitions and handbills in town to stir ancient prejudices. "The Negro will never be satisfied until he moves into the front bedroom of the white man's home," Bowles once said, "and when he tries that a lot of gunpowder will burn."[4]

Crowds of white people gathered daily in front of the Lakeside School, jeering the Black students inside. The school was forced to close, and dozens of reporters arrived to cover the story. Fearing the flames of resistance would spread to other states, the NAACP sent Kenneth to investigate. To grapple with a complicated problem, you needed data, and Kenneth was the man to supply it. His visit to Milford was timely, just a few months before the Supreme Court was to issue a new decision spelling out how the nation's public schools must desegregate.

Mingling with Black patrons at a lunch spot, Kenneth learned they were avid supporters of school integration. He interviewed two male students who'd desegregated the Lakeside School, and both said they liked their white classmates, teachers, and football coach. Grownups in town, they said, were the problem. Later that night, Kenneth traveled to Dover, the state capital, and stood amid a crowd of angry segregationists as state officials buoyed their hopes by announcing that the Lakeside School had no right to admit Black students. Milford's brief experiment with school desegregation was over.

The next night, Kenneth and Black reporter James L. Hicks went to a tiny airport on the outskirts of Milford where white supremacist Bryant Bowles was holding a rally with a large crowd of followers. Cornered and threatened by the crowd, the two Black men fled but another car followed them. Fortunately, Kenneth stopped at a home where someone helped them hide. "There was this one night when I said, 'Well, gee I won't see my wife again, I won't see my children again'," Kenneth recalled. "Because these people were very menacing."[5]

As the struggle for school integration continued in the courts, the Clarks' work with the NAACP was unfinished. Even before the *Brown* ruling in May, the Supreme Court had ordered lawyers from both sides to prepare new arguments on how to desegregate schools: gradually or "forthwith." The justices faced a dilemma: if they ordered desegregation at once, violence might erupt across the South. And if they permitted gradual change, Black pupils could be deprived of better schools for years.

Thurgood Marshall had put Kenneth in charge of a fact-finding project to answer the court's request and document the best way to desegregate schools: at once or gradually. Mamie joined his team of advisers, and they met regularly at Northside Center. The NAACP assigned June Shagaloff, a twenty-five-year-old white staffer, to Kenneth to help. Bright, comely, and committed, Shagaloff moved into the Clarks' office at Northside, where Kenneth found her a phone and a desk to face his. Mamie sat just three feet away in the small office as Kenneth and Shagaloff phoned or wrote to experts and activists across the country for information. They interviewed leaders of cities, churches, universities, and the military to learn how desegregation had worked or failed. The two worked night and day with NAACP lawyers preparing a new legal brief for the Supreme Court. "It was our lives, everything," Shagaloff recalled.[6] She admired Kenneth's mind and liked that he treated her as an equal without flirting. She watched Mamie sitting quietly at her desk at Northside, a gracious though distant figure. "It took me a while to understand that she was reserved and not cold—very unrevealing."

Months later, as Shagaloff and Kenneth sifted through their data, they found that many communities nationwide had embraced desegregation after initially opposing it. School districts in twelve states that sanctioned school segregation—including Arizona, Maryland, and New Mexico—were desegregating. There were models of local leadership—a bishop here, a mayor there—whose strong, moral stands against segregation made all the difference. Kenneth concluded that a gradual approach to desegregation only encouraged resistance. He told Marshall that desegregation had to be swift, equitably enforced, and justified on moral or democratic grounds with the support of community leaders. Having read Kenneth's report, Marshall agreed and used some of the data in a new legal brief awaiting the Supreme Court's decision.

———————

His stature heightened by the *Brown* ruling, Kenneth was in demand as never before. Boards and commissions wanted him as a member, journalists sought him for interviews, and publishers asked him for a book. Strangers wrote him for advice on careers or psychological problems, and students asked for his help with their own versions of the doll test. Colleges, churches, and activist groups in a dozen states invited him to speak, and Kenneth leaped at the chance to spread his gospel of integration. He appeared on radio broadcasts and speaker panels with Marshall.

Meanwhile, Mamie and Ella Baker of the NAACP continued working with Kenneth to desegregate New York City's schools. The board of education paid lip service to the *Brown* ruling but denied that its own schools were segregated. "We have natural segregation here—it's accidental," Superintendent Jansen said, overlooking the fact that bankers, real estate agents, and public officials had restricted African-Americans to Black neighborhoods for decades.[7] Jansen clung to old policies and practices that left the schools in these neighborhoods to stagnate while white schools thrived. He and the board of education wasted five months before even sitting down to talk with Baker and the Clarks.

Finally, the board allowed an independent investigation, and after weeks of study, the Public Education Association reported there was no evidence of rigging attendance zones to segregate the schools, as Kenneth had charged, but that many of his other allegations were accurate. Just 30 percent of the city's schools gave Black and Puerto Rican pupils a solid chance to learn alongside white kids, "a state of affairs which we all should deplore."[8] The report also revealed that schools for students of color were older, poorly equipped, and poorly maintained. The teachers were less qualified and taught few classes for gifted students and too many classes for pupils labeled as "retarded." Math and reading scores for ghetto schools were more than two years behind grade level.

Meanwhile, white parents were fleeing the city's schools while Black and Puerto Rican pupils enrolled in greater numbers. Without white students, school integration was impossible. Still, the Clarks pressed on, and Kenneth praised city educators for each small step they took toward desegregation. He also lauded Black parents for demanding better schools. *New York Post* reporter Ted Poston credited Kenneth with leading the integration crusade, calling him "a prophet without honor in his own home."[9]

Unhappy with the criticisms in the PEA report, the board of education sought an investigation of its own with conservative Superintendent Jansen in charge. The study dragged on for nearly two years, and Kenneth lashed out at Jansen: "We feel that the superintendent is deliberately confusing, delaying, distorting and sidetracking the reports of our commission."[10] Black parents picketed city hall to open white schools to children of color, and white parents held protests to keep them out.

There'd be no cross burnings in Manhattan, but the Clarks were learning that resistance to integration in the North was as stubborn and resourceful as in Dixie.

––––––––

In the spring of 1955, a year after the *Brown* ruling, Kenneth published his first book, *Prejudice and Your Child*. It raised his profile as a public intellectual and spread his ideas on children, race, and integration. He dedicated the book to Kate, age fifteen, and Hilton, three years younger. It was a family project with Mamie, as usual, critiquing the drafts. Kate and Hilton joined in. The book included anecdotes from family life—Hilton's experience at school with white kids touching his hair, for example. The first chapter described the doll test in detail for the general public, and others spelled out what families, schools, and churches could do to undermine segregation.

The reviews were mostly positive. "Dr. Clark has documented a case against discrimination in terms which no Christian, no humanitarian, and indeed no American citizen who honestly faces his own conscience can brush aside," the *Christian Science Monitor* said.[11] Black author J. Saunders Redding wrote that the book offered little news for African Americans. "Who will be surprised—even shocked—are white readers, who form, after all, the basic audience for which *Prejudice and Your Child* is intended."[12] The chief naysayer was psychologist Bruno Bettelheim, who mocked Kenneth as "one of the many liberal sociologists and anthropologists who believe that prejudice is always psychologically harmful to everyone concerned."[13]

Later that spring, the Supreme Court finally issued its decision on how to desegregate the public schools. Dropping the high moral tone of the *Brown* ruling the year before, Chief Justice Earl Warren wrote that many schools faced problems with busing, staffing, and other issues before they could desegregate. Warren ordered "good faith compliance" with *Brown*, but "with all deliberate speed."[14] Again, the court set no deadline for desegregation. In effect, "deliberate speed" meant tapping the brakes, giving the white South more time to resist opening its schools to children of all races. To Marshall and his inner circle, it was as if the court had given them a victory one year and taken it away the next. When the Clarks heard about "Brown II," as it was called, their spirits plummeted.

A wave of massive resistance to *Brown* in particular and integration in general spread like a wildfire across the South as Virginia and other states made school attendance optional and allowed public schools to shut down. Education halted for many Black students, including the Farmville teenagers whom Kenneth had interviewed for the Virginia court case. Their school would remain closed for years to come. Southern states also passed laws giving tuition grants to students at private, all-white academies. Meanwhile, chapters of the White Citizens' Council, a kind of middle-class Ku Klux Klan, cropped up across Dixie to harass integrationists. Fanning the flames was Tom P. Brady, the Mississippi judge who wrote the racist screed *Black Monday*—a reference to the date of the *Brown* ruling. "Black denoting darkness and terror," Brady wrote.[15] "Black signifying the absence of light and wisdom."

Crank mail landed in Kenneth's mailbox. "You stink," a segregationist from North Carolina wrote him.[16] "Everybody knows that it is the Communist Party who is pushing this thing anyway." Ernest van den Haag of New York was more genteel, accusing Kenneth of using a test with the drawings of dolls to mislead the Supreme Court and promote "compulsory congregation" of the races.[17] The Clarks, however, had used real dolls and completed their experiment more than a decade before the *Brown* decision.

Alarmed by the massive resistance in the South, the Clarks entered a new phase of their public lives, a time for experimenting with new tools and tactics to fulfill the promise of the original *Brown* ruling. Their goal, however, was not integration for integration's sake. The reason they'd opened Northside Center, for instance, was not to promote integration but to relieve suffering and expand opportunities for Harlem children. As intellectuals, humanitarians, and community organizers, they'd carry on the struggle to improve the lives of people of color in New York and nationwide, especially children at risk. For the Clarks, integration was a strategy to achieve this goal. Labeled a mere integrationist, veteran activist Rosa Parks once bristled, "I have never been what you would call just an integrationist."[18]

As white resistance to desegregation spread in 1956, Black activists Rosa Parks, E. D. Nixon, and others pushed back in Montgomery, Alabama, where a twenty-seven-year-old newcomer named Reverend Martin Luther King Jr. rose to lead a movement to boycott the city's segregated bus system. For years, Black passengers had to pay up front on a bus, exit, and then reenter by the back door for a back seat. They also had to yield their seat if a white passenger demanded one. Black passengers like Rosa Parks, who one day refused to forfeit her seat, were often arrested, sometimes even beaten. African Americans accounted for three-fourths of the city's bus passengers, and after Parks's arrest, they organized to end the Jim Crow seating. They rallied in churches at night and walked or carpooled in the daytime. And they did this for months. The crusade for integration had finally moved from the courts to the streets.

The Clarks got involved when the activist, church-affiliated Unitarian Service Committee hired Kenneth and sociologist friend Hylan Lewis to investigate massive resistance to integration in the South. Mamie joined their "Lewis and Clark expedition," and on a train heading west toward Alabama, a Black porter approached them and said, "Reverend King is on this train, and I know that you would like to talk with him."[19] Surprised, Kenneth asked Mamie how the porter could possibly know this. "I haven't the slightest idea," she said.[20]

Finding Reverend King sitting by a window in a coach with other Black passengers, Kenneth introduced himself. The young minister said that he'd heard about the Clarks' work on the school segregation cases, and the two men moved to the lounge car where Mamie awaited them. As King told the Clarks about the Montgomery bus boycott, a white conductor interrupted him, shouting, "A dollar forty-three! A dollar forty-three!"[21] For what? Kenneth asked, and the conductor demanded King's train fare. After King handed the white man a ten-dollar bill, the conductor was so enraged his hands shook as he fumbled to make change. King invited the Clarks to his home in Montgomery and returned to his coach.

The Clarks' work began in earnest in Alabama where their friend Hylan Lewis joined them. In Montgomery, they toured the offices of the Montgomery Improvement Association, headquarters of the bus boycott, where an elaborate system of carpools was coordinated. They also visited the Kings in their little white cottage on South Jackson Street, which had been bombed three weeks before while Coretta Scott King was at home with her three-month-old baby. Both escaped unharmed. Kenneth noticed that armed men were guarding the Kings' patched-up cottage. Reverend King, however, seemed cool to the point of detachment and mentioned that his chief concern was the safety of Coretta and their baby. Kenneth promised to raise funds in New York to help the Kings with housekeeping and child care while they were busy with the boycott.

During their two-week tour, the Clarks and Hylan interviewed 150 people in five Southern states, from Atlanta to Memphis, nearly all of them Black. They spoke with people of all walks of life in cities and tiny towns like Tunica and all-Black Mound Bayou in Mississippi. They learned that under massive resistance, Black teachers were forced to sign papers denouncing integration and that activists received death threats at night over the phone. To defend home and family, many had to arm themselves. The Clarks also discovered that even whites were not free in Dixie; the few liberals who dared to support integration lost jobs, businesses, homes, and friends. In his final report on the investigation, Kenneth recommended securing voting rights for Black citizens. If white candidates needed the Black vote, he reasoned, more leaders would court African Americans instead of inciting bigots to oppress them.

Once back at Northside Center, the Clarks passed the hat for the Kings and found other donors to pitch in. When Reverend King arrived in December to give a speech in New York, Kenneth introduced him to the audience: "He has the potential for leadership of the spiritual, ethical, and moral sort that all the American people sorely need."[22] The Kings would return in the spring and sleep in the Clarks' spare room at the top of the stairs in Hastings. And on a winter vacation in Jamaica, the Kings would spend a couple of days with the Clarks renewing their friendship.

———————

After the schools opened in September 1957, massive resistance to desegregation raged out of control in Little Rock, the capital of Arkansas. Governor Orval Faubus had railed against enrolling Black students at revered, all-white Central High School, but nine of them showed up anyway, and a white mob of hundreds jeered the teenagers and attacked reporters. The televised images of the howling mob surrounding and terrorizing a Black girl shocked the world and delighted Soviet propagandists. To restore order, President Eisenhower sent in federal troops.

Soldiers patrolled the school and its grounds daily, and the Little Rock Nine—three boys and six girls—went separately to class and met together only for lunch. In the gym, hallways, and cafeteria, they faced a campaign of terror coordinated by adults. White kids kicked, tripped, body-slammed, and spat on the Black teenagers. The newcomers heard "nigger" so often the word lost some of its sting. White students stepped on the Black girls from behind to make their heels bleed, and any white kid who sympathized with the Blacks was threatened.

Of the nine Black teenagers, Minnijean Brown, sixteen, daughter of a mason and a licensed practical nurse, was the chief target. Tall, big-boned Minnijean—"Big M," the white kids called her—could not lie low. To the chagrin of her history teacher, Minnijean once asked why there was only one page about slavery in the whole textbook.

She paid a price for her pluck. As her mother watched from a car one afternoon, a white boy kicked Minnijean and knocked her down. And when she crossed the cafeteria at lunch with her tray, white boys shoved chairs in her path. She spilled a bowl of chili on them, and her suspension from school made headlines nationwide.

Soon afterward in December, the Clarks traveled to Hot Springs to spend the holidays with Mamie's parents. Instead of relaxing, Kenneth put on his investigator's cap again and headed to Little Rock, fifty miles north, to spend a week gathering data on the Central High crisis. Mamie had introduced him to Daisy Bates, mentor and spokeswoman for the Little Rock Nine, and Kenneth would stay with Daisy and her husband, L. C. Bates. Daisy headed the Arkansas NAACP and with her husband co-owned the *Arkansas State Press*, a crusading Black newsweekly. Greeting the Black couple in their home, Kenneth noticed the broken picture window in the front room—a rock from a vigilante, Daisy explained. Intimidation and threats were routine, she said, and the window would stay broken as a symbol of defiance.

Kenneth met the Little Rock Nine at a Christmas party where the teenagers received gifts from all over the country. Minnijean Brown's mother told him about a funny letter sent to her daughter after the chili incident. It included a ten-dollar check "to buy more plates when needed."[23] When Kenneth asked Minnijean what had caused the notorious chili spill, she smiled and said, "Well, maybe if I held the tray a little tighter it wouldn't have fallen but maybe if I had held it a little looser it would have fallen on them with more force."[24]

After five days of interviews, Kenneth reported widespread

Black support for Daisy's leadership and school integration. None of the Little Rock Nine suffered severe psychological damage, he wrote, and none seemed aware of serious danger, though several had expressed a sense of dread. Cowed by segregationist bullies, several white students were also victims, Kenneth reported. How it all would end, he wasn't sure.

———

Life in the shadow of their celebrated parents was irksome for the Clark children. Kate, age sixteen and thin as a twig in bobby socks and loafers, and Hilton, age thirteen, an avid sports fan, found a novel way to rebel. Raised outside the church by agnostic parents, they walked down to Grace Episcopal Church one day and signed up for confirmation classes. "Nobody urged us," Hilton recalled, "but everybody was shocked and surprised at the time that we were doing it."[25] Their father downplayed the gesture as a ruse to get out of school early once a week for religious instructions.

Like her mother, Kate was an avid reader who studied hard and made the honor roll. She was president of the history club and won an essay contest sponsored by the Daughters of the American Revolution. As her mother had in her youth, Kate insisted on choosing her own college. Her parents preferred one of the elite Seven Sisters colleges for young women, perhaps Radcliffe or nearby Vassar. But Kate preferred Oberlin, the integrated college in Ohio that had played a historic role in Black education. Paging through its viewbook, Kate spotted the photo of the most handsome young Black man she'd ever seen. Oberlin was for her, she told her parents, and they had to give ground.

Kate was eager to put Hastings behind her. She had friends in town but no boyfriend. "It was clear I was considered not dateable," she recalled.[26] "I wasn't going to the parties." These were often held at segregated country clubs, and as long as Kate stayed in Hastings, her social life was on hold. Boys fascinated her, and she found it odd that her mother, a psychologist, had never taught her the facts of life. Kate had learned them instead from a book she found in a girlfriend's home.

Hilton too was on his own when it came to the birds and bees. And unlike his father, he was a Little Leaguer who excelled in sports, even beating his skillful mother at Ping-Pong in the basement rec room. His parents pressed him to earn good grades, but like his dad in youth, Hilton preferred reading the books he loved to studying for tests. Seldom was his report card a cause for celebration. A bright boy with a sense of humor, he wrote about his parents raising him in a giant Skinner box, the device psychologists used to train lab rats. "I wrote a couple of papers about that at school, and they got very offended," he recalled.[27] Suspecting that Hilton was gliding through school by charming his teachers, Kenneth searched for a good prep school.

In the winter of 1958, Hilton and Kate had to make room in their lives for a sixteen-year-old girl coming to live with them: Minnijean Brown of Little Rock. Central High expelled her after a white girl had called her a "nigger" and Minnijean yelled back, "White trash!" Minnijean's expulsion made news nationwide, and the Clarks decided to offer her a home and schooling in New York. Like so many Black couples, the Clarks often sheltered relatives, friends, and others in need for months at a time. Kenneth contacted Minnijean's mother and mentioned he had a daughter about Minnijean's age. She reluctantly accepted the offer, and Kenneth helped arrange a full scholarship for Minnijean at the private New Lincoln School in Harlem, where Kate and Hilton had once attended. The school shared a building with Northside Center, where Mamie could monitor Minnijean's progress.

In February, Minnijean's airplane arrived at La Guardia Field in New York. As she walked down the plane's steps, flashbulbs popped and she faced dozens of reporters amid a crowd of NAACP wellwishers, including the Clarks with Kate. Answering the reporters' questions, Minnijean expressed concern for the Black schoolmates she'd left behind at Central High: "If things keep going as they are, I don't see how they can stand it."[28] Minnijean had become the poster child for the many beleaguered Black students who were among the first to feel the sting of white resistance to school desegregation.

On her first day of class at New Lincoln School in Harlem, reporters took notes and photographers snapped Minnijean's picture alongside smiling white kids. Students of all colors attended New Lincoln, including Indonesian, Indian, and Burmese children—a brave new integrated world for the Arkansas girl. "The most exciting day of my life," she said.[29]

Minnijean shared a bedroom with Kate, who introduced her to friends and helped with her homework. Minnijean found Hilton cute and enjoyed rating rock 'n' roll tunes with him. To Minnijean, life with the Clarks was like living in a glossy magazine. She enjoyed Broadway shows, went bowling, and marveled at the Clarks' dishwasher and shiny green Lincoln sedan. The range and diversity of the Clarks' friends astonished Minnijean: artists, doctors, professors, and other professionals, some of them white, some black, and some of them gay, came by for dinner, drinks, and dancing. There were no "Whites Only" signs in downtown Hastings, and if Minnijean wanted a cherry Coke, she sat at a soda fountain and bought one. White parents asked her to babysit their children.

And yet she wrangled with demons. "She had a lot of trouble, and I felt badly about it," Kate recalled.[30] "There were emotional difficulties. I didn't seem to help her be happier." Minnijean missed her family and grappled with the guilt of knowing that she was the only Black student expelled from Central High and left the others behind to fend for themselves. A product of weak, segregated schools, she now faced rigorous courses alongside white students. "I had none of the skills that they had," she recalled.[31] "I was an ignorant little Southern girl."

On Saturdays, Mamie recruited Minnijean with the rest of the family to help clean the house. Minnijean ironed clothes with Kate and tidied their room while Kenneth served as vacuumer in chief. The two girls washed the dishes and kept Mamie's copper-bottomed pots twinkling. After her daily classes, Minnijean went to Northside Center and watched Mamie help parents and children ill treated by a segregated society. "It wasn't all sweetness and light in that place, in that time," she recalled.[32] Minnijean heard Mamie grinding her teeth: "You'd see her jaw tightening, then she'd stop it. She'd become aware of it."[33] Minnijean attributed Mamie's famously quiet reserve to anxieties broiling within: "I just feel socializing was hard for her."[34]

The Clarks admired Minnijean's exuberance. She often sang in the house and posed no discipline problem whatsoever, but Mamie had to press her to study. Unaccustomed to hitting the books, Minnijean was more interested in singing and pop music. Still, she survived the spring term at progressive New Lincoln, which issued no grades.

In the fall, after segregationists in Little Rock closed the public schools to avoid integrating them, Minnijean returned to the Clarks and her school in Harlem. Family life in Hastings, however, was not the same. Both of the Clarks' children had left to attend other schools: Kate at Oberlin College and Hilton at the private Kent School in Connecticut. Missing them in the big, quiet house, Minnijean stayed in touch by mail.

On her graduation day in the spring, reporters showed up again at the New Lincoln School to cover the story, and in September, she began studying at the Mount Sinai School of Nursing in the city. Looking back on her time with the Clarks, she was grateful for all they'd done for her. "I changed my belief that I had no value," she recalled.[35] "There was never a lecture. It was all by example of what was possible."

The Clarks became empty nesters. "So Mamie and I are right back where we started again—alone," Kenneth wrote a friend.[36] "We feel as if we are rattling around in the house all by ourselves."

ELEVEN

A DAVID AND GOLIATH BATTLE

All over Harlem, Negro boys and girls are growing into stunted maturity, trying desperately to find a place to stand; and the wonder is not that so many are ruined but that so many survive.

—JAMES BALDWIN[1]

Lots of kids at Northside Center "were enough to tear you apart emotionally," Clara Rabinowitz, a psychiatric social worker, once said.[2] Georgie, a tall, thin, preadolescent boy, was one of them. Georgie never seemed the same after discovering the body of a boy who'd hanged himself in a school bathroom. It probably didn't help that Georgie was initially treated as a suspect. Traumatized by the incident, he stole things in school and was eventually expelled. Fortunately, Rabinowitz found a private school willing to admit Georgie.

The problems of troubled kids at Northside ran the gamut. Some were homeless, others needed tutoring or medical care, and still others required psychotherapy. The Clarks, like most of the staff, believed that a blend of child psychiatry, remedial education, and social work was the best way to help kids who suffered the ills of a segregated society. But in the late 1950s, Marion Ascoli, the clinic's chief benefactor, held another view. She favored Freudian psychoanalysis to raise standards and transform Northside into a training center for psychiatrists. But that, the Clarks feared, would only drain money and time for kids and might even kill the clinic.

Tensions that had simmered for a decade between Ascoli and the Clarks came to a slow boil as she and her white allies on the board raised questions about the Black couple's stewardship. A committee report backed by Ascoli attacked the quality of therapy at Northside and called for retraining Mamie to improve her management skills. Ever the soft-spoken diplomat, Mamie first defended her staff and then herself at a board meeting and called the proposal to retrain her "an insultingly interesting concept."[3] But if incompetence were the problem, she added, no consultant could help her. Supporting his wife, Kenneth warned that Ascoli's approach would create a soulless psychiatric clinic led by a father figure from whom all wisdom flowed. Ascoli had met her match in Mamie. "She never complained, she never looked ruffled," Joanne Stern, Ascoli's daughter-in-law, said of Mamie.[4] "And she was like a rock and she was very tough, although she looked frail and kind of like a doll."

Northside had grown sturdy roots on 110th Street in Harlem, serving four hundred clients per year, one in five Puerto Rican and 7 percent of them white. The staff tried new programs, including group therapy, mental-health seminars for the children's teachers, and classes on parenting. Summer reading lessons raised pupil test scores by eight months. Most of the kids seemed to improve at Northside and were discharged. The clinic had a solid reputation in Harlem with the generous support of Black celebrities such as Billie Holiday, Eartha Kitt, and Jackie Robinson.

The clinic's head of psychotherapy, Dr. Stella Chess, shared the Clarks' skepticism about psychoanalysis, especially the fretting about toilet training, thumb-sucking, and weaning. Dr. Chess taught at New York Medical College and conducted path-breaking research in child psychiatry. Eschewing the cool, detached persona of the conventional analyst, Dr. Chess hurried from her home in Riverdale one night to help a child facing an emergency at home in Harlem. Criticized for her eclectic approach, Chess stunned the Northside staff by resigning after eleven years of service. To replace her, board chair Ascoli promoted a man trained in psychoanalysis, Dr. Albert Bryt, and made him Mamie's coequal. Stunned, Mamie stayed at Northside but hedged her career bets by taking a part-time job lecturing at Yeshiva University.

Complaints about Dr. Bryt soon mounted on Mamie's desk. A traditionalist with a British accent, he berated colleagues in public, including another psychiatrist. "Dr. Bryt practically had that man in tears," Victor Carter, the head of social work, recalled, "and this was a grown man."[5] Appearing before the board of directors, Bryt faulted the Clarks' leadership and the staff's record keeping. Parents missed too many appointments, he said, and the clients had to be chosen more selectively, even at the risk of alienating Harlem. He discharged more than one hundred children, replacing them with just forty newcomers. But the harder Bryt pushed, the more frustrated he became. No one bent to his will, and a wave of staff resignations followed.

Meeting again with the clinic's board, Bryt said he could no longer support the way Northside operated. It was too expensive, with too few results, and would function better as a placement agency that sent children elsewhere. At another time and place, Bryt and Ascoli might have prevailed. But this was 1960 in Harlem, and power arrangements between whites and Blacks were shifting worldwide. In Africa, a new nation was born every other month as white colonial regimes were shown the door. In the American South, Blacks were taking to the streets to end segregation. And in Harlem, the paternalism of Ascoli and other whites spurred Black activists to seize control of their own institutions.

After fourteen years of hard work at Northside, the Clarks pondered their options. If they cut Ascoli loose, their clinic could collapse for lack of funds. And if she and Bryt stayed, most of the staff would resign. Employees joined the Clarks at yet another board meeting to threaten a mass resignation. The Clarks warned Ascoli that her money couldn't dictate the clinic's future, so she resigned and withdrew all financial support. Several whites on the board followed suit, but not Ascoli's daughter-in-law, Stern, who said of the losing side, "We just thought they were nuts."[6] Dr. Bryt also resigned and admitted years later to being a bull in a china shop.

Northside faced a steep $100,000 deficit, half its annual budget, and the New Lincoln School, strapped for space, warned that the clinic might have to vacate the building and move. Kenneth negotiated to regain some space, but without an infusion of cash, Northside would close.

So Kenneth turned to James Dumpson, the city's first Black commissioner of welfare, who yanked at the levers of power and found money to keep Northside afloat. Dumpson joined its board and would soon rise to lead it. The Clarks met with foundations and gained still more aid. "They were always fundraising," Stern recalled, "and they were always proselytizing and they were—this was no nine-to-five job, I can assure you."[7]

Sometimes activists have to push back, hard, to preserve prior gains before moving on to higher ground. The Clarks had finally prevailed at Northside Center, but their next move forward would start with another slap at white charity.

———————————

By 1961, desegregation inched along at a millipede's crawl, and the Clarks were disheartened. *Brown* had been the law of the land for seven years, yet only a fraction of the nation's schools had desegregated. Southern stores, motels, cafés, and theaters remained rigidly segregated. Most Blacks couldn't vote. But the Clarks had found a new cause for hope: young people. After Black students in Greensboro, North Carolina, demanded service at a Woolworth lunch counter, a wave of sit-ins forced dozens of cities across Dixie to desegregate their public accommodations—the best thing since the Boston Tea Party, Kenneth said.[8] Impatient with the NAACP's moderate tactics, he applauded the student activism.

The pace of protest accelerated in the spring of 1961 as young activists boarded two buses in Washington and headed south to desegregate bus stations. These were the Freedom Riders, most of them Black students, and their goal was to reach New Orleans by the May 17 anniversary of the *Brown* ruling. But a white mob firebombed one of their buses near Anniston, Alabama, and beat the fleeing activists. Other Freedom Riders were attacked in Birmingham and Montgomery, one of them paralyzed for life, yet most others moved on to Mississippi to face arrest and imprisonment at notorious Parchman Farm, a prison.

As the Freedom Rides continued through July, Kenneth was in Philadelphia to receive the Spingarn Medal, the NAACP's highest award. Cited for "inspired research which contributed significantly to the U.S. Supreme Court decision...banning segregation in public education," he accepted the award while his family, including his nearly seventy-year-old mother, beamed with pride.[9] Kenneth praised the new spirit of activism in the land and said the time for compromise on civil rights had passed: "We cannot partake in the moral hypocrisy and equivocation of gradualism, tokenism and moderation."[10]

———

It all started with a newspaper article that infuriated Kenneth: city hall was working with the Jewish Board of Guardians to provide psychiatric care to kids in Harlem gangs. Outraged that no one had consulted Black leaders or Harlem agencies like Northside, Kenneth denounced the proposal as social welfare colonialism. This upset Jewish friends, some of them Northside donors, and Mamie quietly backed him while he mended fences. Yet Kenneth was adamant: Harlem had to be consulted, and the days of kowtowing to white charity were over. Ever the diplomat, Mamie often felt that he was unnecessarily abrasive.

With Kenneth on its board, the Harlem Neighborhood Association informed Mayor Wagner that the Guardians' proposal had to be scrapped. Wagner was open to suggestions, and Kenneth applied for a federal grant to start a juvenile delinquency program that one day would evolve into a War on Poverty program. With President Kennedy in the White House, there was support for such projects, and activists met with the Clarks at Northside to found Harlem Youth Opportunities Unlimited, or HARYOU. Kenneth's goal was to recruit young Harlemites to help cure what he and other Black scholars called the pathologies of the ghetto, a welter of social ills such as illiteracy, disease, and crime—maladies common to the poor who were denied equal opportunity. Kenneth hoped that HARYOU would buoy young people's self-confidence, rebuild their community, and serve as a national model.

In June 1962, Mayor Wagner held a news conference with Kenneth and more than a dozen Harlem leaders to announce two planning grants for a HARYOU pilot program: $250,000 from the federal government and nearly $100,000 from the city. Wagner said the project would focus on Central Harlem and support nearly two years of planning. If the plans were approved, millions of federal dollars would flow into Harlem as never before. Smoke curling from his cigarette, Kenneth told reporters that HARYOU was not only for delinquents but also the 90 percent of young Blacks on the right side of the law. All were at risk.

Scrambling to get HARYOU up and running from the offices

at Northside, Kenneth tapped Black leaders to serve on an integrated board of directors, including cigar-smoking J. Raymond Jones, "the Harlem Fox," a powerful Harlem Democrat and aide to Mayor Wagner. Kenneth became HARYOU's chair and chief consultant at a salary about double his modest professor's pay. He took a leave of absence from Northside and City College. HARYOU was his baby now.

Kenneth was reinventing his role as a Black activist, setting aside his regular duties to manage a youth program that would pave the way for a multimillion-dollar poverty agency. But management was never his strong suit, and he relied on Mamie's advice to get HARYOU up and running. "At Northside they used to say, 'Don't let Kenneth get involved in the books or the scheduling,'" daughter Kate recalled.[11] "He was an absent-minded professor." He cast about for a professional staff of twenty to establish HARYOU, and Mamie coached him through the hiring process. Most of those he chose were young, university-trained Black men who moved HARYOU into offices on the first floor of the Harlem YMCA.

Kenneth's immediate goal was to write a vivid proposal for a huge federal grant and enlist the aid of young people to collect the data he needed. He aimed to write a compelling document that depicted the maladies of ghetto life, prescribed the remedies, and claimed the federal aid needed to heal Harlem. But there was conflict at the outset. Congressman Adam Clayton Powell Jr., pastor of the Abyssinian Baptist Church, had also secured a federal grant to build his own antidelinquency agency in Harlem, the Associated Community Teams. Kenneth looked askance at ACT, which lacked the heft of his university-trained staff. But Washington officials counted two pilot programs in Harlem as one too many and expected them to merge. Kenneth apparently thought he could finesse the issue, but with Powell holding the federal purse strings as chair of the House Education and Labor Committee, that was unlikely.

To Kenneth, Powell was a political hustler who'd exploit HARYOU for his own ends. Powell, on the other hand, saw Kenneth as a naive, ivory-tower intellectual. And yet the two men had much in common: both were maverick liberals who criticized whites for telling integrationists to go slow. In the 1930s, Powell led street protests against job discrimination citywide, and in Congress, he tormented the Pentagon by blocking aid for segregated military programs. Harlem voters liked Powell and reelected him every two years.

But Pastor Powell was no saint. Tall, trim, and charming, he was a skirt chaser and traveled abroad at public expense with female aides. Though his wife lived in Puerto Rico, he put her on the House payroll and cashed her checks. He took salary kickbacks from his staff and faced charges of tax evasion. Powell always denied wrongdoing and once said, "If it's not illegal, immoral or fattening, I'll do it."[12]

———————

While Kenneth focused on HARYOU, Mamie was busy at Northside with fundraising and cost cutting to stabilize the clinic's shaky finances after Ascoli's departure. Though no longer on the payroll, Kenneth still helped her at Northside by applying for grants and writing papers about the children's academic progress. They both presented papers at a conference in Washington—old hat for Kenneth but not for Mamie, who suffered from stage fright and panicked while presenting her paper. "The first words couldn't come out," her niece, psychologist Evelyn Phipps Boyer, recalled.[13] "It let me know how difficult these things were for her—for her to be out there."

Even so, Mamie was a force at HARYOU, advising Kenneth, helping with committees, and coordinating the work of three Northside staffers to conduct studies for him. By 1963, the HARYOU pilot program was still getting its sea legs but drew more than two hundred participants ages fourteen to twenty-one to lectures on Black history, workshops in the performing arts, and interviews with Harlem residents. The young people held rallies and worked with adults planning a rent strike. They took part in skull sessions on urban problems: crime, drug addiction, corrupt cops, and school segregation. One group renovated a storefront and opened Afro House, a café with coffee and soul music to draw gang members off the streets. "We had a lot of fun around that café we built on 133rd Street," recalled Hilton Clark, who went there after his classes at Columbia University.[14]

HARYOU was not all hope and harmony. "There was turmoil all the time," Hilton recalled. "Kids, hustlers, con artists would come in." Teenagers crowded the offices and strained the patience of adult staffers whose cigarettes disappeared as the youngsters took over their typewriters. Conflict between the HARYOU kids often led to outbursts. "This was prevalent, and it was difficult to run an operation with that kind of feeling," Hilton recalled, "but my father had some good people working with him." Some of the HARYOU youngsters were wary of Kenneth's scholarly demeanor and groused that he was an Uncle Tom doing the bidding of *the man* downtown. To Kenneth, the cynicism was understandable, given that hustlers stood on every other corner in Harlem.

HARYOU was changing Hilton's life. Raised in the suburbs and educated at a prep school, he was back in the Harlem of his early childhood and loving it. At age twenty, he had an Afro and helped organize HARYOU radio shows with guests such as Malcolm X and Bayard Rustin. Hilton joined in the panels on community problems and interviewed Harlemites about life in the ghetto. He was stunned by the squalor he found in some homes: "It was a hell of an education for me, in terms of people's concerns, people's perspectives, people's situations and status."[15]

Hilton got to know Malcolm X and admire his charisma and emphasis on *Black* beauty and *Black* pride, his call to defeat white supremacy "by any means necessary". A budding Black nationalist, Hilton believed that Blacks should control their own businesses and become the dominant force in their neighborhoods. But to the relief of his parents, he'd never become a separatist lashing out at "white devils". Still, Hilton clashed with his father over Black nationalism and early on embraced the emerging term *Black* to describe members of their race. At that time, his father preferred *Negro* and rejected the idea of race as the organizing principle for any community. Kenneth envisioned an integrated Harlem with streets, schools, and businesses shared by all races. He wanted more power for African Americans, but not by any means necessary. Still, he liked Malcolm X, who backed school integration. Kenneth welcomed him to HARYOU's offices and joined Mamie on a student field trip to Malcolm's mosque. Kenneth admired the caring, gentle way Malcolm addressed the young people.

Even so, the Clarks rejected Malcolm's nationalist rhetoric while agreeing with much in his critique of racism. By 1963, race relations were in tatters, and the Clarks' vision of an integrated society was fast going out of fashion, especially among young firebrands like Hilton.

––––––––––––––

Kenneth worked at a manic pace that spring, his life a rushing stream of HARYOU meetings, phone calls, and trips with Mamie to speak in cities such as Cleveland, Baltimore, and Boston. A stomach ulcer put him in the hospital, and his life veered out of control, he told a friend: "Mamie, in her usual wise, calm and quiet way has provided a most effective form of therapy. In the midst of all the confusion, she simply made all the arrangements for us to take a trip to Europe."[16] She needed a change of pace as well.

On July 26, the Clarks boarded the SS *France* in New York for their first transatlantic journey. For five days, they read, napped, lazed on deck chairs, and made new friends. Mamie swam in the pool, and at dawn on the last day of July, they awoke to see the English coast. In London, they saw Langston Hughes's play *Black Nativity* and toured the Tower of London "with its barbarity and its Crown Jewels," Mamie ruefully noted in her travel diary.[17] They made a quick jog to Wales for tea with philosopher Bertrand Russell, a lanky, white-haired pacifist at age ninety-one whose views on power, peace, and civil rights Kenneth admired. Unimpressed by fame, Mamie jotted, "Big deal about going to see Lord Russell."

Crossing the English Channel, the Clarks toured the canals of Amsterdam, dined with friends, and sped off to Rome, where they visited the Forum, the Colosseum, and St. Peter's Basilica twice. "Got flirted on the Spanish Steps," wrote Mamie, still fetching at age forty-five. The Clarks chatted till 3:00 a.m. with Black performer Ada Smith, better known as Bricktop, at her nightclub in Rome.

Moving on to Paris, the Clarks club-hopped with James Baldwin and his entourage, and Mamie had one word for that night: "Crazy." Before heading homeward, the couple toured Versailles, the Louvre, and a community for Jewish persons displaced by World War II.

While criticizing America for its treatment of Blacks, several Europeans the Clarks had met seemed oblivious to bigotry within their own borders. A British man insisted that his country welcomed Pakistani and Caribbean immigrants with open arms. And a French man at a sidewalk café denied that Algerian newcomers were humiliated in France. Moments like these may have reminded the Clarks of what psychologist Alfred Adler once said: "Those who have traveled have found that people everywhere are approximately the same."[18]

———————

The glow from the trip abroad did not last long once Kenneth returned to work. He had to finish his master plan for expanding HARYOU from a small pilot project into a federal poverty program. By the beginning of the new year, 1964, his plan was finally ready. Titled *Youth in the Ghetto*, the six-hundred-page study of Central Harlem documented a delinquency rate double the rest of the city's, an infant mortality rate nearly twice as high, a homicide rate six times greater, and a drug addiction rate nine times greater. Quotations from Harlemites breathed life into the numbers. "The way the Man has us, he has us wanting to kill one another!" one man said.[19] "Dog eat dog, amongst us!"

Youth in the Ghetto was both a cri de coeur and utopian blueprint for change. It called for sweeping reforms in Harlem, especially in the schools that neglected young people and the police force that mistreated them. It also called for replacing the gang culture with a civic youth culture by harnessing the anger and talent of young people. Though it proposed no mixing of races, the report was an integrationist document that aimed to turn Harlem into a community of excellence with good schools and safe streets that people of all races would find attractive.

The HARYOU report outlined a jobs program for hundreds of tutors, trainers, organizers, and counselors in Harlem. Young people would learn skills in fields with job shortages, such as data processing, auto repair, and metal crafts. New jobs centers would find them work. There would also be workshops in the arts, preschools for tots, and after-school centers for students weak in math or reading. A reading mobilization year in the schools would focus on wiping out illiteracy, which Kenneth called the central pathology of the ghetto.

As federal officials required, the report included a one-hundred-page pitch for Powell's ACT program, since both were expected to merge to gain federal aid. After reading the HARYOU section, according to Kenneth, Powell called it brilliant and told him, "With your brains and my power, we'll split millions."[20] Powell saw in Kenneth's plans the makings of a political machine for dispensing jobs that could threaten his Harlem congressional seat. So Powell offered Kenneth a deal: manage a merged HARYOU-ACT program as a junior partner to Powell, who'd fill all the top jobs. Kenneth said no.

Edward Dudley, Manhattan's Black borough president, scolded

Kenneth for antagonizing Powell and his ACT program. "The problem with you, Ken, is that you are negative and hostile toward those people at ACT." Mamie, however, shared her husband's view that HARYOU should operate in the public interest, not a politician's. The Clarks spent many a night at the dinner table talking about the tug of war with Powell. Mamie doubted her husband would prevail. To stay calm, he watered their azalea and rose bushes on weekends and took country drives with her.

In June, Kenneth met with Powell in his Washington office with its plush sofas and chairs, a view of the Capitol dome, and a fancy new phone with lots of shiny buttons on Powell's desk, a gift from President Johnson. Powell warned that no one in Washington sided with Kenneth, certainly not President Johnson or Attorney General Robert Kennedy, who both needed Powell—especially Kennedy, who hoped to run for the U.S. Senate in New York. "See, that's politics," Powell said.[21] "You've got to grow up, Kenneth."

If HARYOU were allowed to go its own way, Kenneth responded, it would serve as a monument to the congressman. Powell brushed the notion aside, and his office phone with all the buttons began to ring. Powell put it on speaker phone, loud, so Kenneth could hear a Kennedy aide on the line. Kenneth heard the man say that Kennedy was indeed siding with Powell on HARYOU. Hanging up, Powell repeated his power-sharing offer, but Kenneth again declined.

Later that day, Kenneth tipped off reporters about his battle with Powell to control HARYOU. Woody Klein of the *New York World-Telegram and Sun* was interested in the story but warned Kenneth of a counterattack from Powell. "That's fine," Kenneth said.[22] "My wife and I put too much into this." When Klein phoned Powell for his side of the story, Powell laughed, denied Kenneth's account of a bribe, and asked how much Klein earned. "You want to come work for me?" Powell asked, according to Klein.[23] "I'll double your salary."

Klein's article about HARYOU landed on the front page under the banner headline, "Powell Turns on Pressure," with a photo of Kenneth and his comment that HARYOU was "the city's last hope to save these children from a wasted life."[24] The *New York Times* followed with a story of its own on the front page, and the dispute stewed for weeks in the white press, which sided with Kenneth. The *New York Post* called him "a courageous fighter as well as an inspired egghead" pitted against "Powell and his henchmen."[25] The Black press mostly avoided the story.

In clerical robes after his Sunday sermon, Powell told reporters that Kenneth was a liar and the Clarks' clinic stood to gain more than $10 million from HARYOU. "You can see there is a lot of money involved."[26] Powell claimed that Kenneth would also make $30,000 a year leading a City College research project funded in part by HARYOU. Kenneth denied the charges and added that the college would pay him just $19,000 to return in the fall and that his $25,000 HARYOU salary would soon run out. Mamie called Powell's charges absurd. She and Northside had served HARYOU without profit, she said. "Finally, my husband is a man of absolute integrity."[27]

Trying to end the feud, Washington officials froze federal aid to HARYOU pending a truce between Powell and Kenneth. If the feud continued, there'd be no new poverty aid at all for Harlem.

Fearing the loss of millions of dollars, four of the nation's Big Six civil rights leaders—Roy Wilkins, Whitney Young, James Farmer, and A. Philip Randolph—all colleagues of Kenneth's, urged him to end the feud. Exhausted and in despair, Kenneth resigned on the last day of July, and Powell took control of the newly merged HARYOU-ACT program. "Clark Quits HARYOU, Deploring Politics," the *New York Times* reported on its front page.[28] Dozens of friends, colleagues, and supporters wrote Kenneth to sympathize, but he was inconsolable. "He didn't understand cynicism," news reporter Klein recalled.[29] "It was shocking to him."

At age fifty, Kenneth felt there was no place in Harlem for him anymore. Several Black leaders and young people at HARYOU had taken Powell's side in the dispute, and Kenneth admitted he'd been bullheaded. "I may have the devil's horns in this story," he told a reporter.[30] "But I had my reasons." The conflict was painful for Mamie, who felt Kenneth had been naive. "He was standing there all alone, you know, waging this war against Adam Powell," she said years later.[31] "I mean, he just couldn't possibly win it. And it was just ghastly. Ghastly. For me."

Kenneth's spirits were low and his energies sapped, but he was too hopeful and persistent to give up. Already he was planning a book about Harlem and a new research center at City College to carry on the struggle for integration and equal opportunity.

TWELVE

JUMP-STARTING HEAD START

If this society of yours is a "Great Society," God
knows I'd hate to live in a bad one.

—FANNY LOU HAMER[1]

O n the morning of July 16, 1964, an off-duty white cop shot and
killed a fifteen-year-old boy at a Harlem apartment building.
As protesters gathered at the police station two days later, officers
waded into the raucous crowd with flailing nightsticks. For six days,
rioters shattered windows, looted shops, and skirmished with police
on corners and rooftops in Harlem. Thousands of rounds were fired,
hundreds of people were arrested, and a Black man was killed. The
rioting spread to Brooklyn and Rochester before crossing the state line
into Jersey City, Paterson, and Elizabeth, New Jersey. Philadelphia
exploded in August. It was the first of the long, hot summers of the
1960s. Early in the century, white terrorists motivated by hatred or

profit fomented race riots in Black neighborhoods. But these ghetto rebellions were the eruption of Black rage suppressed for generations.

The Clarks were shocked but not surprised by the mayhem in combustible Harlem. Whites, however, were stunned by the flickering images of burning buildings and looted shops on their TV screens night after night. To them, the riots seemed mistimed in President Lyndon Johnson's Great Society after he signed the 1964 Civil Rights Act to integrate stores, motels, pools, and other public accommodations nationwide.

The ferocity and scale of the riots fired a new sense of urgency in official Washington, which finally seemed willing to fight poverty in the ghettos—a willingness the Clarks seized upon to further the Black struggle, especially on behalf of children. A power couple at the height of their influence, they took on new projects that stretched the limits of their energy and talents.

It was the social event of the winter season in 1965: tea for four hundred in President Johnson's White House, and among the guests were actress Gina Lollobrigida and the wives of the capital's movers and shakers. They all squeezed into the East Room to hear the First Lady launch a new War on Poverty initiative, Project Head Start. Lady Bird Johnson called for volunteers to save preschool children "lost in a gray world of poverty and neglect, and lead them into the human family."[2] The children were so deprived, she said in her Texas drawl, "why, some of them don't even know their own names."

If Mamie recoiled at the paternalism, it was understandable.

She was one of the few Black people that day in the East Room and on Head Start's steering committee, the dozen or so psychologists, doctors, and educators charged with designing a preschool program for the nation's neediest children. "The national media covered the White House tea as a 'society' event rather than a 'news' event," wrote Yale psychologist Edward Zigler, coauthor of two books about Head Start.[3] "This was fortunate because it provided Head Start with the image of being a nice, respectable program."

The push for Head Start began in the shabby New Colonial Hotel, the Washington headquarters of Sargent Shriver, the ebullient white liberal who'd married into the Kennedy clan of Camelot fame, raised five kids, and headed both the War on Poverty and the Peace Corps. Only eighteen states had kindergartens at the time, and none had prekindergartens. Discovering a surplus of federal funds, Shriver pushed to invest them in Head Start, a preschool program for needy children. Other poverty programs he oversaw, like Powell's new HARYOU-ACT, were accused of harboring radicals and tossing money at social problems. But Head Start was intended for the youngest of the deserving poor, and Shriver put Dr. Robert Cooke, his family pediatrician, in charge. Cooke turned to a dozen professionals for help, Mamie among them, and they formed the Head Start steering committee with no staff at all to help them. "That committee really did all the work," Shriver once said.[4] Briefed in Washington, Mamie and her colleagues learned they had just a few weeks to design the summer program before it opened for eight weeks. Some called it Project Rush-Rush.

Cooke scheduled workshops for the twelve committee members

in Washington and New York to write guidelines for the Head Start centers across the nation. As a Black Woman, Mamie felt the weight of her new duties and spoke out against the use of medical and psychological records to follow the children through life. "Mamie Clark shot down the suggestion to screen children for retardation because she felt IQ testing would discriminate against minority children," recalled Zigler, a committee member who differed with Mamie over the term *cultural deprivation* to describe the plight of minority children.[5] "Once again, Clark led the opposition," Zigler wrote, acknowledging that Mamie was right because every child has a culture, though maybe not the favored one.[6]

Mamie also opposed hiring education professors to teach parents how to raise their children. The professors, Mamie warned, would likely disparage Black culture. She faced another debate at home. Kenneth said that even if Head Start centers were well run, they'd only frustrate kids moving on to dismal ghetto schools. Mamie shot back that at least they'd have one good educational experience, and it could serve as a model for public schools. Head Start's ideals—that kids needed structure and security, a sense of family and community in a setting conducive to learning—were Mamie's, the same values that shaped Northside Center.

Within weeks, the committee submitted its recommendations for Head Start, and some sounded as if they'd come straight from Northside, including that the pupils should get medical, dental, and eye care for ailments that hamper learning. The committee recommended no formal curriculum but plenty of play to enhance verbal and social skills and encourage a positive attitude toward learning—playing with dolls and puppets, for instance, or taking part in skits. The local centers should serve meals, and in keeping with the War on Poverty's stress on "maximum feasible participation of the poor," parents should play a key role in the centers and perhaps hold jobs there. Some of Mamie's colleagues argued that Head Start should begin as a tiny pilot project, but Shriver said no, that President Johnson was thinking big, Texas size, to seize the political moment. "We're going to write Head Start across the face of this nation so that no Congress and no president can destroy it," Shriver vowed.[7] When Johnson met with the Head Start committee in the Rose Garden, he stressed the importance of learning: "If it weren't for education, I'd still be looking at the southern end of a northbound mule."[8]

As summer drew near, thousands of applications for new Head Start centers arrived in Washington—far more than expected, even though communities had to foot 20 percent of the cost. Hundreds of volunteers also arrived in the capital to help, and thousands more would show up at about three thousand Head Start centers in churches, schools, and community halls. By July, enrollment projections vaulted from one hundred thousand to nearly six hundred thousand children, and the project's budget soared from an estimated $10 million to $70 million.

Mamie inspected Head Start centers that summer to assess their progress. She found the quality uneven and saw that parents were seldom involved beyond menial tasks like kitchen work. Unfortunately, most seemed unprepared for work at a higher level, she reported. To Mamie, poverty was a matter of degree, because in some upstate areas, the children seemed more capable than others she'd observed closer to home: "So that what was poor in Niagara Falls, and what they were calling poor, to me was quite sophisticated."[9] That fall, she and her colleagues were summoned back to Washington to fine-tune Head Start, which was evolving into a year-round program, perhaps the most popular in the War on Poverty. In decades to come, conservatives in Congress would repeatedly try to kill Head Start but in vain.

Meanwhile, Mamie took on another major project to improve the lot of the poor and minorities. In dire need of space at Northside and lamenting the slums nearby, she moved to replace them with new homes and offices for her clinic and other Harlem agencies. The blighted, four-block site she targeted was just up the street from Northside at 110th Street and Fifth Avenue, then known as Frawley Circle. Near Central Park, it bordered three neighborhoods often at odds: Central Harlem, mostly Black; East Harlem, Puerto Rican; and the white Upper East Side. Meeting at Northside with volunteers, Mamie formed a committee to move the project forward. She formed subcommittees to research the housing, educational, and cultural issues raised by the project. Kenneth headed the education group and drew on his contacts at city hall and the state capital in Albany to secure the funds and public approval needed for the project. Mamie gained a grant to hire an executive director for the project: Barry Jackson, an architect and city planner. She assigned him an office at Northside to work on the plans and drawings.

The Clarks met with Mayor Wagner to enlist his support. Touting Frawley Circle as "the gateway to Harlem," Mamie described her dream: an integrated town center with modern offices and hundreds of new apartments in an area where thirty-five hundred people now lived in squalor. New businesses would replace seedy old shops. The project would bring jobs, money, and construction to Harlem and spur other development there. Partnerships with universities, medical centers, and arts institutions would draw new services and cultural events to Harlem for all races and classes. Hers was an integrationist dream, and Mamie proposed a new name for the stretch of 110th Street where it would take shape: "Central Park North."

The Clarks' meeting with Mayor Wagner and other politicians yielded no promises, so they met with them again and again, with few results. City Councilman J. Raymond Jones gained council support for a street sign labeled Central Park North that was ceremoniously raised at the corner of Fifth Avenue and 110th Street. "Frankly, the name change of itself is not going to do a damn thing," Kenneth told a *New York Times* reporter.[10] Mamie was more upbeat. "We want the place to look like Central Park South," a very nice place, she added.

Frawley Circle was no Central Park South. Mamie found litter-strewn gutters and a ramshackle hotel with so many people streaming in and out it could have used a revolving door. Drug addicts monopolized the sidewalk benches, and she was horrified by the decay she found in the tenements. Many residents were destitute and on welfare, though some were from solid, working-class families with high hopes and children in private schools. All, however, feared the loss of their homes to slum clearance. But for Mamie, the status quo was unacceptable.

To gain the neighbors' support, she met with the president

of the 110th Street Block Association who'd attacked the project. "We can't be antagonistic towards each other, we've got to help each other," Mamie said.[11] She asked Jackson, executive director of her Central Park North committee, to explain the project to neighbors at a block association meeting. Jackson drew heavy flak at the session, but undaunted, Mamie recruited two precocious teenagers to reach out to residents and help organize their block meetings. The boys joined adult volunteers who mingled with the neighbors to report their concerns.

Mamie encountered either indifference or hostility at every turn: from neighbors, block leaders, and city hall. But she had Kenneth and loyal colleagues on her side. She also had charm, tact, and an iron will. A few Harlem leaders joined her crusade, among them Elaine Gaspard, a mother and grassroots activist; former Manhattan borough president Hulan Jack, who lived nearby; and Reverend Apolonio Melecio of La Hermosa Church. Mamie appealed to their hopes for decent housing, jobs, and business opportunities for all races and classes at the gateway to Harlem. Having heard all the objections—that urban renewal was "Negro removal," that she was one of the fancy people cashing in on Harlem's despair—Mamie blocked out the static and embraced a colossal struggle for years to come. "This was a huge thing in her life," daughter Kate recalled.[12] "This was a battle to get those buildings built."

Teaching classes while founding a research center at City College would have been challenging enough for most professors, but

Kenneth took on another big assignment that fall: writing a book about Harlem for Harper and Row. Drawing on a half century of his life and work in Harlem as well as the trove of data in the *Youth in the Ghetto* report, he aimed to write a powerful book about segregation in Northern cities and improve the lot of African Americans.

Kenneth knew his subject cold and wrote swiftly and passionately about what he called the pathologies of the Harlem ghetto: crime, drugs, and disease. The lack of medical care, sanitation, employment, and quality education. The rampant mental illness and waste of so many young lives. He also touched on ghetto life in Boston, Philadelphia, Chicago, and other big cities. His relentless focus on a grim topic sent Kenneth's spirit plummeting. "He was so depressed about what he had to write he couldn't bear it, really," his editor, Jeannette Hopkins, recalled.[13] While they pored over his manuscript in her thirteenth-floor apartment one afternoon, Kenneth frightened Hopkins by saying he felt like jumping from her window. "I said to him, 'Not out of my apartment,'" she recalled. "He laughed when I said that."

Throughout the winter of 1965, Mamie read each of Kenneth's chapters and offered suggestions and encouragement. In spite of Hopkins's warnings against doing so, Kenneth aimed more jabs at Powell in the book, titled *Dark Ghetto*. He dedicated it "To Mamie, Who Has Endured And Given Much." Gunnar Myrdal, his famous Swedish friend, wrote the foreword, and the book was in the stores by May.

Dark Ghetto was dark indeed. The prologue offered page after page of bitter comments from Harlemites raging against the segregated way of life. "I'm not a man, none of us are men!" one said.[14] "I don't own anything. I'm not a man enough to own a store; none of us are." Kenneth offered his unvarnished observations on controversial topics such as Black self-hatred, families without fathers, and class conflict between African Americans. He argued that structural racism—bad cops, chaotic schools, lily-white unions, and rapacious commercial interests—had turned Harlem into a segregated colony with whites controlling even the numbers racket.

Dark Ghetto was well-timed amid the urban riots of the 1960s. It sold well and drew glowing reviews, and critics called it a classic. Newspapers and magazines published long excerpts, and translated editions sold in about a dozen countries, including Japan, Hungary, and Norway. Black writer Jervis Anderson praised the book for looking squarely at ghetto life and all but defying optimism: "It is an indictment that is not easy to stand up and take."[15]

But Kenneth's emphasis on self-hatred and psychological damage did not go down well with other Black critics. And his criticism of Powell, already drawing fire in the press for financial irregularities at HARYOU-ACT, rekindled the HARYOU controversy. One of Powell's aides, C. Sumner "Chuck" Stone, lashed out: "Whites read and applaud the Kenneth Clarks because they reaffirm their prejudices, buttress their subconscious hatreds, involve Negroes in a diversionary pursuit of morality and tell them what they want to hear."[16] White columnist Murray Kempton, however, sided with Kenneth: "Powell is an ambassador from the Negro to government. Clark is an ambassador from the Negro to the public conscience."[17]

The unkindest cut for Kenneth came from novelist Ralph Ellison, often a guest of the Clarks, who charged that Kenneth had "an investment in negative propaganda as a means of raising funds" and likened him to the character in Herman Melville's Confidence Man who "blackened his face and twisted his limbs and then crawled about the ship deck whimpering like a dog begging and catching coins in his mouth."[18] Kenneth shot back, "I think Ralph Ellison needs more contact with Negroes, needs to feel more anger."[19]

Exhausted by overwork, Kenneth suffered again from stomach ulcers. To help him relax, Mamie arranged a month's break first in Hot Springs and then the Caribbean before his summer stint teaching at Harvard. While in Hot Springs, Mamie gave a graduation address at her alma mater, the Langston School, and it did not go well. Her topic was success, but she looked terribly nervous and fixed her gaze on one corner of the auditorium. "She was criticized by some in the faculty," recalled retired Black teacher Elmer Beard.[20] Whenever the famous Clarks were in Hot Springs, the word spread quickly, and Black neighbors welcomed the couple. "They were such prominent people, and my parents would say, 'Oh, Kenneth and Mamie will be home, and we're going to the dance,'" recalled Edward Wesson, the son of hotel workers in town.[21]

Returning home from Arkansas, the Clarks headed next for Montego Bay in Jamaica, where they often vacationed with Black friends from New York, especially NAACP attorney Robert Carter and Dr. John Moseley. Kenneth enjoyed drinks and joking about sex in these rare, unguarded moments, often wondering aloud if he should leave America and its racial problems for a tranquil life in

Jamaica. But Mamie reminded him that the island had its own social problems and he'd end up trying to solve them.

Back in New York, the success of *Dark Ghetto* secured Kenneth's reputation as the nation's most prominent Black scholar and public intellectual. On stage, on television, and in print, he came across as a soft-spoken but blunt critic of white racism. Baffled by Black rage and urban riots, whites asked him why there was so much conflict in an era of progress in civil rights. Kenneth suggested that a brutally repressed minority seldom rebels, but easing the boot from its neck can have the opposite effect. He predicted that the flames from ghetto revolts would burn hotter before cooling. Often asked if he too had prejudices—a question Kenneth regarded as naive—he suggested that racism in America left no one unscathed.

He offered bitter medicine to Black audiences as well. Kenneth said there was some comfort in segregation, but as it diminished, Blacks would face the anxieties of a competitive, integrating society. "To be the first Negro who is offered a job in a company brings a sense of triumph but also the dread of failure."[22] Kenneth argued that Black colleges were weak and had to raise standards to survive. Black teachers had to improve their skills, and Black institutions in general needed to compete with others on a single standard of excellence or face collapse.

Magazines pressed Kenneth for articles, publishers asked him to write books, and foundations offered him money. Black leaders summoned him to their conclaves, and he was invited to the White House to present his views. In one month that fall, he left the state eight times to give speeches and made headlines wherever he spoke. He raised the eyebrows of whites by urging them to get over their fear of miscegenation and clinging to color prejudice in a mostly nonwhite world. He startled Black activists by declaring street protests a tactic of the past that sapped energy better spent on careful organizing. To young militants brimming with outrage, Kenneth sounded terribly conservative.

In bridal gown and veil, Kate Clark, age twenty-four, walked down the aisle with her father at St. Philip's Episcopal Church in Harlem. In the pews were three hundred friends and relatives, including civil rights activists from two generations: old friends such as Whitney Young of the Urban League and Roy Wilkins of the NAACP but also young friends of the twenty-four-year-old groom, Black activist Donald Harris, including Julian Bond and John Lewis, stalwarts of the civil rights movement in Dixie. Kate's wedding photo appeared in the *New York Times* with a headline noting, "Bride is Escorted by Her Father, Former HARYOU Chairman"[23]—hers a rare Black face on the society page.

Kate's romance with Harris, a civil rights worker from New York, had begun with their correspondence while he was in jail for a protest he led in Americus, Georgia. Trying to integrate the movie theater there, Harris was stunned by a cop's cattle prod and sentenced to three months in jail for insurrection. The charge carried a maximum penalty of death by electric chair.

The Clarks admired Harris for his courage but never wanted Kate or Hilton to face the homicidal racism of the South. Impatient with her graduate work at Smith College in 1964, Kate had talked of shelving it all to fight for civil rights in Mississippi. Her father said no, insisting that she finish her education instead. So Kate helped set up new offices for the civil rights movement near Boston and helped with fundraising. Meanwhile her beau, young Harris, continued his work in Georgia. One night when James Baldwin was in the Clarks' home for drinks and conversation, Harris and Kate announced their engagement.

More rebellious than Kate, Hilton often wrangled with his father over his activism at Columbia. Kenneth wanted him to spend more time on books and less on activism. Some of their arguments ended in sullen silence that lasted weeks, and their differences surfaced in news stories. His father told the *New York Post* that Hilton was considering law school—"That is, if he can stay in his classrooms long enough."[24] And when Hilton was arrested at a Schaefer brewery protest over job discrimination, he told reporters that he couldn't discuss it, that his father opposed the protest. Still, Hilton insisted on doing his part, even working and living for a time with Fanny Lou Hamer, godmother to Black civil rights workers in Mississippi.

At first, Kenneth opposed Hilton's efforts to found the Student Afro-American Society at Columbia, which explored Black identity and fought student apathy. But after reflecting on his own alienation at Columbia in the 1940s, Kenneth endorsed Hilton's group by writing an essay on racial identity for its magazine, the *Black Student*. Hilton followed with an essay strikingly similar in subject and style to his father's. Hilton told a reporter that his father's article might seem more objective, "But I think he pulls too many punches."[25]

Hilton was independent, outspoken, and a trifle stubborn—a slivery chip off the old block.

Kenneth had dreamed of building a dynamic research center at City College with top scholars working to solve urban problems, but the college declined to provide even a typewriter and two parking spots for his miniscule staff. Purchasing an IQ test took months, and Kenneth was besieged by requests for expense vouchers and budget data. More interested in teaching, writing, and activism than in shuffling paperwork, he quit the research job after one semester and requested a year's leave of absence.

Once the news was out, the Field Foundation approached Kenneth about founding a bigger, private research center where there'd be no need for a voucher in triplicate to buy a box of paper clips. Intrigued, Kenneth envisioned a think tank like the RAND Corporation, but instead of serving corporations or the government, his would serve the poor. He'd think about it.

Exhausted by his work on *Dark Ghetto*, Kenneth badly needed his leave of absence. Mamie too was overwhelmed. After two years of fruitless toil on the gateway-to-Harlem project, her committee was running out of funds. She begged the members for cash to keep it afloat. Northside, as always, also needed money, and Kenneth donated his *Dark Ghetto* royalties to the clinic. The total came to about $50,000, quite a windfall in the 1960s, and Mamie sent him a thank-you note. "Love you madly," she wrote, adding her initials.[26] "More Love."

THIRTEEN

BLACK POWER

If America don't come around, we're going to burn
America down, brother.

—H. RAP BROWN[1]

I t was June 5, 1966, a sunny day in Mississippi, when James
Meredith, in work boots and short sleeves, walked along a highway
on his March Against Fear. The Black activist who once faced white
mobs to desegregate the University of Mississippi was marching
toward the capital, Jackson, 220 miles away. Suddenly, there was a
gunshot, and Meredith fell, shrieking in pain. While he recovered in
a hospital, Dr. Martin Luther King Jr. joined dozens of young Black
activists to resume Meredith's march on the same highway.

Along the way one night, Stokely Carmichael, the militant new
chair of the Student Nonviolent Coordinating Committee, told his
followers that it was time to stop begging for civil rights. "We want

Black Power!" he said, thrusting his forefinger downward.[2] "That's right. That's what we want, Black Power." The phrase rippled through the crowd and soon crossed the lips of millions nationwide. Fed up with the shootings and beatings in the Southern crusade for integration, young Blacks embraced separatism. They wanted communities run by Blacks, businesses owned by Blacks, and schools controlled by Blacks. Carmichael and comrades like H. Rap Brown talked openly of getting guns or tearing up cities. They purged white activists from their ranks, and the interracial alliance that powered the civil rights movement unraveled.

The Clarks feared that Black Power was hardening into a separatist dogma for the young, and Mamie argued that leveler heads had to speak out. To many Black leaders of the Clarks' generation—Dorothy Height, Roy Wilkins, Whitney Young, Bayard Rustin, and A. Philip Randolph—Black Power was folly, and all five signed a statement denouncing it. In articles and speeches, Kenneth lambasted Black Power as a mindless fad of youth—a slogan, not a strategy: "It is a desperate retreat from the hope of national integration into the blind alley of racial segregation under the guise of racial pride and defiance."[3]

The Clarks had learned at Howard University that race was an arbitrary concept, that Black chauvinism was as bad as white chauvinism, and that integrating all classes and colors was the best way forward. Even so, Kenneth conceded that after decades of brutally enforced segregation, Black Power was an understandable overreaction, a sign of mental health, as the young took fierce pride in their race. But he preferred a different path to power, arguing that

Blacks in politics and business needed better training, networking, and data—not just to gain power for themselves but to secure civil liberties and help the poor. He believed that a dynamic new research center could fuel the next phase of the Black struggle. For years, whites of wealth and power had built think tanks to mold public opinion and promote their own interests, so why not build a think tank for the poor? Unlike at HARYOU, this time, he'd rely on professionals instead of the young to propel the struggle forward. Still, he'd never deviate from the message of his Howard professors and W. E. B. Du Bois: wield disciplined intelligence as a weapon to smash segregation and secure equal rights and opportunity.

On his leave from City College, Kenneth approached foundations to support a new research center where integrated groups of students, scholars, and activists could study urban problems and find solutions. Given his prestige and connections—and the threat of urban riots yet to come—the Field Foundation offered Kenneth $1.5 million over five years to open the Metropolitan Applied Research Center (MARC). The Ford Foundation followed with another $700,000—hardly small change at the time. Other foundations chipped in.

As Kenneth envisioned it, MARC would focus on social maladies in New York City but branch out to help heal the nation. To stay free and independent, his think tank would accept no government aid. Fellowships would bring scholars and activists together, including mainstream leaders like Dr. King but also Black Power advocates like Floyd McKissick and Roy Innis of the Congress of Racial Equality, or CORE. On neutral ground, they'd write, debate, and hone new strategies to build a better society. A publications department would release books and reports on urban ills by MARC scholars. To groom young activists, there'd be internships, conferences, and other training. MARC would become the nation's first Black think tank but integrated with whites in key positions, many of them women. His new board of directors included white labor mediator Theodore Kheel as well as renowned Black leaders such as Bayard Rustin and A. Philip Randolph, who'd organized the March on Washington three years before. Kenneth moved MARC into new offices on Fifty-Eighth Street in Manhattan.

Mamie helped to get MARC up and running, just as Kenneth helped her at Northside and with her gateway-to-Harlem project. In March 1967, he held a press conference to unveil his new venture. The story landed on the front page of the *Washington Post*, and a *New York Post* headline put it this way: "Brain Trust Here to Study Problems of the Deprived."[4]

Bitter quarrels over Black Power and the Vietnam War split the nation's civil rights leaders soon after MARC opened its doors, and as its leader, Kenneth served as peacemaker. Nearly half a million GIs were in Vietnam, and U.S. warplanes were bombing the North Vietnamese capital of Hanoi and hamlets in South Vietnam. In the spring of 1967, horrified by photos of Asian children maimed in the air raids, Dr. King took a bold stand against the war from the pulpit of the Riverside Church near Harlem. King called the U.S. government "the greatest purveyor of violence in the world today."[5] Demanding a withdrawal from Vietnam, he got a standing ovation in the pews, but the white press hit him hard. Some Black leaders, including Roy Wilkins of the NAACP, objected that King had angered President Johnson and diverted attention from civil rights. Kenneth silently sided with King.

In May, MARC sent a limousine to whisk King to the Clarks' home in Hastings for a secret summit meeting. More than a dozen of the nation's Black leaders showed up to air their differences, including Wilkins, Black Power advocate McKissick of CORE, Dorothy Height of the National Council of Negro Women, Whitney Young of the Urban League, and a representative from Carmichael's militant Student Nonviolent Coordinating Committee. They met in the Clarks' sun-filled library of book-lined walls.

Kenneth opened by suggesting ways that MARC could help the Black leaders, and McKissick called for more such meetings to set goals and avoid sniping at each other in the press. King chimed in that MARC might cover the travel costs. The meeting's tone sharpened once Wilkins suggested that some in the room were encouraging riots by forecasting them in the press. Bristling, McKissick defended his right to expose the explosive conditions in the ghettos. And when King added that militarism and monopoly capitalism should be criticized, Wilkins asked if King had a timetable for defeating these evils, and how would it help the poor? The leaders bickered over Vietnam, draft resistance, and venting their disputes in newspapers. As their host and mediator, Kenneth tried to calm them by summing up their differences and emphasizing points of agreement. He called for another session in two weeks to discuss ways of dealing with urban unrest over the summer, especially in Cleveland, which was on the verge of a riot just as a promising Black candidate, Carl Stokes, was running for mayor.

On June 13, as riots racked Boston, Cincinnati, and Tampa, Kenneth convened a calmer, second summit for Dr. King and the other Black leaders to unite and quell urban riots. Sensing a need for more fence-mending, Kenneth held other leadership meetings that summer, including one at his mother's home in Queens to bring Black Power advocates such as Carmichael and H. Rap Brown together with mainstream civil rights leaders.

Kenneth's standing with the nation's Black leadership had never been greater. He was an adviser, mediator, and valuable link to well-heeled donors, and a charming one at that. "He wasn't the kind of person that folks saw as a rival," recalled George Dalley, an aide to Kenneth at MARC.[6] "Nobody felt he was doing these things to gain stature."

Cleveland kept its cool that summer and elected Stokes as mayor, but Newark, a few miles from New York, erupted. After police beat a Black cabdriver, storefronts burst into flames, gunshots rang out, and the rioting lasted for days. Twenty-six people were killed, and Kenneth walked the charred, rubble-strewn streets, sickened by what he saw. Another clash with cops led to four days of pillaging in Detroit. Police and National Guard troops patrolled the streets, and bullets again streaked the darkness. Forty-three people were slain this time and nearly seven hundred buildings damaged or destroyed. Scores of other riots erupted in the most violent summer yet.

Groping for solutions, President Johnson tapped Illinois Governor Otto Kerner to lead a commission to investigate the riots. The panel included just two Blacks: moderates Roy Wilkins and Senator Edward Brooke of Massachusetts. Kenneth viewed the commission as a public-relations gimmick and ignored its invitations to testify. After Mamie pressed him to attend, he finally faced the commissioners and testified that there had been too many reports on race riots over the last half century. They all sounded alike and accomplished nothing. "I must again in candor say to you members of this commission that it is a kind of Alice in Wonderland—with the same moving picture re-shown over and over again, the same analysis, the same recommendations, and the same inaction."[7] He continued:

> *This society knows, I believe—and certainly the leaders of the society must know—that if human beings are confined in ghetto compounds of our cities and are subjected to criminally inferior education, pervasive economic and job discrimination, committed to houses unfit for human habitation, subjected to unspeakable conditions of municipal services, such as sanitation, that such human beings are not likely to be responsive to appeals to be lawful, to be respectful, to be concerned with the property of others.*

The rioting would continue, Kenneth warned, because America refused to muster the resources equal to the problem. Assailing the nation's "planlessness" and neglect of its cities, he said the ghetto was America's only plan. Politicians weren't the only ones to blame, he argued. Churches, labor unions, and even schools and colleges maintained a segregated society. "That is my opinion—and I think that the data will back this up."

If there was any hope, Kenneth said, it lay in developing serious initiatives, without gimmicks, to produce real change in the lives of Black people. Whenever America was serious about a goal—building the atomic bomb or rebuilding postwar Europe—it mobilized the resources to achieve it, he said. Human intelligence could resolve the race problem—America lacked only the will, Kenneth said. It was his finest hour as a public intellectual.

The Kerner Commission's compelling final report, a bestseller, issued its famous warning that America was moving toward two societies: one Black, one white—separate and unequal. Drawing data from Kenneth's *Dark Ghetto* and other sources, the report called for eliminating segregation, improving urban schools, retraining police, and other major reforms. In its hard-hitting conclusion, the Kerner report quoted Kenneth's Alice-in-Wonderland prediction that its findings would result in little or no change. Washington columnist Drew Pearson observed: "Dr. Clark was prophetic. For the Johnson Administration has proceeded to pour lukewarm water over the commission's recommendations for immediate massive action."[8]

Percy Sutton, Manhattan's Black borough president, spotted a sign one day that said, "White politicians *won't* do anything for the Negro, and Negro politicians *can't*." Tired of hearing that Black politicians were Uncle Toms, Sutton told Kenneth that it killed confidence in Black elected officials and something had to be done. Kenneth responded by securing a training grant to bring them together for a three-day conference in Chicago. At a time when their numbers had surged to 700 nationwide, about 250 arrived at the National Conference of Negro Elected Officials in September 1967. They were from big states and small, many of them mayors or members of city councils and school boards, to debate hot topics such as the war, urban riots, and Black Power. They attended workshops on applying for business loans, fundraising for community projects, and running voter drives. Among those attending were U.S. Representative John Conyers of Michigan and Georgia lawmaker Julian Bond. The conference was a success, and the participants asked to convene again.

Kenneth made it happen two years later and led more than two hundred leaders to the White House Rose Garden and stood beside the new law-and-order president, Richard Nixon, to introduce each one. Some of them later said they should have picketed the White House instead of shaking Nixon's hand, but Kenneth responded that engaging the adversary was a necessary part of the political process. Opening their conference at the Hilton Hotel, Kenneth took an oblique swipe at Nixon by criticizing politicians who spout law-and-order rhetoric. A *Chicago Daily Defender* headline summed it up this way, "Dr. Kenneth B. Clark Lays It On Line in DC" [9] The civil rights movement was not dead, Kenneth said; it just moved to a higher plane with Black elected officials in charge instead of self-appointed activists.

Like W. E. B. Du Bois decades before him, Kenneth was bringing Black leaders together to cultivate leadership for the struggles ahead. To build the infrastructure for a revitalized movement, he had

MARC publish directories of the nation's African American scholars and officeholders so they could form networks and share data more easily. Kenneth's staff organized separate conferences to bring the nation's Black professionals in law, business, and education together. MARC supplied data and technical assistance to new Black mayors, including Kenneth Gibson of Newark and Richard Hatcher of Gary, Indiana. He helped revitalize or build other organizations for Black leaders, including the One Hundred Black Men in New York City and the Joint Center for Political and Economic Studies, a Washington think tank. "Kenneth really saw there had to be something after all the marching and the dying were over," historian Roger Wilkins recalled.[10] "There had to be things in place that could make things move in a richer and deeper way." George Dalley, chief of staff to Kenneth at MARC, recalled, "He was a leader of leaders."[11]

Mamie worried as Kenneth's stature grew and demands on his time and energy mounted. Along with running MARC, giving speeches, and appearing regularly on television news shows, he returned to teaching, though only part-time, at City College. His jabs at Black Power drew hate mail from Black nationalists, and several showed up at the college to berate him. As he walked in Manhattan one day, a Black driver pulled up, shook his fist, and said, "We're gonna get you, you son of a bitch."[12] Young militants ridiculed Kenneth as an Uncle Tom, but the Black press still covered his work, and Black leaders phoned him for help. As he juggled meetings and appointments, the strain showed on his face. His staff fretted about Kenneth's health, and so did Mamie, who whisked him off to the Caribbean to relax from time to time.

They were often seen out on the town together: at Northside fundraisers, Mayor John Lindsay's inaugural ball, and an awards ceremony for President Johnson at the Waldorf Astoria. The Clarks dined in the homes of Governor Nelson Rockefeller and U.S. Senator Jacob Javits, both liberal Republicans. Mamie's profile rose right along with Kenneth's. Columbia University jointly awarded them its Butler Medal for their humanitarian work and offered Mamie a board seat at the Teachers College. The New York Public Library and Haverford College invited her to join their boards as well. Her reputation spread as a psychologist, administrator, and mother with sound advice on raising children in a bigoted society. She told a reporter that giving foreign dolls in native dress to a child—not just white dolls—was a good way to broach the topic of prejudice. "The Other Dr. Clark," the *New York Post* called her, and photographers from both *Vogue* and *Family Circle* magazines trained their cameras on Mamie.[13] The Black press had never lost interest in her or Northside Center. In the *Amsterdam News*, columnist Betty Granger Reid wrote, "Dr. Mamie Phipps Clark deserves every accolade we can garner."[14]

Mamie redoubled her efforts to rebuild Northside's deteriorating neighborhood. Time and again, she met with city, state, and federal officials to fund her gateway-to-Harlem housing and office complex. Mayor John Lindsay made promises and issued press releases but little more, and Mamie was exasperated. Finally, Governor Rockefeller signed a law creating the Urban Development Corporation, an agency to fund urban renewal projects, and put Kenneth on its board. Once Kenneth learned the ropes, he could advise Mamie on which ones to pull to gain the financing she needed. But major hurdles loomed. The Young Lords, a militant Puerto Rican group, denounced Mamie's project, picketed Northside Center, and threatened to barricade its doors. The situation was volatile, and Mamie met with the Young Lords. Meanwhile, she faced a huge $100,000 deficit at the clinic and the doubling of its rent.

Early in 1968, after vacationing with Mamie in Bermuda, Kenneth prepared to move MARC into a three-story townhouse at 60 East Eighty-Sixth Street. It was owned by the Bronfmans of the Seagram's fortune, who one day would give him the building. The front door was made of brass, and an elevator led to Kenneth's new office on the third floor where a portrait of his hero, W. E. B. Du Bois, hung on the wall. Tall African sculptures stood at both sides of Kenneth's desk. His new headquarters augured a fresh start.

———

Riots, assassinations, and daily protests over the Vietnam War and civil rights made 1968 a turbulent year for the Clarks and the nation. In the spring, Kenneth assumed the role of peacemaker again when Howard students seized university buildings and asked him, as a trustee, to hear their demands. When word spread that federal marshals would sweep the campus, he met with both the protesters and administrators in overnight talks that averted bloodshed.

Two weeks later, his other alma mater, Columbia, erupted in similar protests. Hearing that H. Rap Brown and other militants were headed there, Kenneth hurried to a dormitory occupied by about one hundred Black students. He tipped them off that police were coming to their building just in time for the students to line up, leave their building, and face an orderly arrest. Like the Howard protesters, Columbia's Black students had few illusions about white cops. In the meantime, white protesters in other buildings defied the police, and Kenneth watched in horror as hundreds of cops with clubs and fists flying tore through their buildings. They beat students and dragged them down stairways, and Kenneth begged two officers to stop harassing them. About 150 people were injured, including reporters and professors who were merely observing.

Meanwhile, the nation was mourning the death of Dr. King, who had been gunned down in Memphis by a white man. The Clarks were heartbroken. Choking up, Kenneth told a *New York Times* reporter, "You have to cry out in anguish for this country...weep for this country."[15] Black Power advocate Stokely Carmichael, who admired King, had lashed out in fury: "Black people know that they need to get guns."[16] Riots broke out in more than one hundred cities, including Chicago and Washington, but not Harlem, where Kenneth inspected the streets at night and saw police showing restraint. In the morning, he stood and grieved for King with City College students at city hall, their heads bowed in silence till the clock chimed at noon.

The city was racked by turmoil again in the fall, when the Clarks were swept up in the biggest and longest teachers' strike in American history. The conflict pitted teachers against parents and Jewish persons against Blacks. The Clarks cast their lot with minority parents who opposed the strike. The issue wasn't teacher pay; it was community control of urban schools, a hot topic nationwide as minorities demanded a say in their children's education. In New York City,

Black and Puerto Rican parents had little leverage with the byzantine school bureaucracy and nearly sixty thousand unionized teachers. The Clarks hoped that a decentralized system of community boards headed by civic leaders and parents would improve the schools.

But for Albert Shanker, the United Federation of Teachers president, it was easier to deal with one board of education than dozens of boards with power over teachers. Working in city schools was a stressful, low-paid, often thankless job, and the teachers, full of the rebellious spirit of the times, demanded more power and better working conditions. "Listen, I don't represent children," Shanker once said.[17] "I represent the teachers."

State officials had allowed three new community boards on an experimental basis: one in Harlem, where the Clarks were intimately involved, and the others in the Lower East Side and the Ocean Hill-Brownsville section of Brooklyn. The latter board served a community that was chiefly Black, Puerto Rican, and poor, and it proved the most combustible. It dismissed hundreds of teachers and principals, many of them Jewish persons who'd spoken out against community control.

The strike dragged on for weeks, and nearly all the city's teachers and a million students were out of school. Some Black instructors, however, joined with liberal whites who broke through the picket lines to teach some classes. The crowds were raucous, and ethnic slurs flew from all sides. Cops struggled to keep the peace, and the whole city was tense. As journalist I. F. Stone put it, "The Mason-Dixon line has moved north, and the Old Confederacy has expanded to the outer reaches of the Bronx."[18]

Mamie organized volunteers to cross the picket lines and

teach children while Kenneth used MARC to organize the Union of Concerned Parents. With Mamie as secretary-treasurer, the UCP led a publicity campaign slamming the teacher strike in radio spots, newspaper ads, a newsletter, and even a sound truck in the streets. "Save Our Children" fliers and "Flunk Shanker" buttons circulated. Kenneth joined in negotiations with Mayor Lindsay, Shanker, and state educators from Albany. Twice they reached settlements that later unraveled as the militant Ocean Hill-Brownsville board, with Rhody McCoy as administrator, refused to reinstate the dismissed teachers. McCoy appeared at rallies with a raised, clenched fist, the Black Power salute.

The Clarks tried to distance themselves from the extremists trying to break the strike. "We want the participation of all concerned parents but not the dominance of any one group such as the militants," Mamie said. She ordered the withdrawal of an inflammatory *UCP News* item, and at a sensitive point in negotiations, Kenneth quietly pressed the Ocean Hill-Brownsville militants to cool it. Still, he drew flak from Jewish persons for not condemning the radicals. "The Jewish community felt estranged," MARC aide Dalley recalled.[19] "That was a big deal."

Late in November, after weeks of negotiations, Kenneth showed up at Gracie Mansion for a final round. More than twenty-four hours later, a deal was finally struck, and the strike was finally over. The Clarks and their allies came out on the short end. The intransigent Ocean Hill-Brownsville board remained suspended while its fired teachers got their jobs back. All teachers in the illegal strike were compensated for lost pay, a huge victory for Shanker.

The struggle between powerful teacher unions and minority parents in troubled city school systems would flare up, die down, then erupt again and again in New York and nationwide—a perennial conflict that begs for a solution.

—————

With the turbulent year behind them at last, Mamie arranged a month-long trip to Scandinavia, not just to relax but for a glimpse of more orderly societies renowned for protecting families and the needy—in contrast to what she and Kenneth saw as the planlessness of America. On July 29, 1969, they boarded the MS *Bergensfjord*, and daughter Kate was at the pier in Manhattan with her little ones to wave goodbye: baby Natalie and Scott, a toddler. A grandmother at age fifty-one, Mamie was sad when the ship pulled away and left the children behind.

Under cloudy skies, Mamie napped and rested before mingling with other passengers, most of Scandinavian descent. "We have invaded W.A.S.P. territory but are receiving a friendly welcome," she wrote in her travel diary.[20] The next morning, she slipped in the shower and injured her right leg. Kenneth helped her to the ship's infirmary for X-rays and learned that his blood pressure was high again. Exasperated, Mamie jotted, "He simply has to take his medicine."

The Clarks arrived on August 5 in Kristiansand, a tidy Norwegian city of sun, fjord, and flowers where they toured a Lutheran church built in 1040 and marveled at the gravestone carvings. Their tour guide pointed with pride to symbols of Norway's generous social welfare system—a handsome school, hospital, and apartment buildings—all built for the people, he said.

Two days later in the capital city of Oslo, the Clarks marveled at more flowers and fountains while eating hot dogs for lunch in a park. Mamie found a doctor to wrap her throbbing leg. "Marvelous, warm hospital," she noted. Kenneth wanted to see Oslo's neighborhoods, and a cabdriver who called himself a radical promised to show him slums, but every building and street that he drove by was tidy. "Great emphasis on housing and needs of all age groups," Mamie wrote. "No true slum areas."

The Clarks took a train and streaked down to Stockholm, the capital of Sweden, to see their old friends Gunnar and Alva Myrdal and chat about the social welfare system they'd helped build there. Later, while Mamie took the pressure off her leg, Kenneth visited neighborhoods and the ombudsman's office that investigated complaints about social services. Moving on to Copenhagen, the Clarks toured a daycare center, a nursing home, and more neighborhoods. Near drizzly Amsterdam, they admired modern, high-rise homes with a view of cows in a pasture.

Before leaving Europe, the Clarks pondered what they'd seen in Scandinavia: the sleek trains, the efficient schools and hospitals, the dignified homes of working families, and the ombudsmen's offices to help citizens. Why all this collective concern for each person's well-being? Was it just because of the long winters or Sweden's racial homogeneity? Discounting the latter, Kenneth concluded that any affluent nation that wanted a civil society could have one.

The Clarks' ship ventured homeward through thick fog and placid seas and arrived in New York on September 3. Both Hilton and Kate awaited them at the pier with little Scott and Natalie again. They all headed for home in Hastings, and ending her diary, Mamie wrote, "Marvelous reunion."

FOURTEEN

OPENING A GATEWAY TO HARLEM

Until twenty million black people are completely inter-
woven into the fabric of our society, you see, they are
under no obligation to behave as if they were. What
I am saying is that whether we like the word or not,
the condition of our people dictates what can only be
called revolutionary attitudes.

—LORRAINE HANSBERRY[1]

Well into their fifties, their energies flagging, the Clarks talked
wistfully of retiring. By 1970, the optimism they'd shared after
the *Brown* ruling was a bittersweet memory. And yet they pressed
on, Mamie struggling to build her gateway-to-Harlem complex on
Fifth Avenue and Kenneth projecting his integrationist views on
race, politics, and education from MARC's offices in New York, Los
Angeles, and the nation's capital. He was also president of the prestigious American Psychological Association.

As the idealism of the 1960s faded in a new decade, the nation's politics veered rightward. Kenneth accused President Nixon of cutting antipoverty aid and blocking equal opportunity in jobs and housing. Nixon expanded the Vietnam War by bombing Cambodia that spring, and when American students rose up in protest, four were shot and killed at Kent State University in Ohio and two at Jackson State, a Black college in Mississippi. In a riot in Augusta, Georgia, police killed six Black men. Meanwhile, the FBI continued a campaign of repression against the Black Panthers that had led to fatal shoot-outs and the imprisonment of several members—a shameful episode in the bureau's checkered history. Lamenting the tenor of the times, Black historian Roger Wilkins wrote, "Even from my pessimism of 1967 I could not have anticipated a country as desolate as the America of 1970 seemed to me to be."[2]

Meanwhile, whites in the North adopted the tactics of Black activists, suing, boycotting, and picketing to keep minorities out of predominantly white schools and neighborhoods. Self-proclaimed experts like Arthur Jensen and William Shockley cherry-picked statistics to claim that Blacks were intellectually inferior. And Nixon aide Daniel P. Moynihan, a liberal sociologist, recommended "benign neglect" of Blacks, rupturing his relationship with Kenneth.[3] Other liberals turned conservative or shifted their focus from civil rights to the antiwar, feminist, or environmental movements. But the Clarks held their ground, on the center left, immersed in the struggle for integration and the improvement of Black lives nationwide.

A dozen staff members burst into Mamie's office one day at Northside Center as she met with visitors. Protesting low pay and poor working conditions, the workers demanded a union and used the word *hell* to underscore the message. Mamie shot back, "You not only showed me such gross disrespect, but you also cursed."[4] Labor unions had long turned their backs on African Americans, and after the teachers' strike two years before, *union* was a dirty word to the Clarks. Local 1199's union drive at Northside came just as Mamie was making headway on her gateway-to-Harlem project. She was busy with lawyers, architects, and others to prepare the site for construction. To build out and furnish new offices for the clinic, she scrambled to raise $1.5 million, but Northside's future was now in jeopardy.

The next shot fired in the staff rebellion, a letter from Local 1199, revealed that most of the thirty-five rank-and-file workers had signed union cards. In the mandatory election that followed, the union won the right to bargain for all of them. The Clarks worried about a strike, the cash needed to cover higher union wages, and the prospect of heading a clinic that served a union instead of the children of Harlem. To the young, rebellious staffers, this smacked of paternalism.

Northside's board formed a negotiating team that included Kenneth and Herbert Prashker, an attorney for airlines in labor disputes. Kenneth seethed at the bargaining table as the union talked tough and demanded a union shop where the workers had to join and pay dues. Mamie kept her counsel while he warned his fellow board members that a union shop could kill the clinic. "This is a nonnegotiable item for Northside," he said, threatening to resign with Mamie.[5] But board member Robert Carter, who'd guided Kenneth through *Brown* as an NAACP lawyer, said the union wouldn't change all that much. Some board members agreed and liked that Local 1199 had ties to the late Dr. King and organized minority hospital workers for years.

The board remained divided for months as the contract talks dragged on. Finally, Mamie broke her silence at a meeting. Noting that all the clinic's administrators and ten of the thirty-five workers opposed a union shop, she said, "It is my firm personal conviction that a decision in favor of a union shop is a decision against the best interests of the children and families we serve."[6] But when the board met again in the spring of 1971, attorney Prashker presented a tentative agreement stating that current staffers need not join the union but all new hires would have to join and pay dues. In the first year, wages would rise by only $8,000 with no increase in benefits. Impressed, the board voted nineteen to three to approve the deal, and the Clarks, unlikely to gain a better one, accepted the decision. Recognizing the stress that Mamie endured for months, the board gave her extra vacation time to recoup. With the union aboard, life at Northside would never again be so informal or intimate. Still, good work could continue there.

And so it happened that a couple of days before Christmas in 1974, Mamie savored a long-delayed victory. It was sunny but cold when she gathered at a Harlem street corner with Mayor Abraham Beame and other dignitaries in winter coats. They'd all come to snip the ribbon for Schomburg Plaza, the huge new housing and office complex that she dedicated ten years of her life to build at Fifth Avenue and 110th Street.

Mamie's integrationist dream had finally emerged from its chrysalis: twin octagonal towers soaring thirty-four stories with new homes for Harlem families. In an adjacent building were new offices for Northside Center. Reading from prepared remarks, she celebrated the $26 million plaza as a symbol of renewed ties between Harlem's Black and Puerto Rican communities. The complex was named for renowned bibliophile Arthur Schomburg, who was both Black and a native of Puerto Rico. More than a monument of mortar and steel, Mamie said, Schomburg Plaza embodied a sense of pride and determination to replace slums with decent homes.

Her clinic's new offices in the complex had brightly painted walls and corridors lined with artworks by Black artists Charles Alston, Jacob Lawrence, and Raymond Saunders. There was a spacious new library and three rooms for classes or meetings. The whole family had helped to make Mamie's dream a reality. With contacts in high places, Kenneth had been indispensable. Daughter Kate had raised funds as a member of Liaison, a volunteer group, and Hilton touted his mother's achievement in an article he wrote for the *New York Age*.

In a black winter coat and karakul fur hat, Kenneth was in the small, shivering crowd watching Mamie speak. She, not he, was at center stage with the grandees of New York City, most of them men, celebrating her achievement. Kenneth was the family visionary who tried to cure all the world's ills at once and by every means possible: teaching, writing, speaking, peacemaking, and inventing one scheme

THE CLARKS IN THEIR STUDY
IN HASTINGS, CIRCA 1970

after another to combat segregation and pursue equal opportunity. But no mortal could do all these at once and well. Mamie, however, conserved her energies and focused relentlessly on a couple of goals: stabilizing Northside Center and erecting Schomburg Plaza one step at a time over the last decade. She was the manager and master of detail in the family—a study in quiet, tactful, indomitable persistence. And whatever she built endured. Kenneth was so proud of her that he nominated Mamie for the Spingarn Medal, the NAACP's highest honor. She'd never win it, but his nomination was a clear sign, if she'd ever needed one, of his devotion.

Schomburg Plaza, however, was no Camelot. Mamie had gained six hundred homes for Harlem families with problems that lacked a fairy-tale ending. New homes buoy new hopes, yet many residents of the bulldozed old tenements never saw the inside of a new high-rise apartment. The Clarks knew this and regretted it.

Unlike Mamie, Kenneth savored no big victory in the 1970s, and the first of several setbacks had been set in motion in January 1970.

That was when Anita Allen, the Black school board president in Washington, DC, had sought his help to transform her city's troubled school system. Would he do it for free, in the national interest?

Everything in his background had prepared Kenneth for the task, including his work to integrate and improve New York City schools over two decades as well as his experience since 1966 as the first Black member of the powerful state Board of Regents, which set the standards for all schools, public or private, even the universities. As a regent, Kenneth was ahead of his time in demanding basic skills for all students and releasing test scores to hold public schools accountable. He'd built a solid reputation as a no-nonsense school reformer, but MARC advisers warned that it would be tarnished in Washington, a school system in turmoil. But rarely did Kenneth spurn a request for help, and here was his chance to reshape a predominantly Black school system in crisis and make it a model for the nation. He promised Allen that MARC would charge only for expenses and present her with a blueprint for action by June. Though weary and perilously overworked, he vowed to devote a fourth of his time to the project.

Kenneth raised $33,000 in private funds for the task, but an early sign of trouble emerged when school board dissidents predicted that he'd undermine a school superintendent yet to be hired. The *Washington Evening Star* commented, "Kenneth Clark is hardly a minor figure in this field. And given the terms of his proposal, what is there possibly to lose?"[7]

Washington's schools had fallen a year and a half behind other big-city districts in test scores and had soaring absenteeism, dropout, and teacher-turnover rates. School buildings were shabby, and teachers lacked curriculum and professional oversight. School board meetings were often interrupted by shouts, taunts, and once by bongo drums as Allen gaveled for order. The divided school board was the laughingstock of Washington, but it was no joke that 94 percent of the system's 146,000 pupils were Black, the highest in the nation.

As promised, Kenneth's blueprint for action was ready in June. Newspapers called it "the Clark Plan." It proposed a literacy drive in its first year, with every elementary and junior high school forming a team to ensure that reading and math were taught well. Teacher pay would be linked to pupil test scores, and to raise expectations for students, social promotion and grouping by ability would be scrapped. Test scores would be released to the public. If properly taught, Kenneth argued, all normal children could learn, including poor kids without a father at home. There was something in the plan to offend everyone, but surprisingly, all but one school board member backed it. Even the top candidate for school superintendent said he liked it. Black, thirty-six, and from Detroit, Hugh Scott called Kenneth one of his heroes.

But middle-class parents complained that the Clark Plan was a boot-camp approach to education without art or music. And a civic group complained that parents and teachers should have more say in the plan. School board member Charles Cassell opposed Kenneth's call for correcting Black English, which Cassell said damaged a child's identity. Union president William Simons, who represented seventy-eight hundred teachers, most of them Black, charged that Kenneth's vow to have students reading at grade level in a year was a hoax. Simons threatened that if faculty pay was linked to students' test scores, teachers would hand out the correct answers.

MARC's office in Washington coordinated the Clark Plan, and Kenneth arrived from New York on occasion to promote it on television and in public meetings. He belatedly conferred with leaders of the Washington Teachers Union, but days before the schools opened for the fall, superintendent-designate Scott, announced, "I have some concerns about the Clark Plan," adding he was "fairly noncommittal about it."[8] The Clark Plan appeared doomed.

Kenneth lost his composure and lashed out, urging parents to rise up and save his plan. He berated his Black critics as "educational racists" who shackled young minds.[9] School board dissident Cassell, who was Black, shot back, "He's just another racist as far as I'm concerned."[10] The racially tinged feuding escalated, and columnist William Raspberry of the *Washington Post* exclaimed, "If only the parents could take Scott, Clark and the school board by the scruff of the neck and tell them: Cut it out and do something for the children!"[11]

Kenneth's reform plan flunked out in its first semester, and he resigned as a consultant before Christmas. He'd reached the bitter conclusion that Black educators in Washington, like their white counterparts in New York, valued pay, job security, and power more than students' futures. For decades to come, others would try to work their magic in Washington and end up making mistakes of their own. There would be a measure of progress, but the school system's most intractable problems would remain.

Kenneth returned to Washington with Mamie nearly a year later for the annual meeting of the prestigious American Psychological

Association on Labor Day weekend. In the last hours of his one-year term as APA president, he prepared for his farewell address. Normally, he'd ask Mamie to read it first and offer criticisms, but he knew she'd hate it. Instead, he showed a draft to two colleagues, and both shook their heads. His editor at MARC, Jeannette Hopkins, recalled, "I told him I thought it was dangerous."[12]

Kenneth figured that his APA colleagues expected a lecture on race, but he preferred another topic close to his heart: nuclear disarmament. He'd never forgotten the human toll that a single American bomb had taken on the Japanese city of Hiroshima, and he'd been active at City College in the antinuclear movement. In Kenneth's view, world leaders were insecure beings vying for power with others to fortify their egos. History was a gory chronicle of warring tribes and nations, and now Nixon's expanded war in Southeast Asia pitted white allies in the West against people of color in the East. Three million would be slaughtered. Kenneth called the tribal impulse to dominate other people "The Pathos of Power," the title of his APA address.

Approaching the hotel lectern to face his colleagues, Kenneth began reading the rather dull, donnish opening of his address. It was enough to make eyelids droop, but the audience perked up once he called for research on drugs to pacify the heads of state for the world's nuclear powers. "This form of psychotechnological medication would be a type of internally imposed disarmament," he said.[13] Drug testing was needed first, however, and compulsive criminals might volunteer for the clinical trials.

After he left the lectern, irate colleagues showered Kenneth with questions: Was he serious? Using a drug to disarm world leaders? He repaired to the hotel suite where Mamie held a reception, and over drinks into the wee hours that night, Kenneth discussed his speech with friends and colleagues but not yet with Mamie. Later, after the others had left, he finally asked for her opinion. "I'll tell you," Mamie answered but said nothing more about it that night.[14]

As Kenneth drove her to Union Station the next day, Mamie said she was ready to talk: "Why the hell do you want to save mankind?"[15] Maybe human beings were not worth saving, she said, noting that ours wouldn't be the first species to perish and that speeches were no guarantee of survival. At a loss for words, Kenneth carried her suitcase toward the train and asked why she insisted on going home so soon. "Because I want to be with the grandchildren over the Labor Day holiday," she said. Kenneth said that was why he'd given the speech—for their grandchildren and for everyone else's. That sounded lame, even to him, and Mamie boarded her train and headed home alone, more interested in family than tilting at windmills in Washington.

Back at his hotel, Kenneth met with his critics and told them that a debate over his provocative proposal was all he'd wanted. And that was what he got. News of his speech made the front pages of the nation's leading newspapers: "Kenneth Clark Asks New Drugs to Curb Hostility of Leaders," the *New York Times* reported.[16] The *Washington Post* declared, "Dr. Clark Wants to Prevent Holocaust."[17] An avalanche of journalistic invective rumbled on for months after his "peace-pill" speech. Hundreds of columnists and editorial writers weighed in—even at the *Devils Lake Journal* in North Dakota and the *Crowley Signal* in Louisiana. Nasty letters piled up in his mailbox. "You're sick! Incurably sick!" one read.[18] In Chicago, Vice President Spiro Agnew berated Kenneth and psychologist B. F. Skinner for their theories on mind control and freedom—"drivel," Agnew said.[19]

But Kenneth doubled down, writing a *Newsweek* column on nuclear disarmament and publishing his provocative APA address in *Pathos of Power*, a book of his essays. Maurice Carroll of the *New York Times* called the book "every bit as dreadful as its pretentious title."[20] Kenneth's APA address was a fiasco that marred an otherwise distinguished career as a public intellectual. If he'd shown his speech first to Mamie—his closest, most diplomatic, and loyal adviser—the outcome likely would have been different.

Defeated in crusades to improve predominantly Black schools in Washington and New York, Kenneth shifted tactics again and reimmersed himself in the struggle for school integration—a stand popular with Black parents. One of the most divisive issues to emerge in the 1970s prompted the change: busing to achieve school integration. "I am an unreconstructed integrationist," Kenneth declared.[21] "My position, if anything, has hardened."

With courts ordering cities to desegregate their schools, the struggle for integration shifted from the South to the North, where white parents blocked buses and marched in the streets. During the presidential primaries in 1972, George Wallace, the segregationist ex-governor of Alabama, railed against "forced busing." Wallace won Democratic primaries not only in Southern states like Florida and North Carolina but also in Michigan, where white mothers in Pontiac chained themselves to the gate of a school bus depot and marched with signs that said "Nigger, go home."[22] The Ku Klux Klan entered the fray, and ten buses were firebombed. In a televised address, President Nixon called for a moratorium on court orders for busing, arguing that Black families too disliked busing. The NAACP Legal Defense and Education Fund disagreed in a report titled, "It's Not the Distance, 'It's the Niggers.'"[23]

After Nixon's speech, Kenneth forged a coalition of Black, Puerto Rican, and civil liberties groups to support busing. Releasing a MARC fact book on the topic, he told reporters that 40 percent of the nation's pupils rode buses to schools but less than 3 percent to integrate them. The number of Black students in desegregated schools was surging in the South but dwindling in Northern cities, he said. To persuade Nixon to drop his antibusing policy, Kenneth met in the White House with George Schultz, one of the president's most trusted aides. Schultz was cordial but not encouraging, citing heavy pressure from Northern members of Congress.

In New York's capital city, Albany, where Kenneth served on the Board of Regents, state lawmakers followed Washington's lead and banned the mandatory assignment of students to integrate schools. The lawmakers also pressed the regents and liberal Education Commissioner Ewald Nyquist to curb busing for integration. As his fellow regents tilted to the right, Kenneth cut against the grain. He was outraged that in the middle-class, Canarsie section of Brooklyn, white parents turned buses away for six weeks and kept Black and Puerto Rican pupils out of school. White parents told reporters that minority kids were unruly, not interested in learning, and lived in public housing. Kenneth called for an investigation and a state takeover of the city's schools, but his calls went unheeded.

Looking alarmingly thin and haggard after a long hospitalization for a brain seizure, Kenneth talked of retiring soon at sixty. His doctor prescribed medication to prevent more seizures and ordered him to cut his work hours and stop driving. Mamie was frightened. While Kenneth recuperated, Black leaders held a Brotherhood Reception in his honor at the Advertising Club on Park Avenue. About three hundred attended, including U.S. Representative Charles Rangel, Vernon Jordan of the National Urban League, and ex-HUD Secretary Robert C. Weaver. In a full-page photo spread, the *Amsterdam News* declared, "The Big Town Turns Out To Toast Ken Clark!"[24]

Despite doctors' orders to slow down, Kenneth still skirmished with conservative regents, even testifying against them in a Buffalo school integration case. Whenever his fellow regents argued that busing encouraged white flight, he countered that the real issue was enrolling children of color in white schools. The press coverage embarrassed the white regents, and several regarded Kenneth as ungrateful. Regent Clark was caught in the crossfire between genteel racists and Black separatists, *New York Post* columnist James A. Wechsler wrote, "But he has held his ground with a rare blend of dignity and valor."[25]

Acting under court orders in 1975, Education Commissioner Nyquist ordered Buffalo and four other city school districts to desegregate. Kenneth was pleased, but other regents were furious. They scrapped their old pro-busing policy, barred quotas to integrate schools, and urged parents to appeal busing orders. Tired of Nyquist's support for integration, the regents fired him a year later—clear evidence to Kenneth that even in a Northern, progressive state like New York, the white majority would do all it could to keep students of color out of lily-white schools.

Upset by his monthly bouts with the regents in Albany, Kenneth usually returned to Hastings in a snit. Mamie tried to calm him but urged him to stay the course. If he resigned as a regent, she once said, who else would take up the struggle?

———————

By 1975, Kenneth was under the gun at MARC. The declining stock market curbed the generosity of foundations, and race relations in America seemed as troubled as ever. White donors no longer held high hopes for integration. "There was a sense of discouragement," recalled George Dalley, an aide to Kenneth at MARC.[26] "They felt a little bit betrayed, that the [Black] community wasn't properly thankful."

Kenneth was floundering at MARC. He'd fallen hopelessly behind in his costly, time-consuming "Two Cities" project, a book-length study of race in Newark and White Plains, New York. The Ford and Field Foundations, MARC's top two donors, warned that if it was to survive, he had to slash expenses. Kenneth confided to Gunnar Myrdal that neurological problems had sapped his strength: "During the past year I have become aware that I have much less physical stamina and psychological energy than I had a few years ago."[27] Kenneth notified the foundations of his pending retirement.

As financial support dwindled for MARC, Kenneth cut the

payroll and relied on federal grants to keep the doors open—a move that he once said would compromise its independence. He struggled to finish the Two Cities study, which he often claimed was in its final stages. "Ken's challenge, which he never really met, and he articulated it, was to write another *Dark Ghetto*," Dalley recalled.[28] "I know he shied away from it, because he didn't think he could ever really match what he did before."

The Field Foundation, which had given MARC $2.1 million over nine years, lost all patience with Kenneth. Executive director Leslie Dunbar wrote him that instead of embodying an idea, MARC embodied a man, Kenneth, who failed to delegate responsibility and build a strong staff. He'd taken MARC too far afield with projects in far-flung cities while shouldering other duties at City College, the APA, the Board of Regents, and, most recently, planning a book with Myrdal on race in America. At a time of financial stringency, Field would no longer fund MARC at its current level.

Dunbar's scathing critique lacked a jot of praise for Kenneth's leadership in bringing quarreling civil rights leaders together, encouraging Blacks to run for office, or overseeing MARC studies of police shootings, Black adoptions, poverty programs, and other issues. But in truth, Kenneth was forever leaving MARC to fly off and give speeches, show up on television, or write for magazines and journals. Too often, he enlisted the staff in a new crusade before finishing his last one. MARC was adrift, and Mamie had helped to get it back on track, but with scant success. Responding to Dunbar, Kenneth admitted that management was not his strong suit and that he was overwhelmed by the Two Cities project. In fact, he'd never finish it.

Succeeded by Charles V. Hamilton, the political scientist who'd written *Black Power* with Stokely Carmichael, Kenneth retired at age sixty-one from both MARC and City College. His colleagues at the college gave him a warm send-off, and so did the staff at MARC. Hamilton immediately laid off a third of the staff at MARC. Within months, it would close for good.

Celebrating Kenneth's long career, more than five hundred guests showed up at the Hotel Pierre on Fifth Avenue for a black-tie dinner sponsored by the New York Civil Liberties Union. Its leader, Ira Glasser, called Kenneth "one of the most persistent civil rights leaders in the past 20 years."[29] Among the guests were friends and allies such as Julian Bond, ex-Attorney General Ramsey Clark, and Black mayors Kenneth Gibson of Newark and Richard Hatcher of Gary, Indiana. Still thin and haggard, Kenneth listened nervously as the speakers heaped praise on his achievements. When it was his turn to rise and speak, he grew somber and lamented that too many of his best efforts had come to naught. He called them "glorious defeats."[30]

FIFTEEN

QUIET COURAGE

Sometimes as I sit communing in my study I feel that death is not far off. I am aware that it will overtake me before the greatest of my dreams—full equality for the Negro in our time—is realized.

—MARY MCLEOD BETHUNE[1]

H aving days free to write in his sun-streaked library and nights to read by the fireside was Kenneth's retirement fantasy. But at sixty-one in the summer of 1975, even though his health was fragile, he wasn't ready for the life of a hermit scholar. Instead, he was starting a consulting firm in the former MARC building he owned on the Upper East Side. Kenneth sought clients and banks loans while doing a little reading, writing, and puttering over the roses in Mamie's garden, but once the frost and flurries arrived, he steeped himself in his new business. Without foundations to please or student papers to grade, he was content. "Needless to say, my 'retirement' is keeping me busier than ever," he wrote to a friend, "but I find this new venture most exciting."[2]

One reason for opening the firm was to provide work and income for his whole family, especially Hilton, who'd completed his bachelor's degree but opted out of Columbia's law school. Politics in Harlem, where Hilton lived with his wife, Catherine, was his new passion. A member of the Malcolm X Club of Independent Democrats, Hilton seldom clashed now with his father over Black nationalism. Instead, they tussled over the family business. "It was difficult because I was my father's son and didn't look upon him with the same sense of awe that others did," Hilton told the *Amsterdam News*.[3] Catherine, a former executive assistant at MARC, offered secretarial services through a subsidiary of the Clark firm in the same building.

Clark Associates would be more than a money-maker for family, friends, and colleagues. Reinventing himself yet again, Kenneth was building another vehicle to push for integration and equal opportunity. He saw no conflict between the role of activist and entrepreneur. Back in the fashionably left 1960s, liberals gasped when Kenneth had called business

THE CLARKS OF CLARK ASSOCIATES
CONSULTING FIRM, CIRCA 1976

the last hope of minorities. In his view, the U.S. military stood out for integrating its work force while schools, government, and businesses dawdled. It was time for the private sector to get with it, and he wanted to help.

Kenneth believed that business offered hope for integration because executives were pragmatic, required an efficient workforce, and understood that trapping the poor in ghettos hobbled the nation's treasury and economy. His goal was to train employers to recruit women and minorities and build a diverse society while turning a profit. He'd coach them on new federal rules for affirmative action and equal opportunity. But to ensure his firm's integrity, Kenneth had clients sign an opt-out clause. If they were just trying to tweak their images by hiring a Black firm, he'd rip up their contracts. "We're not going with the white-washers," he said.[4]

The Clarks promoted their grand opening with an art exhibit and reception. Mamie invited 750 guests, including friends, former colleagues, and 117 Black news organizations. Kenneth asked artist friend Charles "Spinky" Alston to borrow artworks from young Black artists, and a publicist he hired spread the word that the new firm's client list included IBM, AT&T, the Bermuda Islands, Joseph E. Seagram & Sons distillers, and pollster Louis Harris.

Each morning, Mamie woke Kenneth before 6:30 a.m. for the drive into the city to face a workday of recruiting Black candidates for corporate jobs, resolving labor conflicts with employers, and analyzing public opinion polls. A streak of gray parted the front of Kenneth's hair now, and the brown barnacles of aging flecked his face, yet he mustered the energy to write articles, give speeches, and work with the Congressional Black Caucus and other groups. He continued to court controversy, pouncing on sociologist Nathan Glazer's new book, *Affirmative Discrimination*, for attacking affirmative action programs. Kenneth denounced Daniel P. Moynihan, a candidate for the U.S. Senate, reminding New Yorkers that Moynihan had called for the "benign neglect" of Blacks and ridiculed Third World nations.

Kenneth also made headlines by backing Roy Wilkins in a dispute with the fractious board of the NAACP. Wilkins had already agreed to retire, but the board demanded he leave at once. Kenneth saw Wilkins as a tepid moderate but someone who'd done his best. Wilkins was retiring anyway—why crush an old man's heart? Wilkins held a nuanced view of Kenneth as well, once calling him "an irascible egghead and enemy of the status quo of racial segregation."[5] Kenneth no longer looked so fondly on the NAACP. He saw his younger self as a cautious moderate who'd refrained from clashing with allies. "Then I was a Negro," he said. "Now I'm Black."[6]

Clark Associates was an activist firm. Kenneth hired an integrated team of researchers to fly with him to South Africa and investigate whether Seagram & Sons distillers would help the apartheid regime and harm Black workers by operating there. And on a federal contract during the bicentennial year of 1976, he delivered brutally honest lectures about the sorry state of U.S. race relations. At the Army War College in Pennsylvania, he argued that America was founded in slavery and that racism held our political, economic, and moral belief systems in a firm grip.

Kenneth gave a similar address at the University of Munich in

West Germany and ventured into town afterward to see champion boxer Muhammad Ali at a news conference. Ali was facing British challenger Richard Dunn that night, and Kenneth was amused to see Ali in martial arts garb while joking and entertaining reporters. Spotting Kenneth, Ali introduced him as his personal psychologist and gave him a free ticket to the fight that night. Kenneth later watched Ali put his white opponent away in the fifth round.

Kenneth's return to West Germany to address military officers in the fall was not as much fun. German customs officers ordered him to step aside for a narcotics check, and he refused to open his luggage. Hours later, the U.S. military police arrived and resolved the conflict. A German official said Kenneth "fit the description of several Black drug dealers from America who pass through the airport regularly, and we weren't about to take chances."[7]

Both the city and the state of New York neared financial collapse in the late 1970s and slashed aid for Northside Center to the core. To keep the doors open, Mamie halted several projects, including an after-care program for kids from hospitals. Appealing to friends and other donors, she pulled out all the stops to raise cash. Superstars like Muhammad Ali, Bill Cosby, and Stevie Wonder joined the Clarks' celebrity friends at Northside fundraisers. Among them were pro golfer Arthur Ashe, musician Lionel Hampton, and actors Ruby Dee, Ossie Davis, and Diahann Carroll. The celebrities schmoozed and signed autographs for Northside donors at high-profile venues like the Tavern on the Green and Studio 54, the popular disco club. Seven hundred guests showed up at the Windows on the World restaurant in the World Trade Center to celebrate the clinic's thirtieth anniversary, and Mamie was blasé about the glitterati surrounding her that night. "I guess we knew a lot of people to begin with," she told the *New York Times*.[8] "Some of them developed, philanthropically—whether they had money or time to give."

In an era when boardrooms were finally opening to minorities, Mamie was in demand as a director of the ABC television network, Union Dime Savings Bank, Mount Sinai Medical Center, and other institutions. She set her own rules for board membership: if allowed to make a solid contribution, she'd stay and help, but if her seat was just a token or if the duties didn't play to her strengths, she'd move on. She cared little for the highfalutin social scene and used board seats to advance the cause of minorities. At the New York Public Library, she promoted the Schomburg Collection of books and artifacts of the African diaspora. At the Museum of Modern Art, she pressed for the inclusion of Black artists and access for young, underprivileged museum-goers. And after her appointment to the Palisades Interstate Park Commission, she argued for the equitable treatment of minority business vendors. She moved confidently among the white elite. As the daughter of a hotelier, Mamie knew that the bathtub rings and strewn underwear of the rich and famous were much the same as everyone else's.

While on the board of ABC, Mamie got free passes to attend the 1976 Summer Olympics in Montreal with Kenneth. Watching the boxing, track, and field events, Kenneth marveled at the African Americans who'd won so many medals. He wished the rest of

America accepted Blacks as well as the sports world did. When he started to gripe about the tribalistic flag-waving and chanting in the stands, Mamie upbraided him: "Kenneth, stop this, stop this. Think of it in terms of young people who are excellent in particular sports without regard to their nation."[9] This was classic Mamie, accepting humanity pretty much as it was, while Kenneth groped for an elusive ideal. Despite his laments to the contrary, he joined in the Olympic chauvinism: he was darned proud of those African American medalists.

Back in New York, the stresses of Mamie's work life appeared on her face. In her sixties and the fourth decade in the same demanding job, she looked weary and thin with bags under her eyes. Driving through Harlem with her daughter one day, Mamie broached the topic of retiring and asked if Kate would take charge of Northside. "Mother, you know how much I hate mental health," Kate responded.[10] Soon afterward, Mamie opened her search for a successor.

To ensure the clinic's solvency in the fall of 1979, Mamie's friends and colleagues planned a series of tributes and fundraisers marking her retirement after thirty-three years on the job: a disco dinner for seven hundred at the Astoria World Manor in Queens, a Congressional Black Caucus breakfast in Washington, and Northside's annual fundraiser at Lincoln Center. Finally, the Tower Suite was packed for her retirement party on the forty-eighth floor of the Time-Life Building. Mamie's three grandchildren were present, as was Michelle Craig, a child at Northside Center, who read a poem she'd written for Mamie. When it was her turn at the microphone,

Mamie froze. "She hated public speaking," Kate recalled.[11] "She was nervous, nervous, nervous." Blood trickled from a nostril, and Mamie never spoke that night.

With the consulting firm operating to his satisfaction, Kenneth ramped up his outside activities despite Mamie's warnings. He took on a demanding travel and speaking schedule and wrote articles to encourage integrating the nation's workforce and schools. He criticized Black economist William Julius Wilson's book *The Declining Significance of Race*, which stressed social class over race as an obstacle to Black achievement. But race still mattered, Kenneth argued, and it mattered the most.

Lauding him as a civil rights crusader, the Joint Center for Political and Economic Studies, the Washington think tank he'd cofounded, dedicated its tenth anniversary celebration to Kenneth and arranged an Oval Office visit with President Carter. Though busy with a historic peace agreement between Egypt and Israel, Carter took the time to chat and shake Kenneth's hand. "You're very persistent," Carter said.[12] More than a thousand people showed up that night for the Joint Center's gala honoring Kenneth. Among the guests were Washington Mayor Marion Barry, who was wrestling with a teachers strike, and children's advocate Marian Wright Edelman, who lauded Kenneth as a man who "stays angry and keeps working for Blacks—and so should we."[13] In response, Kenneth decried the psychological genocide of racism and reminded his affluent audience that the poor trapped in ghettos outnumbered the Blacks entering the middle class.

Meanwhile, Mamie was alarmed by the disarray in the family firm and attributed it to Kenneth's activism. To right the ship, she took a first-floor office and got to work with Kate. "Administratively, it was a mess," Kate recalled.[14] "She was trying to straighten out all the grants and give it focus." Even the offices were messy, and Mamie led a cleanup drive. She helped prepare reports and plan events but had no interest in working full-time. She had her own life at home with three grandchildren minutes away at Kate's home in Hastings. Mamie yearned to travel and spend more time with friends and family at their cottage in Cape Cod, but Kenneth usually begged off, citing business and other duties. Tired of spending nights reading alone at home while he was at meetings, Mamie told him it was time to live a little, not just work, and they quarreled over this. "Mamie has almost given up on me in terms of any social life," Kenneth wrote a friend.[15] "I keep telling her that things will improve and that we will be able to see friends and go to the theatre and do a little travelling as soon as I feel more confident about the business. She really doesn't believe me, but I will insist on proving that she's wrong."

Instead of trimming his commitments, Kenneth cofounded a polling firm with his friend Percy Sutton. Data Black was Kenneth's brainchild and a subsidiary of his firm and Sutton's Inner City Broadcasting Corporation, which included a dozen Black radio stations nationwide. Kate served as Data Black's executive vice president, and Hilton helped as well. "Black people are tired of whites telling them what to think," Hilton told the *Amsterdam News*.[16]

Kenneth had persuaded Sutton that with 11 percent of the population, Black people needed polls that reflected their views. Data

Black would hire African Americans to question twelve hundred others nationwide about busing, housing, schools, and affirmative action. Data Black would break down the results by subgroups, such as Southern or middle-class Blacks. The first poll was ready in January 1980. "Polls Show Blacks See Return of Racism," the Black-owned *Pittsburg Courier* reported.[17] The front page story noted that 41 percent of the Blacks questioned had experienced job discrimination.

The Clarks used Data Black to prepare an article for *Ebony* magazine that touched on their early research with dolls. Titled "What Do Blacks Think of Themselves?," it was the first article they'd done together in decades.[18] It featured a classic 1947 Gordon Parks photo showing a Black boy choosing between a brown doll and a white one at Northside. Based on the Clarks' poll results, the article explored whether Black adults in 1980, despite the gains of the civil rights era, still harbored doubts about their race, much as Black kids had revealed them by preferring a white doll back in 1940. An *Ebony* headline offered this answer: "Important new study by renowned psychologists indicates 'progress' and continued internal conflicts about color."

The Clarks' poll focused on Black preferences in skin color, romantic partners, dolls, and other topics. To avoid false, self-protective answers, they asked Black adults how *other Blacks* thought, as in, "Are Blacks more or less proud of being Black now than they were in the 1940s and 1950s?" Ninety percent answered that African Americans were prouder now, reflecting a surge in race pride since the 1960s. Another poll item stated, "Blacks with traditional Black features are less attractive than Blacks who look more like Whites." Forty-three percent disagreed, and 41 percent expressed ambivalence or rejected African American features. Men reported 10 percent more dissatisfaction than women. Asked whether other Black parents bought brown dolls for their children, 71 percent responded negatively. Just 38 percent of Black women said yes. The poll also asked which was preferable: a Black doctor or a white one, a Black lawyer or a white one? Again, the answers were discouraging, and together with the other data they gleaned, the Clarks concluded "the majority of Blacks still appear to be burdened by racial self-doubt."

Each fall, the Clarks went to Washington for the Congressional Black Caucus weekend. Daughter Kate also attended with her husband, Donald, taking in the speeches, cocktail hours, and festive meals for Black movers and shakers. Surprised to see her father alone on the caucus weekend in September 1982, Kate asked why her mother was absent. "She had a chest X-ray," Kenneth said, vaguely mentioning a problem.[19] "It's all right."

Symptoms of laryngitis had bothered Mamie for some time, and her doctor prescribed antibiotics. When the symptoms remained, she got an X-ray. In the hospital for more tests, she learned that inoperable lung cancer had spread to her vocal cords—this, less than two years after retiring. Mamie began a series of overnight hospital stays for blood transfusions and chemotherapy that left her weak and barely able to function. "Kenneth," Mamie said, "I couldn't have got a piddling form of this disease, could I?"[20] She regained her strength after most treatments, but her skin color darkened and her hair fell out. She lost so much weight her legs were like broomsticks. Kenneth told her doctors they'd got it all wrong: he, not Mamie, was the chain-smoker. She'd quit smoking years ago and never missed a doctor's appointment. Kenneth clung to hopes for her recovery. "As you probably suspect, Mamie's spirits and courage remain high," he wrote a friend.[21] "Ironically, she has expressed to the doctors her concern about me. Needless to say, we will do everything we can to conquer this insidious affliction."

Citing monthly hospitalizations and regular treatments, Mamie resigned from several boards but continued her work with the Museums Collaborative, the advocacy group she led as board president. She also helped raise funds for Northside and continued with the family business. Kenneth seemed in denial about her condition, jetting off to conferences and giving speeches as in the past. "He just refused to accept the idea she was fatally ill," Kate recalled.[22] "He kept going to work and night meetings as before—didn't change his pace at all."

Kenneth was busy waging a one-man campaign to protect the gains of the civil rights era under heavy attack in the 1980s. He feared that the progress in voting, employment, and integration in general would be reversed much as the rights of freed slaves were discarded after Reconstruction in the 1870s. Kenneth resented President Ronald Reagan, who'd launched his election campaign in Neshoba County, Mississippi, to reassure whites who clung to states' rights. This was where three civil rights workers had been executed and buried in an earthen dam, one of the worst atrocities of the 1960s. In his campaign, Reagan complained of welfare queens in Cadillacs and strapping young men with food stamps. An avuncular former actor, he was popular with whites—not so much with Blacks. As ex-First Lady Rosalynn Carter said, "I think he makes us comfortable with our prejudices."[23]

Working with historian John Hope Franklin, Kenneth met with dozens of scholars and activists at a series of conferences in Racine, Wisconsin, and Tarrytown, New York, to develop a blueprint for renewed Black activism. Among those attending were Coretta Scott King, Jesse Jackson, and sociologist William Julius Wilson. The Clark and Franklin report, titled "A Policy Framework for Racial Justice," called for reforms in education, the economy, and society at large to rescue the Black "underclass," a buzzword of the 1980s. The study drew scant attention.

As the Reaganaut tide rose, Kenneth still tried to plug the dyke by meeting with the leaders of the NAACP and the National Urban League and begging them to play a more activist role. They resisted him, and he irked the leaders with his jabs at them in articles and speeches. Kenneth pleaded with Black professionals at conferences to get more involved in social issues, but the protest spirit of the 1960s had subsided, and he no longer had the bully pulpit of MARC. When a reporter reminded Kenneth that he'd called for curbing street protests back in the late 1960s, Kenneth deadpanned, "The moral there is: Don't listen to college professors."[24]

As her health declined, Mamie bid a silent farewell to old friends. At lunch with Leighla Whipper Ford, her matron of honor back in 1938, they reminisced about their Howard days when the Clarks eloped. "I didn't know it was meant as a goodbye," Ford recalled of their lunch date.[25] Russia Hughes, a family friend and assistant in the Clark firm, was surprised when Mamie beckoned her into an office one day to chat about Hughes's two sons. Usually Mamie was all business. "I remember it as a very touching time for me because she was so friendly, so close," Hughes recalled, "and you see, she was not the kind of person who wanted to show her closeness all the time by giving me a hug."[26]

Mamie drew closer to her daughter as well. At Mamie's urging, Kate had quit her job with a scholarship agency to help stabilize the family business. They talked often in the office and went out together for lunch. They drew closer still after illness forced Mamie to stay home. Tumors had formed in her brain and on her body, one of them a painful, lemon-sized mass on her hip. No longer able to walk, she was moved from the bed she'd shared with Kenneth into the adjoining room with a hospital bed. As nurses cared for Mamie at home, Kate remained by her mother's side. They enjoyed the most intimate talks of their lives together, reminiscing about the grandchildren and old times with friends and recalling their spats over the years. They set them aside. "It was just like talk, talk, talk—a different woman," Kate recalled.[27] Despite agonizing pain, Mamie seldom complained or took painkillers. She insisted on remaining aware and in control. When Kate asked if she feared death, Mamie said she worried more about Hilton and Kenneth, who seemed haunted by her predicament.

To avoid upsetting her husband, Mamie asked her two children to help plan her funeral. She wanted her burial to come first at nearby Mount Hope Cemetery, then a tiny secular service at Mercy College—both pastoral settings along the Hudson River. She asked that a handful of speakers recount her life, Hilton chief among them. Leveling with Kenneth, Mamie lamented that he was quietly raging inside against the injustice of her fate. "Kenneth, we can't complain," Mamie said.[28] "No one promised us eternity." Theirs had been an effective life, she added, but looking back on their activism together, they commiserated for the millionth time about the unkept promise of the *Brown* ruling and the fact that more children were in segregated schools now than ever before—and the dark ghettos were even darker. Mamie had one request for Kenneth: to be strong and continue his work. "Look," she said, "you've got to keep on."[29]

A week before his sixty-ninth birthday, Mamie canceled a chemotherapy treatment and arranged a visit from John Moseley, one of their closest friends, who shared Kenneth's birth date, July 24. Though weak and in pain, Mamie sat upright in a chair that day and asked the two men to join her in birthday toasts with a piña colada. She'd sipped only a little, so Kenneth rose after a while to take her glass. "No, you can't do that!" she said in mock horror.[30] "That's my glass, and I'm going to finish it."

Mamie's condition worsened steadily over the next three weeks, and on August 11, 1983, shortly after midnight, she died at age sixty-six. Hilton and Kate followed her last wishes to the letter, except for shifting her memorial service from a small college auditorium to the spacious Riverside Church, where Dr. King had delivered his famous antiwar address. The change allowed Northside families from nearby Harlem to attend. Hundreds of mourners packed the church pews to honor Mamie, and Hilton delivered the eulogy. Kenneth had prepared one but never delivered it. He'd asked that Duke Ellington's "Sophisticated Lady" be played at the service—he loved to think of Mamie that way—but Kate and Hilton ruled it out as too treacly. Instead, Mamie's favorite chorus from Handel's *Messiah* thundered through the church at the service's end: *Hal-le-lu-jah! Hal-le-lu-jah! Hal-le-lu-jah!*

STRUGGLING ON

If you can't run, walk; if you can't walk, crawl, but
keep moving forward.

—REVEREND MARTIN LUTHER KING JR.[1]

Kenneth lost more than a wife of forty-five years. He lost a colleague
and confidante, an editor for his articles and speeches, an adviser
to clarify issues and question his motives. When he was in over his
head, Mamie was the one who'd given him a talking-to, rolled up her
sleeves, and made phone calls to rearrange his schedule and lighten
his burden. Kenneth also lost the partner who'd ensured that his suits
were dry-cleaned and his doctor appointments kept. But more important, he lost his muse and the mother of his two children, the emotional
ballast that had given him the confidence to struggle on. Losing Mamie
was like losing a vital organ. "With Mamie gone, the living was gone,"
his friend John Heyman recalled.[2] "There was nothing left."

In the months after Mamie's death, Kenneth was inconsolable. Perhaps he felt guilty that fumes from his chain-smoking might have caused her lung cancer, or maybe he regretted his infidelities of the past. A packrat, he kept a cache of intimate letters from a California woman who'd signed many of them "G." Whatever the reason, Kenneth ceased writing and giving speeches. He dragged himself mornings to his office in Manhattan and slept alone at night in his big, darkened house on a hill in Hastings. He now realized how much his productivity had depended upon Mamie. "I would say he was clinically depressed," psychologist friend Dr. Stephen Berger recalled.[3] "I tried to get him interested in writing his autobiography, and he laughed at me." Kenneth was tempted to shutter the family business, but the memory of Mamie's warning lingered: "Look, you've got to keep on."

In the spring of 1984, thirty years after the *Brown* ruling, Kenneth began reaching out to the world, though never again with the vigor of his days with Mamie. He celebrated the anniversary by speaking in five states and dedicating his remarks to Mamie and her role in *Brown*. He raised money for a scholarship in her memory and appeared regularly at Northside events and board meetings. He began a series of talks at John Jay College on crime, race, and the nation's broken criminal justice system. Working with Hilton in the family firm, he conducted a study of bias against minorities and women in the U.S. Postal Service. He worked to maintain integration at Starrett City in Brooklyn, the nation's largest private rental housing complex. But by his seventies, Kenneth was tired and in a pit of grief. He left the Board of Regents, closed his offices in Manhattan, and rented a smaller space in Hastings, where he put his framed photo of W. E. B. Du Bois back on the wall.

In 1986, after Kate had taken charge at Northside and Hilton had joined the city council, Kenneth carried on the best he could, teaching part time at Mercy College, working in his new office, and writing the occasional speech, article, or book review. He joined the board of the Woodrow Wilson International Center for Scholars in Washington. There were dinners with friends and book parties for Toni Morrison and Charlayne Hunter-Gault. He traveled often to receive awards and honorary degrees. He even made a trip to China. Every winter, he spent time with friends in Jamaica and joined them for summer stays at his cottage in Cape Cod. Journalists and scholars often interviewed him for insights into the civil rights era, and several observed that Kenneth was haunted by the plight of our cities and the substandard schooling of minority children. The South, once a belated leader in school integration, was heading in the opposite direction. "We call this resegregation," Kenneth said.[4]

He suffered strokes and fainting spells in his eighties and had a pacemaker implanted to cope with a heart condition. He could no longer drive his Lincoln and had to lean on a caregiver while walking. A failing memory left him grumpy and in low spirits. Hilton monitored his father's caregivers, drove him to appointments, and oversaw the household. Prominent friends dropped by to visit Kenneth—activist Vernon Jordan and scholar John Hope Franklin among them—and many left saddened. June Shagaloff Alexander, an NAACP colleague, recalled, "It was awful to see this man who was an intellectual and whose mind was part of his essence, sitting in that chair in his immaculate clothes with the television going, droning on and on."[5]

Despite illness, despair, and a sense that the struggle for racial justice had come to naught, Kenneth lived more than two decades after Mamie's death—long enough to see a small stack of books, dissertations, and journal articles about their work, and long enough to see two made-for-TV movies about their role in *Brown*. On May 1, 2005, after hospital stays and a stint in a nursing home, Kenneth Bancroft Clark died at home of cancer. He was ninety. His funeral was held in the church of his early youth, St. Philip's Episcopal in Harlem. He was buried at Mount Hope Cemetery in Hastings in a grave next to Mamie's.

The Clarks were ordinary people who'd done extraordinary things and left a solid legacy, and Mamie was in no small part responsible. If not for her research in graduate school at Howard, they never would have developed a doll test. For decades after her death, countless children would continue to benefit from her leadership at Head Start and Northside Center. Thousands of Harlemites would call Schomburg Plaza their home.

Kenneth's attempts to build something lasting had largely failed: HARYOU, MARC, and his consulting firm had perished. Then again, his lofty goals were bound to exceed his grasp: rebuilding Central Harlem, reforming Washington's schools, gaining national support for integration and busing. Even so, he'd left his mark. Like scholar-activist W. E. B. Du Bois, Kenneth had brought Black leaders together and paved the way for the struggle ahead in government, business, and society. He was a leader of leaders. He'd also put urban school reform on the nation's agenda for generations to come and informed millions of Americans as a public intellectual in an era of wrenching racial conflict. He'd inspired thousands of students in his teaching career, and the principles he'd helped enshrine in the *Brown* decision would long animate the resistance to school segregation.

By the 1980s, public officials had moved on to politically safer issues, and the debate over school integration all but vanished. Today, in reaction to the growing racial and economic isolation in our daily lives, the issue has reemerged. On a balmy day in 2019, a racially diverse crowd of teenagers stood in the heart of Times Square in T-shirts stamped "Integrate NYC," the name of their organization.[6] Some held signs that said, "65 Years Later Retire Segregation," a reference to the *Brown* ruling. The students lamented the lack of diversity and equity in their education. "The mission is to have real integration in schools," Jace Valentine, a high school senior in Brooklyn, told a reporter.[7] "More resources for everybody." Of the 895 slots available to study at elite Stuyvesant High School that year, just seven went to Black students. The city's mayor, the school chancellor, and grassroots groups, including white parents, were pushing for school integration.

Similar groups have emerged nationwide, including Integrated Schools, founded in 2015 in Los Angeles. Dozens of chapters have sprung up, from Oakland, California, to New Haven, Connecticut. Parents of all races take part in the organization's book clubs, podcasts, happy hours, and online discussion groups to promote the benefits of integrated classrooms.

Even so, cynicism about the aftermath of the *Brown* ruling

abounds. "I mean I cannot see that it's changed anything," Black playwright Lorraine Hansberry once said.[8] Thurgood Marshall's prediction in 1954 that America would integrate within five years was clearly wrong. In 1988, 44 percent of Black students in the South attended majority-white schools, but by 2011, after a series of conservative Supreme Court rulings, the number plummeted to 23 percent.

And yet there's been major progress since the *Brown* litigation of the 1950s—progress seldom acknowledged. Black pupils no longer have to use outdoor latrines or drink water from a bucket with a dipper. High school instruction for Black students, once rare outside cities in Southern and border states, is universally available today. And with the demise of dual school systems, predominantly white schools no longer turn away Black students living in their attendance zones. Gains like these were won by Black parents who risked their lives and lost jobs, businesses, and homes for working with activists like Thurgood Marshall and the Clarks.

The Clarks' doll test, a project begun in their twenties, has had an extraordinary impact on our society. Filmmakers, journalists, scholars, and museum curators still pay tribute to their research and role in *Brown*. Televised movies like *Separate But Equal* (1991), *Simple Justice* (1993), and *Thurgood* (2011) have reminded us of the doll test and the struggle against school segregation. In 2016, the new National Museum of African American History and Culture opened in Washington with a permanent exhibit on *Brown* that features a brown and a white baby doll from Northside Center and the Clark family. A museum in Topeka, Kansas, where the original *Brown* case was tried in federal court, has a similar doll exhibit.

Hundreds of researchers have followed in the Clarks' footsteps with doll tests and racial-identity studies of their own, not only in states across our nation—from Hawaii to Massachusetts—but also in Australia, New Zealand, Trinidad, and the Republic of South Africa. The earliest of the American studies, in the 1950s, largely confirmed the Clarks' findings, and the researchers recorded what the children told us. "I don't want to be colored," said Dianne, a four-year-old, in a 1952 study.[9] "This morning I scrubbed and scrubbed [my skin] and it came almost white." In 1987, Black psychologist Darlene Powell Hopson made headlines by revealing that two-thirds of the Black children she tested preferred white dolls. Early in this century, sixteen-year-old Kiri Davis, a Black student, filmed a doll test of her own that went viral on the internet. Fifteen of the twenty-one Black kids she questioned preferred a white doll to a brown one, "because it is Black," as one child put it.[10] "Even though the kids are that young," Kiri said, "they were kind of, they were kind of like mirrors showing what society values, and they knew at that stage that it wasn't them."

In the late 1960s, an era of Black pride, a number of researchers began to question the validity of doll tests in general and the Clarks' in particular, arguing that their approach was makeshift, statistically flawed, or based on the false notion that Black kids who picked a white doll rejected their own race. In 1968, H. J. Greenwald and D. B. Oppenheim conducted a doll study in New York City that introduced a third doll, of mixed race, which most of the light-skinned children preferred, reducing the overall preference for a white doll to only 13 percent. Two years later in Lincoln, Nebraska, a study using the Clarks' methods found that only 30 percent of the Black children tested preferred a white doll, compared with the Clarks' finding of 67 percent. "First, times may be changing," the researchers concluded.[11] They attributed their hopeful results in part to a two-year Black pride campaign in their university town.

The most ardently anti-Clark of the new generation of researchers is Black scholar William E. Cross Jr., who attacked the doll test as simplistic and based on a negative thesis of "self-hatred." In his 1991 book, *Shades of Black*, Cross faulted the Clarks for not recognizing the sustaining power of Black solidarity and culture: "The Clarks saw Negroness as a *stigma*."[12]

After the *Brown* ruling, many if not most researchers included white kids in their testing, and the results were often unsettling. In 2010 and again in 2012, the CNN television network hired experts to explore the racial preferences and attitudes of both white and Black children and aired them on the *Anderson Cooper 360* program. Shown drawings of five frolicking children ranging in hue from white to brown to black, a little blond girl with white ribbons in her hair picked a drawing of a Black child as the "bad" one in the group. Why? "Because she's a lot darker." Asked to point to a "mean" child, the white girl again pointed to a Black child. Why? "Because she's way darker." And asked to point to an ugly child, the white girl selected a Black child once again, "Because she's like, um, a lot darker."[13] When asked to choose a drawing of a "nice" child, she chose the drawing of a light-skinned child. Watching this, the little girl's mother sniffled and teared up in front of CNN's camera. "I'm crying," she said in a Southern accent. "I think it's just because she's not exposed... We've not talked about race." The CNN studies found that white parents seldom discuss race with their children.

Kenneth had long argued that white children, not just Black kids, were damaged by segregated schooling. White students who neither know nor compete with Black students often feel superior to them and are ill equipped to deal with a world that is mostly nonwhite.

The legacy of Kenneth and Mamie Phipps Clark is more than their doll test and historic role in *Brown*. The Clarks left us their shining example of persistence, of unflagging struggle against bigotry in the face of implacable resistance. They fought for racial justice long before it was fashionable and at great personal cost. And they remained in the struggle as long as health would allow—long after many of their contemporaries had given up in despair, expatriated, or retreated to a comfortable life among the privileged elite.

The Clarks also left us two questions that we as a nation have never answered: How much damage has segregation inflicted on children over the years, including white children? And *what are we going to do about it?* We may be searching for the answers until the last days of our great republic.

READING GROUP GUIDE

1. Had you heard of the doll test before reading? Did that include any information about Kenneth and Mamie? What were you most surprised to learn about their lives and work?

2. Do you think the differences in Kenneth's and Mamie's upbringings influenced their later work? How so?

3. How was the field of psychology shaped by its earliest white practitioners? How does diversity within a field prevent biased findings?

4. Mamie's parents were staunchly against her marriage to Kenneth. What was their reasoning? Why wasn't the young couple willing to wait? Do you think there was a compromise besides the secret wedding?

5. What do the findings of the doll test tell us about internalized prejudice? Why do you think the Clarks delayed publishing them when they first completed the study?

6. How would you describe Mamie's relationship with her segregationist mentor, Dr. Garrett? Why did she seek his mentorship? How did she handle his assumptions about her career?

7. How did Kenneth's own mental health challenges influence the Clarks' work and family?

8. Discuss the relationship of the Black and Jewish communities during the Clarks' careers. How did their shared experiences bring the communities together? What obstacles did the two groups face while trying to collaborate?

9. Why do you think the Clarks faced so much criticism from within the Black community when their research and other projects (like *Dark Ghetto*) gained public attention?

10. While presenting reports on his research and testifying in court, Kenneth was careful not to attribute children's feelings of racial inferiority solely to segregated schooling. Why was this so important to him?

11. Despite their own national activism, the Clarks did little to solicit better treatment for their own children in integrated schools and discouraged the kids from becoming involved in activist groups. Where do you think that disconnect comes from?

12. The author leaves us with two key questions: How much damage has segregation inflicted on children over the years, including white children? And what are we going to do about it? How would you answer those questions?

A CONVERSATION
WITH THE AUTHOR

How did you first hear of Kenneth and Mamie Clark? What prompted you to tell their story?

When I was a seventeen-year-old college freshman, a professor described the Clarks' doll test in my 8 a.m. child psychology class. The anecdote was so fascinating it stuck with me. Over the next two decades, I followed Kenneth's career as a public intellectual in the pages of the *New York Times* and finally met and interviewed him when I was an education writer for another newspaper. This was shortly after Mamie had died, and Kenneth told me that losing her was like losing a vital organ. That's when I first sensed that I wanted to tell their story, a story of romance, research, and social activism set against the backdrop of American history.

You cite a plethora of interviews and a great deal of the Clarks' personal correspondence. What did your research process look like?

I began my research by collecting everything the Clarks had said or written, including their dissertations, articles, interviews, and oral histories. I also interviewed their elderly friends, colleagues, and relatives, then in their eighties, to ensure that their memories of the Clarks would still be fresh. I travelled all over the country tracing the Clarks' footsteps, including a month-long stay in Mamie's hometown of Hot Springs, Arkansas. I spent many hours sifting through

Clark-related documents in archives along the way, especially in their college town of Washington, DC, where the Library of Congress keeps the Clarks' papers, a trove of nearly five hundred boxes that included their fascinating love letters.

Despite its success, the doll test was a harrowing undertaking for the Clarks, especially Kenneth who saw the students' distress firsthand. Were there any parts of your research that you found especially emotionally challenging?

I found it very moving to read the test sheets that Kenneth kept on each child who took the doll test. In his penciled notes, between quotation marks, appear the statements that the children made, some of them denying they were Black and others saying they felt rejected by parents or siblings solely because they were darker. Another wrenching experience was interviewing adult African Americans so traumatized by racism and discrimination in their past that they wept during my interview with them. Their memories and feelings were still raw decades after the painful events they described.

In many histories, *Brown v Board of Education* is the last word on integrating schools, but in *What the Children Told Us*, you demonstrate the lengthy struggle that followed to put the law into effect. What do we lose when we teach history only through landmark victories?

We lose the sense that landmark victories are never the last word. They are abstract gains in social policy that require blood, sweat, tears, and a continuing struggle by activists to ensure that solid improvements are made in average people's lives. The federal Voting Rights Act of 1965, for example, was a landmark piece of legislation. But today it's under fire in state legislatures across the country. Without passionate, organized resistance, all of us could lose our democracy.

The Clarks were well-known in their own time, but many may hear about them for the first time by reading *What the Children Told Us*. What do you hope readers will take away from the Clarks' story?

I hope they see that the Clarks were ordinary people like ourselves who did extraordinary things to improve the lives of others. I want readers to see that the Clarks were passionate about their work and kept at it even at the expense of their health and comfort. In a love letter to Kenneth a week or two before they were married in secret, young Mamie wrote that she hoped they'd "live by the side of the road and be a friend to man." We should appreciate that the Clarks were true to Mamie's vision.

SELECTED BIBLIOGRAPHY

BOOKS

Abbott, Shirley. *The Bookmaker's Daughter: A Memory Unbound*. New York: Ticknor & Fields, 1991. Reprint. Fayetteville: University of Arkansas Press, 2006.

Allbritton, Orville E. *Leo and Verne: The Spa's Heyday*. Hot Springs, Arkansas: Garland County Historical Society, 2003.

Anderson, James D. *The Education of Blacks in the South, 1860–1935*. Chapel Hill: University of North Carolina Press, 1988.

Anderson, Jervis. *A Philip Randolph: A Biographical Portrait*. New York: Javanovich, 1973. Reprint. Berkeley: University of California Press, 1986.

Anderson, Jervis. *Bayard Rustin: Troubles I've Seen, a Biography*. New York: HarperCollins, 1997.

Anderson, Jervis. *This Was Harlem: A Cultural Portrait, 1900–1950*. New York: Farrar Straus Giroux, 1982.

Ashmore, Harry. *Hearts and Minds: A Personal Chronicle of Race in America*. Cabin John, Md.: Seven Locks Press, 1988.

Ashmore, Harry, ed. *The Negro and the Schools*. 2nd ed. Chapel Hill: University of North Carolina Press, 1954.

Baldwin, James. *Notes of a Native Son. 1955. Reprint*. New York: Bantam Books, 1972.

Banaji, Mahzarin R. *Blind Spot: Hidden Biases of Good People*. New York: Delacorte Press, 2013.

Banks, William M. *Black Intellectuals: Race and Responsibility in American Life*. New York: W.W. Norton. 1996.

Bates, Daisy. *The Long Shadow of Little Rock*. 1962. Reprint. Fayetteville: University of Arkansas Press, 1986.

Beals, Melba Pattillo. *Warriors Don't Cry*. New York: Washington Square Press, 1995.

Billingsley, Andrew. *Black Families in White America*. 1968. Reprint. New York: Simon & Schuster, 1988.

Bjork, Daniel W. *B. F. Skinner: A Life*. New York: Basic Books, 1993.

Blackmon, Douglas. *Slavery by Another Name: The Re-enslavement of Black People in America from the Civil War to World War II*. New York: Doubleday, 2008.

Bottome, Phyllis. *Alfred Adler: A Portrait from Life*. New York: Vanguard Press, 1957.

Branch, Taylor. *At Canaan's Edge: America in the King Years, 1965–68*. New York: Simon and Schuster, 2006.

Branch, Taylor. *Parting the Waters: America in the King Years, 1954–63*. New York: Simon and Schuster, 1988.

Branch, Taylor. *Pillar of Fire: America in the King Years, 1963–65*. New York: Simon Schuster, 1998.

Brinkley, David. *Washington Goes to War*. 1988. Reprint. New York: Ballantine Books, 1996.

Brisbane, Robert H. *Black Activism: Racial Revolution in the United States, 1954-1970*. Valley Forge, PA: Judson Press, 1974.

Brooks, Roy L. *Integration or Separation? A Strategy for Racial Equality*. Cambridge, MA: Harvard University Press, 1996.

Brown, Claude. *Manchild in the Promised Land*. New York: Macmillan, 1965.

Brown, Dee. *The American Spa: Hot Springs, Arkansas*. Little Rock, AR: Rose Publishing Co., 1982.

Burrows, Edwin G. and Mike Wallace. *Gotham: A History of New York City to 1898*. New York: Oxford University Press, 1999.

Carter, Robert L. *A Matter of Law: A Memoir of Struggle in the Cause of Equal Rights*, New York: The New Press, 2005.

Cary, Francine Curro. *Urban Odyssey: A Multicultural History of Washington, D.C.* Washington DC: Smithsonian Institution Press, 1996.

Clark, Kenneth B. *Dark Ghetto: Dilemmas of Social Power*. 1965. New York: Harper & Row, 1967.

Clark, Kenneth B. *Pathos of Power*. 1974. Reprint. New York: Harper & Row, 1975.

Clark, Kenneth B. *Prejudice and Your Child*. 1955. Reprint. Middletown, CT: Wesleyan University Press, 1988.

Clark, Kenneth B., ed. *The Negro Protest: James Baldwin, Malcolm X and Martin Luther King talk with Kenneth B. Clark*. Boston: Beacon Press, 1963.

Clark, Kenneth B. and Talcott Parsons, eds. *The Negro American*. 1965. Reprint. Boston: Beacon Press, 1967.

Clark, Kenneth B. et al. *A Possible Reality: A Design for the Attainment of High Academic Achievement for Inner-City Students*. New York: Metropolitan Applied Research Center, 1970.

Coleman, William T. Jr. with Donald T. Bliss. *Counsel for the Situation: Shaping the Law to Realize America's Promise*. Washington, D.C.: Brookings Institution Press, 2010.

Cooper, Wayne F. *Claude McKay: Rebel Sojourner in the Harlem Renaissance*. New York: Schocken Books, 1987.

Cottroll, Robert J., Raymond T. Diamond, and Leland B. Ware. Brown v. Board of Education: *Caste, Culture, and the Constitution*. Lawrence, KS: University Press of Kansas, 2003.

Cross, William E. Jr. *Shades of Black: Diversity in African-American Identity*. Philadelphia: Temple University Press. 1991.

Cruse, Harold. *The Crisis of the Negro Intellectual*. New York: William Morrow, 1967.

Dyja, Thomas. *Walter White: The Dilemma of Black Identity in America*. Chicago: Ivan Dee, 2008.

Eisinger, Chester E. *The 1940's: Profile of a Nation in Crisis*. New York: Doubleday, 1969.

Fast, Howard. *Being Red*. New York: Houghton Mifflin, 1990.

Franklin, John Hope. *Mirror to America: The Autobiography of John Hope Franklin*. New York: Farrar, Straus and Giroux, 2005.

Garrow, David J. *Bearing the Cross: Martin Luther King, Jr., and the Southern Christian Leadership Conference*. 1986. Reprint. New York: Vintage Books, 1988.

Gatewood, Willard B. *Aristocrats of Color: The Black Elite, 1880–1920*. 1990. Reprint. Bloomington: Indiana University Press, 1993.

Gillon, Steven M. *Separate and Unequal: The Kerner Commission and the Unraveling of American Liberalism*. New York: Basic Books, 2018.

Gitlin, Todd. *The Sixties: Years of Hope, Days of Rage*. New York: Bantam Books, 1987.

Goodman, Mary Ellen. *Race Awareness in Young Children*. Cambridge, Mass.: Addison-Wesley Press, 1952.

Gordon, Fon Louise. *Caste & Class: The Black Experience in Arkansas, 1880–1920*. 1995. Reprint. Athens: University of Georgia Press, 2007.

Gossett, Thomas F. *Race: The History of an Idea*. Dallas: Southern Methodist University, 1963. Reprint. New York: Oxford University Press, 1997.

Graham, Lawrence Otis. *Our Kind of People: Inside America's Black Upper Class*. New York: Harper Collins, 1999.

Grant, Colin. *Negro with a Hat: The Rise and Fall of Marcus Garvey*. New York: Oxford University Press, 2008.

Green, Constance McLaughlin. *The Secret City: A History of Race Relations in the Nation's Capital*. Princeton, N.J.: Princeton University Press, 1967.

Greenberg, Jack. *Crusaders in the Courts: How a Dedicated Band of Lawyers Fought for the Civil Rights Revolution*. New York: Basic Books, 1994.

Greenberg, Lynn Cheryl. *"Or Does It Explode?": Black Harlem in the Great Depression*. New York: Oxford University Press, 1997.

Guthrie, Robert V. *Even the Rat Was White: A Historical View of Psychology*. Second edition. Boston: Pearson Education, 2004.

Halberstam, David. *The Children*. New York: Random House, 1998.

Halberstam, David. *The Fifties*. New York: Random House, 1993.

Hamilton, Charles V. *Adam Clayton Powell Jr.: The Political Biography of an American Dilemma*. New York: Atheneum, 1991.

Harris, Eddy L. *Still Life in Harlem*. New York: Henry Holt, 1996.

Harris, Leonard and Charles Molesworth. *Alain L. Locke: Biography of a Philosopher*. Chicago: University of Chicago Press, 2008.

Haygood, Wil. *King of the Cats: The Life and Times of Adam Clayton Powell, Jr.* New York: Houghton Mifflin, 1993.

Henry, Charles P., ed. *Ralph J. Bunche: Selected Speeches & Writings*. Ann Arbor: University of Michigan Press, 1995.

Hickey, Neil and Ed Edwin. *Adam Clayton Powell and the Politics of Race*. New York: Fleet Publishing Corp., 1965.

Horn, Margo. *Before It's Too Late: The Child Guidance Movement in the United States, 1922–1945*. Philadelphia: Temple University Press, 1999.

Horst, Heather A. and Andrew Garner. *Jamaican Americans*. New York: Chelsea House, 2007.

Howard, David. *Kingston (Jamaica): A Literary and Cultural History*. Interlink Books: North Hampton, MA, 2005.

Hubbard, Vincent K. *A History of St. Kitts: The Sweet Trade*. Oxford, England: Macmillan Caribbean, 2002.

Ione, Carole. *Pride of Family: Four Generations of American Women of Color.* New York: Avon Books, 1991.

Jackson, John P. Jr. *Social Scientists for Social Justice: Making the Case against Segregation.* New York: New York University Press, 2001.

Jacoby, Tamar. *Someone Else's House: America's Unfinished Struggle for Integration.* New York: Free Press, 1998.

James, Rawn Jr. *Root and Branch: Charles Hamilton Houston, Thurgood Marshall, and the Struggle to End Segregation.* New York: Bloomsbury Press, 2010.

Janken, Robert Kenneth. *Rayford W. Logan and the Dilemma of the African-American Intellectual.* Amherst: University of Massachusetts Press, 1993.

Jaspin, Elliot. *Buried in the Bitter Waters: The Hidden History of Racial Cleansing in America.* New York: Basic Books, 2007.

Jefferson, Margo. *Negroland.* New York: Pantheon Books, 2015.

Johnson, James Weldon. *Black Manhattan.* New York: Alfred A. Knopf, 1930. Reprinted with a new introduction by Sondra Kathryn Wilson. New York: Da Capo Press, 1991.

Jordan, Vernon E. Jr. with Annette Gordon Reed. *Vernon Can Read! A Memoir.* New York: PublicAffairs, 2009.

Joseph, Peniel E. *Stokely: A Life.* New York: Basic Civitas, 2014.

Kahlenberg, Richard D. *Tough Liberal: Albert Shanker and the Battles over Schools, Unions, Race, and Democracy.* New York: Columbia University Press, 2007.

Kendi, Ibram X. *Stamped from the Beginning: The Definitive History of Racist Ideas in America.* New York: Nation Books, 2016.

Kirk, John A. *Beyond Little Rock: The Origins and Legacies of the Central High Crisis.* Fayetteville: University of Arkansas Press, 2007.

Klarman, Michael J. *Brown v. Board of Education and the Civil Rights Movement.* New York: Oxford University Press, 2007.

Klein, Woody, ed. *Toward Humanity and Justice: The Writings of Kenneth B. Clark, Scholar of the 1954* Brown v. Board of Education *Decision.* Westport, CT: Praeger, 2004.

Klineberg, Otto. *Race Differences.* New York: Harper & Bros., 1935.

Kluger, Richard. *Simple Justice: The History of* Brown v. Board of Education *and Black America's Struggle for Equality.* 1975. Reprint. New York: Vintage Books, 1977.

Kozol, Jonathan. *Death at an Early Age: The Destruction of the Hearts and Minds of Negro Children in the Boston Public Schools.* Boston: Houghton Mifflin, 1967.

Krosney, Herbert. *Beyond Welfare: Poverty in the Supercity.* New York: Holt, Rinehart, and Winston, 1966.

LaNier, Carlotta Walls with Lisa Frazier Page. *A Mighty Long Way: My Journey to Justice at Little Rock Central High School.* New York: Random House, 2009.

Lemann, Nicholas. *The Promised Land: The Great Migration and How It Changed America.* New York: Alfred A. Knopf, 1991.

Lewis, Catherine M. and Richard J. Lewis. *Race, Politics, and Memory: A Documentary History of the Little Rock School Crisis.* Fayetteville: University of Arkansas Press, 2007.

Lewis, David Levering. *W.E.B. DuBois: Biography of a Race, 1868–1919.* New York: Henry Holt and Company. 1993.

Lewis, David Levering. *When Harlem Was in Vogue.* 1981. Reprint. New York: Oxford University Press, 1989.

Lewis, Michael. *The Undoing Project: A Friendship That Changed Our Minds.* New York: W.W. Norton, 2017.

Locke, Alain, ed. *The New Negro: Voices of the Harlem Renaissance.* New York: Atheneum, 1925. Reprinted with an introduction by Arnold Rampersad. New York: Atheneum, 1992.

Logan, Rayford W. *Howard University: The First Hundred Years, 1867–1967.* New York: New York University Press, 1969.

Mann, Peggy. *Ralph Bunche: UN Peacemaker.* New York: Coward, McCann & Geoghegan, 1975.

Manning, Kenneth R. *Black Apollo of Science: The Life of Ernest Everett Just.* New York: Oxford University Press, 1983.

Markowitz, Gerald and David Rosner. *Children, Race, and Power: Kenneth and Mamie Clark's Northside Center.* Charlottesville: University Press of Virginia, 1996.

Martin, Waldo E. Jr., ed. Brown v. Board of Education: *A Brief History with Documents.* Boston: Bedford/St. Martin's, 1998.

Massey, Douglas S. and Nancy A. Denton. *American* Apartheid: *Segregation and the Making of the Underclass.* Cambridge, MA: Harvard University Press, 1993.

McCullough, David. *The Path Between the Seas: The Creation of the Panama Canal, 1870–1914,* New York: Simon & Schuster, 1977.

McKay, Claude. *A Long Way from Home: An Autobiography.* New York: Lee Furman, 1937. Reprint. New York: Harcourt Brace Jovanovich, 1970.

McKay, Claude. *Home to Harlem.* New York: Harper & Bros. 1928. Reprint. Boston: Northeastern University Press, 1987.

Metropolitan Applied Research Center. *A Relevant War Against Poverty: A Study of Community Action Programs and Observable Social Change.* New York: Metropolitan Applied Research Center, 1968.

Moorehead, Caroline. *Bertrand Russell: A Life.* New York: Viking, 1992.

Morris, James McGrath. *Eye on the Struggle: Ethel Payne, the First Lady of the Black Press.* New York: Amistad, 2015.

Morrison, Toni. The Bluest Eye. 1970. Reprint. New York: Penguin Books, 1993.

Myrdal, Gunnar. *An American Dilemma: The Negro Problem and Modern Democracy.* 1944. Reprint. New York: Harper & Row, 1974.

Nyman, Lawrence. *Recollections: An Oral History of the Psychology Department of the City College of the City University of New York.* New York: City College, 1976.

Orfield, Gary et al. *Dismantling Desegregation: The Quiet Reversal of* Brown v. Board of Education. New York: New Press, 1996.

Osofsky, Gilbert. *Harlem: The Making of a Ghetto: Negro New York, 1890–1930.* 1963. Second edition. New York: Harper Torchbooks, 1971.

Parker, Matthew. *Panama Fever: The Epic Story of One of the Greatest Human Achievements of All Time—the Building of the Panama Canal.* New York: Doubleday, 2008.

Patterson, James T. Brown v. Board of Education: *A Civil Rights Milestone and Its Troubled Legacy.* New York: Oxford University Press, 2001.

Perkins, Myla. *Black Dolls: An Identification and Value Guide, 1820–1991*. Paducah, KY: Collector Books, 1993.

Perry, Imani. *Looking for Lorraine: The Radiant and Radical Life of Lorraine Hansberry*. Boston: Beacon Press, 2018.

Philogene, Gina, ed. *Racial Identity in Context: The Legacy of Kenneth B. Clark*. Washington, DC: American Psychological Association, 2004.

Platt, Anthony. *E. Franklin Frazier Reconsidered*. New Brunswick, NJ: Rutgers University Press, 1991.

Polsgrove, Carol. *Divided Minds: Intellectuals and the Civil Rights Movement*. New York: W.W. Norton, 2001.

Porter, Judith D.R. *Black Child, White Child: The Development of Racial Attitudes*. Cambridge: Harvard University Press, 1973.

Rainwater, Lee and William L. Yancey. *The Moynihan Report and the Politics of Controversy*. Cambridge, MA: MIT Press, 1967.

Rampersad, Arnold. *Ralph Ellison: A Biography*. New York: Knopf, 2007.

Reed, Roy. *Faubus: The Life and Times of an American Prodigal*. Fayetteville: *University of Arkansas Press*, 1997.

Roberts, Gene and Hank Klibanoff. *The Race Beat: The Press, the Civil Rights Struggle, and the Awakening of a Nation*. New York: Alfred A. Knopf, 2006.

Sarat, Austin, ed. *Race, Law, & Culture: Reflections on* Brown v. Board of Education. New York: Oxford University Press, 1997.

Sarratt, Reed. *The Ordeal of Desegregation: The First Decade*. New York: Harper & Row, 1966.

Schlesinger, Arthur M. Jr. *Robert Kennedy and His Times*, Vol. 1. New York: Houghton Mifflin and Co., 1978.

Schoener, Allon, ed. *Harlem on My Mind: Cultural Capital of Black America, 1900–1968*. New York: Random House, 1968. Reprint. New York: New Press, 2007.

Silberman, Charles E. *Crisis in Black and White*. New York: Random House, 1964.

Sinnette, Elinor Des Verney. *Arthur Alfonso Schomburg: Black Bibliophile & Collector*. Detroit and New York: New York Public Library and Wayne State University Press, 1989.

Southern, David W. *Gunnar Myrdal and Black-White Relations: The Use and Abuse of* An American Dilemma, *1944–1969*. Baton Rouge: Louisiana State University Press, 1987.

Stockley, Grif. *Daisy Bates: Civil Rights Crusader from Arkansas*. Jackson, MS: University Press of Mississippi, 2005.

Steele, Claude M. *Whistling Vivaldi and Other Clues to How Stereotypes Affect Us*. New York: W.W. Norton, 2010.

Stokes, John A. with Lois Wolfe. *Students on Strike: Jim Crow, Civil Rights, Brown, and Me*. Washington, D.C.: National Geographic, 2008.

Tatum, Beverly Daniel. *"Why Are All the Black Kids Sitting Together in the Cafeteria?" and Other Conversations about Race*. 1997. Reprint. New York: Basic Books, 2003.

Theoharis, Jeanne. *A More Beautiful and Terrible History: The Uses and Misuses of Civil Rights History*. Boston: Beacon Press, 2018.

Theoharis, Jeanne. *The Rebellious Life of Mrs. Rosa Parks*. 2013. Reprint. Boston: Beacon Press, 2015.

Traub, James. *City on a Hill: Testing the American Dream at City College*. Reading, MA: Addison-Wesley Publishing Co., 1995.

Urquhart, Brian. *Ralph Bunche: An American Life*. New York: W.W. Norton & Company, 1993.

Walter, John C. *The Harlem Fox: J. Raymond Jones and Tammany, 1920–1970*. Albany: State University of New York Press, 1989.

Warren, Robert Penn. *Who Speaks for the Negro?* New York: Random House, 1965.

Watkins, T.H. *The Hungry Years: A Narrative History of the Great Depression in America*. 1999. Reprint. New York: Henry Holt, 2000.

Watson, Goodwin, ed. *Civilian Morale*. New York: Houghton Mifflin, 1942.

Weatherby, W.J. *James Baldwin: Artist on Fire*. 1989. Reprint. New York: Dell, 1990.

Weiss, Nancy J. *Whitney M. Young, Jr., and the Struggle for Civil Rights*. Princeton, NJ: Princeton University Press, 1989.

Whayne, Jeannie M. et al. *Arkansas: A Narrative History*. Fayetteville: University of Arkansas Press, 2002.

Whitman, James Q. *Hitler's American Model: The United States and the Making of Nazi Race Law*. Princeton, NJ: Princeton University Press, 2017.

Whitman, Mark, ed. *Removing A Badge of Slavery: The Record of Brown v. Board of Education*. Princeton, NJ: Markus Wiener Publishing, 1993.

Wilkerson, Isabel. *Caste: The Origins of Our Discontents*. New York: Random House, 2020.

Wilkerson, Isabel. *The Warmth of Other Suns: The Epic Story of the Great Migration*. New York: Random House, 2010.

Wilkins, Roger. *A Man's Life: An Autobiography*. New York: Simon and Schuster, 1982.

Wilkinson, J. Harvie III. *From Brown to Bakke: The Supreme Court and School Integration: 1954–1978*. New York: Oxford University Press, 1979.

Williams, Juan. *Thurgood Marshall: American Revolutionary*. New York: Three Rivers Press, 1998.

Wilson, William Julius. *The Truly Disadvantaged: The Inner City, the Underclass, and Public Policy*. 1987. Reprint. Chicago: University of Chicago Press, 1990.

X, Malcolm. *Malcolm X Speaks*. 1966. Reprint. New York: Grove Press, 1980.

Zigler, Edward and Susan Muenchow. *Head Start: The Inside Story of America's Most Successful Educational Experiment*. New York: Basic Books, 1992.

Zigler, Edward and Jeanette Valentine, eds. *Project Head Start: A Legacy of the War on Poverty*. New York: Free Press, 1979.

ARTICLES

Clark, Mamie Phipps. "Mamie Phipps Clark," in *Models of Achievement: Reflections on Eminent Women in Psychology*, edited by Agnes N. O'Connell and Nancy Felipe Russo, 270-276. New York: Columbia University Press, 11983.

Du Bois, W.E.B. "Does the Negro Need Separate Schools?" *Journal of Negro Education* 4, no. 3 (July 1935): 32.

Frazier, E. Franklin. "The Pathology of Race Prejudice," *Forum*, vol. 77, no. 6 (June 1927): 857.

Hall, Mary Harrington. "A Conversation with Kenneth B. Clark," *Psychology Today*, vol. 2, no. 1 (June 1968): 19–25.

Hentoff, Nat, "The Integrationist," *New Yorker*, August 23, 1982, 37–73.

"History of Psychology: The Contributions of Kenneth B. and Mamie Phipps Clark," *American Psychologist*, vol. 57, no. 1 (January 2002): 20–59.

Houston, Charles H. "Don't Shout Too Soon," *Crisis 43*, no. 3 (March 1936), 79, 91.

Locke, Alain. "Harlem: Dark Weather-Vane," *Survey Graphic*, 25, no. 8 (March 1936): 457–462, 493–495.

Long, Howard Hale. "Some Psychogenic Hazards of Segregated Education of Negroes," *Journal of Negro Education*, 4, no. 3 (July 1935), 336–350.

National Park, U.S. Department of the Interior. "African-Americans and the Hot Springs Baths," https: //nps.gov/articles/000/african-americans-and-the-hot-springs-baths.htm.

Van den Haag, Ernest. "Social Science Testimony in the Desegregation Cases—A Reply to Professor Kenneth Clark," *Villanova Law Review*, 6, no. 1 (Fall 1960): 71.

Washington, George S., ed. *Hot Springs National Park Souvenir Program*. Woodmen of Union. Box 10, Alfred E. Smith papers, University of Arkansas, Fayetteville.

THE CLARKS' JOINTLY PUBLISHED ARTICLES

"The Development of the Consciousness of Self and the Emergence of Racial Identification in Negro Preschool Children." *Journal of Social Psychology*, vol.10, no. 4 (1939): 591–599.

"Emotional Factors in Racial Identification and Preference in Negro Children." *Journal of Negro Education*, 19, no. 3 (1950): 341–350.

"Racial Identification and Preference in Negro Children." *Readings in Social Psychology*, edited by Theodore M. Newcomb and Eugene L. Hartley. New York: Henry Holt, 1947, 169–178.

"Segregation as a Factor in the Racial Identification of Negro Pre-school Children: A Preliminary Report." *Journal of Experimental Education* (December 1939): 161–163.

"Skin Color as a Factor in Racial Identification of Negro Preschool Children." *Journal of Social Psychology*, 11, no. 1 (1940): 159–169.

"What Do Blacks Think of Themselves?" *Ebony* (November 1980): 176–182.

NEWSPAPERS

Afro-American (Baltimore and Washington, D.C.)
Arkansas Democrat (Little Rock)
Arkansas Gazette (Little Rock)
Charleston (SC) *News and Courier*
Chicago Defender
Hastings (NY) *News*
Hilltop (Howard University)
Hot Springs (AR) *Echo*
Hot Springs (AR) *New Era*
New York Age
New York Amsterdam News
New York Daily News
New York Herald Tribune
New York Post

New York Times
New York World-Telegram & Sun
People's Voice (New York City)
Pittsburg Courier
Richmond (Va.) Times-Dispatch
Sentinel-Record (Hot Springs, AR)
Topeka (Kansas) Daily Capital
Washington Daily News
Washington Post
Washington Evening Star
Wilmington (Dela.) *Journal-Every Evening*

PERIODICALS
Bison (Howard University yearbook)
Crisis (NAACP magazine)
Ebony
Hot Springs City Directory
Jet
Journal of Negro Education
Journal of Social Psychology
Record, Journal of the Garland County (Arkansas) Historical Society
Stylus (Howard University literary magazine)

THESES
Clark, Kenneth B. "Some Factors Influencing the Remembering of Prose Material." *Archives of Psychology*, no. 253. Columbia University dissertation, July 1940.

Clark, Kenneth B. "The Attitude of Negro College Students Toward Their Parents," master's thesis, Howard University, May 12, 1936.

Clark, Mamie Phipps. "An Investigation of the Development of Consciousness of Distinctive Self in Pre-School Children," master's thesis, Howard University, May 12, 1939.

Clark, Mamie Phipps. "Changes in Primary Mental Abilities with Age." *Archives of Psychology*, no. 291. Columbia University dissertation, May 1944.

Ferguson, G.O. "The Psychology of the Negro: An Experimental Study." *Archives of Psychology*, no. 36. Columbia University dissertation, April 1916.

Keppel, Ben Gareth. "The Work of Democracy: Ralph Bunche, Kenneth B. Clark, Lorraine Hansberry and the Cultural Politics of Racial Equality." University of California, Los Angeles, dissertation, 1992.

COLUMBIA UNIVERSITY ORAL HISTORIES
Kenneth B. Clark
Mamie Clark

REPORTS

Arkansas History Commission. "Public Secondary Schools for Negroes in Arkansas," 1935.

Clark, Kenneth B. and John Hope Franklin. "The Nineteen Eighties: Prologue and Prospect." Washington, D.C.: Joint Center for Political Studies, 1981.

Clark, Kenneth B. et al. "Youth in the Ghetto: A Study of the Consequences of Powerlessness and a Blueprint for Change." New York: Harlem Youth Opportunities Unlimited, Inc., 1964.

Department of Education. *Negro Schools in Arkansas: 1927–28.* Little Rock: Department of Education, 1929.

The Kerner Report: The 1968 Report of the National Advisory Commission on Civil Disorders. New York: Pantheon Books, 1968.

Mass Violence in America: The Complete Report of Mayor LaGuardia's Commission on the Harlem Riot of March 19, 1935. Reprint. New York: Arno Press, 1969.

NAACP Legal Defense and Education Fund. "It's Not the Distance, It's the Niggers: Comments on the Controversy over School Busing." New York: NAACP Legal Defense and Education Fund, Division of Legal Information and Community Service, 1972.

Public Education Association. "Status of the Public School Education of Negro and Puerto Rican Children in New York City," 1955.

U.S. Civil Rights Commission. *Five Communities: Their Search for Equal Education,* Clearinghouse Publication No. 37, Washington, DC: U.S. Government Printing Office, 1972.

Witmer, Helen Leland and Ruth Kotinsky, eds. *Personality in the Making: The Fact-Finding Report of the Midcentury White House Conference on Children and Youth.* New York: Harper & Row, 1952.

ARCHIVES

Library of Congress, Rare Book and Special Collections Division, Washington, DC Kenneth B. Clark papers and Ralph Ellison papers.

Moorland-Spingarn Research Center, Howard University, Washington, DC E. Franklin Frazier papers and Works Progress Administration papers. Also papers of Judge J. Waties and Elizabeth Waring and transcript of *Briggs v. Elliott,* U.S. District Court, Eastern District of South Carolina, 1951. Box 110–25, Folder 761.

National Archives at Philadelphia. Transcript of *Davis v. Prince Edward County School Board.* U.S. District Court, Western District of Virginia, 1952.

National Archives, Washington, D.C. Transcript of *Brown v. Board of Education of Topeka, Kansas.* U.S. District Court, District of Kansas, 1951. Also *Belton vs. Gebhart* transcript, Delaware Court of Chancery, 1952.

New York Public Library, Manuscripts and Archives Division. Northside Center for Child Development papers.

University of Arkansas Libraries, Fayetteville, Arkansas. Special Collections Division. Alfred E. Smith papers.

NOTES

ABBREVIATIONS
Names
KBC—Kenneth Bancroft Clark
MKP—Mamie Katherine Phipps (maiden name)
MPC—Mamie Phipps Clark (married name)

Collections
LOC—Library of Congress, Manuscript Division, KBC papers
HC—KBC's Hastings-on-Hudson (NY) collection
OC—Kate Harris's Osprey (Florida) collection
CUOH—Columbia University Oral History
HHS—Hastings (NY) Historical Society
NCCD—Northside Center for Child Development
NYPL—New York Public Library
GCHS—Garland County (Arkansas) Historical Society
UARK—University of Arkansas (Fayetteville)

Newspapers
Af-Am—Afro-American (Baltimore)
AG—Arkansas Gazette
CD—Chicago Defender
DD—Daily Defender (Chicago)
ES—Evening Star (Washington, D.C.)
HSE—Hot Springs Echo
HSNE—Hot Springs New Era
NYAN—New York Amsterdam News
NYHT–New York Herald Tribune
NYP—New York Post
NYT—New York Times
PC—Pittsburgh Courier
SR—Sentinel-Record (Hot Springs, AR)
WDN—Washington Daily News
WP—Washington Post

Interviews cited below were conducted by the author unless otherwise noted. When a series of quotations have clearly come, one after the other, from the same source, such as MPC's travel diary, a KBC speech, or dialogue in court testimony, only the first quotation is cited below.

EPIGRAPH

1 It is easier to build strong children: Nicholas Kristof column, *NYT*, January 8, 2016.

PROLOGUE: THE DOLL TEST

1 One's reputation: Claude M. Steele, *Whistling Vivaldi: And Other Clues to How Stereotypes Affect Us* (New York: W. W. Norton, 2010), 46.

2 Give me the doll: Kenneth J. test sheets, October 3, 1930 [sic], LOC, Box 45, Folder 3.

3 That's a nice color: Helen N. test sheets, October 4, 1940, LOC, Box 45, Folder 2.

4 I look brown: Edward D. test sheets, October 29, 1940, LOC, Box 45, Folder 1.

5 No—I'm a white girl: Phyllis J. test sheets, October 29, 1940, LOC, Box 45, Folder 2.

6 Yes, I would like to be white: Joan W. test sheets, October 23, 1940, LOC, Box 45, Folder 1.

7 Because people call me black: Juanita R. test sheets, October 24, 1940, LOC, Box 45, Folder 1.

8 black: Caleb D. test sheets, October 7, 1940, LOC, Box 45, Folder 3.

9 sumpin' like me: Kermit L. test sheets, October 23, 1940, LOC, Box 45, Folder 3.

CHAPTER 1: THE DOCTOR'S DAUGHTER

1 Black folks aren't born: Melba Pattillo Beals, *Warriors Don't Cry* (New York: Washington Square Press, 1995), 6.

2 My only fear for her: Dr. Harold H. Phipps to Alfred E. Smith, September 24, 1934, Alfred E. Smith Papers, University of Arkansas (Fayetteville).

3 Shut up!: MKP to KBC, July 17, 1934, LOC, Box 1, Folder 1.

4 It was a hot street: Hilda Martin, telephone conversation with the author, June 20, 2008.

5 She was vibrant: Billie Allen, telephone conversation with the author, June 27, 2008.

6 The sisters were real kind: Ida Fort Thompson, in discussion with the author, Hot Springs, AR, May 13, 2008.

7 I would say I learned most of it: MPC, CUOH, May 25, 1976, 5.

8 Harris was hoisted: "Negro Lynched," *Hot Springs New Era*, August 1, 1922, 1.

9 It takes days: MPC, CUOH, 8.

10 It wears on you: Evelyn Phipps Boyer, in discussion with the author, Washington, DC, November 10, 2007.

11 The teachers were really patient with us: Thomas Anderson, in discussion with the author, Hot Springs, AR, May 16, 2008.

12 The school was poor: MPC, CUOH, 10.

13 You had to be right with Granddaddy: Evelyn Phipps Boyer, in discussion with the author, Washington, DC, December 6, 2008.

14 something that has never happened: "What Are You Saying Sophs?" *Langston Maveric*, April 22, 1932, in MKP scrapbook, LOC, Box 11, 1.

15 Displaying a versatility: "Fine Tribute Paid to Young Musician," *Hot Springs Echo*, n.d., MKP scrapbook, clipping, LOC, Box 11.

16 We had certain access: MPC, CUOH, 4.

17 Miss Mamie Katherine Phipps: *Hot Springs Echo*, n.d., MKP scrapbook, clipping, LOC, Box 11.

18 JUST DROP ME A LINE: MKP scrapbook, LOC, Box 11.

19 He had to be one of the most difficult: KCH, in discussion with the author, Hastings, NY, February 5, 1996.

20 They did little dances: Dorothy Logan, in discussion with the author, Hot Springs, AR, May 28, 2008.

21 And I'm telling you: KCH, in discussion with the author, Osprey, FL, June 11, 2007.

22 Most Popular: MKP scrapbook, awards, LOC, Box 11.

23 Because we want better spirit: KBC form letter, n.d., Glenda Marie Watson Collection, Austell, Georgia.

24 He was not the best looking dude: Leighla Whipper Ford, in discussion with the author, Kingston, NY, April 14, 1994.

25 Have you seen Mamie Phipps?: KBC to MPC, July 8, 1935, LOC, Box 1, Folder 4.

26 I don't think you're so hot: KBC to MPC, July 8, 1935, LOC, Box 1, Folder 4.

27 There isn't very much going on: KBC to MPC, April 25, 1935, LOC, Box 1, Folder 1.

28 He and Mamie fit like a shoe: Leroy Weekes, telephone conversation with the author, March 11, 1994.

CHAPTER 2: THE SON OF A SEAMSTRESS

1 De ole sheep, dey know de road: Dudley Randall, ed., *The Black Poets* (New York: Bantam Books, 1981), 32.

2 Frankly these two months: MKP to KBC, February 26, 1936, LOC, Box 1, Folder 6.

3 some degree of Oedipus: KBC, "The Attitude of Negro College Students Toward Their Parents" (master's thesis, Howard University, May 1936), 52.

4 our thesis: MKP to KBC, March 21, 1938, LOC, Box 3, Folder 1.

5 From the moment of landing: Logan Marshall, *The Story of the Panama Canal* (John C Winston, 1913), 77.

6 Don't dance: Miriam Clark Austin, interview by Michael Meyers, New York City, October 30, 1977, transcript, 10, LOC, Box 6, Folder 9.

7 Kind friends: Austin, interview transcript, 18.

8 What a fine young man: KBC, in discussion with the author, Hastings, NY, April 24, 1993.

9 We did a lot of stickball: Dr. John Moseley, in discussion with the author, New York City, February 17, 1996.

10 Some of them looked: Moseley, discussion.

11 Mothers! give your children: Marcus Garvey Jr., "Garveyism: Some Reflections on Its Significance for Today," in *Marcus Garvey and the Vision of Africa*, ed. John Henrik Clarke (New York: Random House, 1974), 377.

12 Don't ever let this happen again: Austin, interview transcript, 21–22.

13 have race: Austin, interview transcript, 21–22.

14 God has no hands: Austin, interview transcript, 21–22.

15 The pulse of the Negro world: Alain Locke, ed., *The New Negro* (1925; repr. New York: Touchstone, 1997), 14.

16 I don't think you should: KBC, "Dealing with the Culturally Different" (speech), Washington, DC, March 22, 1978, transcript, 2, HC.

17 People were sleeping in subways: Arnold Rampersad, ed., *The Life of Langston Hughes* (New York: Oxford University Press, 1986), 1:175.

18 The fact is that this community: Beverly Smith, "Harlem—The Negro City," *New York Herald Tribune*, February 10, 1930.

19 Kenneth, this won't bother us a bit: KBC, interview by D. Lydia Bronte, transcript, 5, LOC, Box 194, Folder 3, September 18, 1990, 11.

20 protective insensitivity: James Moss, "Utilization of Negro Teachers in Colleges in New York State," 1957, 118, LOC, Box 190, Folder 4.

21 Yes, you're going: KBC, CUOH, 62.

22 Put a period there, Mr. Clark: KBC, CUOH, 68.

23 We use artificial proms: *Hilltop*, editorial, March 3, 1933, 2.

24 Those were tight times: Weekes, conversation.

25 They made fun of me: KBC, in discussion with the author, Hastings, NY, July 13, 1993.

26 Living in the nation's capital: Peggy Mann, *Ralph Bunche: UN Peacemaker* (New York: Coward, McCann & Geoghegan, 1975), 87.

27 Get up, get up!: KBC, CUOH, 82.

28 Get out of here: Moss, "Utilization of Negro Teachers," 128.

29 A gift of Providence: KBC, "Big Shots in Miniature," *Hilltop*, February 3, 1933, 3.

30 laboring under the delusion: KBC, "Biased or Unbiased Reports?" Insert. *Hilltop*, January 19, 1933.

31 I am just coming from elections: KBC to Miriam Clark, May 17, 1933, OC.

32 our old school Negro leaders: KBC, "Looking Backward," *Hilltop*, January 19, 1934, 2.

33 There must be room: KBC, interview by Lawrence Nyman, July 1, 1975, transcript, 14–15, HC.

34 For Members Only: "Members Only Sign is Posted in House Cafe," WP, March 17, 1934, 1.

35 We are citizens and we can go: "Negro Students Rush Congress Restaurant In Vain Effort to Test Rule Barring Race," *NYT*, March 18, 1934, 1.

36 You are the damned n——: "Cops Hold Lily-White Lines in Capitol Cafes," *Afro-American* (Baltimore), March 24, 1934, 1.

37 Take their names off: KBC, "Racial Progress and Retreat," in *Race in America: The Struggle for Equality*, ed. Herbert Hill and James E. Jones Jr. (Madison: University of Wisconsin Press, 1992), 8.

38 Negro Students Rush Congress: *NYT*, March 18, 1934, 1.

39 Unless we can weed Communism: "Kick Out H.U. Students and Prexy—Blanton," *Afro-American* (Baltimore), March 24, 1934, 1.

40 We ought to be giving these young men medals: KBC, CUOH, 77.

41 MY DEAR FELLOW STUDENT: KBC form letter, n.d., Glenda Marie Watson Collection, Austell, Georgia.

42 Marry the girl: Hylan Lewis, in discussion with the author, New York City, June 16, 1994.

43 Lament in Ebony: KBC, "Lament in Ebony," *Hilltop*, March 31, 1937, 2.

44 Shortest Short Story: MKP, "Shortest Short Story," *Hilltop*, March 31, 1937, 2.

45   My dear Dr. Phipps: KBC to Dr. Harold H. Phipps, June 9, 1937, LOC, Box 5, Folder 4.
46   Our object with regard to Mamie: Dr. Harold H. Phipps to KBC, July 19, 1937, LOC, Box 5, Folder 4.
47   First, it means anticipation: MKP to KBC, August 20, 1937, LOC, Box 2, Folder 3.

CHAPTER 3: THE SECRET WEDDING

1   Them's the only two people: August Wilson, *Two Trains Running* (New York: Plume, 1992), Act 2, Scene 5.
2   The negro is an example: Georg Wilhelm Friedrich Hegel, *Lectures on the Philosophy of World History*, trans. H. B. Nisbet (Cambridge: Cambridge University Press, 1975), 177.
3   It is generally recognized: U.S. Army War College, "The Army War College Studies Black Soldiers," SHEC: Resources for Teachers, accessed November 3, 2021, https://shec.ashp.cuny.edu/items/show/808.
4   And in view of all the evidence: G. O. Ferguson, "The Psychology of the Negro: An Experimental Study," *Archives of Psychology* 36, (April 1916): 125.
5   All our best psychologists: "Digest of Public Opinion on Jewish Matters," *Jewish Daily Bulletin*, January 28, 1927, https://www.jta.org/archive/digest-of-public-opinion-on-jewish-matters-179.
6   I stayed quite a while: MKP to KBC, September 30, 1937, LOC, Box 2, Folder 4.
7   Kinder keep up with him: Katie Phipps to MKP, August 22, 1938, LOC, Box 10, Folder 2.
8   none too good for you: Miriam Clark to MKP, September 27, 1937, LOC, Box 10, Folder 2.
9   Hope that they know: KBC to MKP, October 11, 1937, LOC, Box 10, Folder 2.
10   So that leaves us together: KBC to MKP, October 13, 1937, LOC, Box 2, Folder 5.
11   Gee, Mamie, darling: KBC to MKP, October 18, 1937, LOC, Box 2, Folder 5.
12   I wish for you good health: MKP to KBC, October 19, 1937, LOC, Box 2, Folder 5.
13   As I told you on the phone: MKP to KBC, November 2, 1937, LOC, Box 2, Folder 6.
14   I am the legitimate father: Phyllis Bottome, *Alfred Adler: A Portrait from Life* (New York: Vanguard Press, 1957), 156.
15   Every neurosis can be understood: Bottome, *Alfred Adler*, 114.
16   Those who have traveled: KBC, "Implications of Adlerian Theory for an Understanding of Civil Rights Problems and Action," *Journal of Individual Psychology* 23, no. 2 (November 1967): 181–90.
17   there is nothing in the brain or blood: Otto Klineberg, *Race Differences* (New York: Harper & Bros., 1935), 348.
18   One page says: MKP to KBC, December 17, 1937, LOC, Box 2, Folder 6.
19   general hipness: MKP to KBC, January 29, 1938, LOC, Box 2, Folder 7.
20   Sometimes I wonder: MKP to KBC, January 6, 1938, LOC, Box 2, Folder 7.
21   Daddy was there: MKP to KBC, January 18, 1938, LOC, Box 2, Folder 7.
22   My philosophy of life: MKP to KBC, January 18, 1938, LOC, Box 2, Folder 7.
23   You will excuse me: Arthurton Clark to KBC, January 25, 1938, LOC, Box 1, Folder 1.
24   Your idea about speaking: MKP to KBC, February 23, 1938, LOC, Box 2, Folder 7.
25   Please speak to Frazier: KBC to MKP, February 24, 1938, LOC, Box 2, Folder 7.
26   Well, are you married yet?: KBC to MKP, March 9, 1938, LOC, Box 3, Folder 1.

27 I felt like a contented cow: MKP to KBC, March 8, 1938, LOC, Box 3, Folder 1.

28 the inferiority complex of Negroes: KBC to MKP, March 16, 1938, LOC, Box 3, Folder 1.

29 If you want to lighten: KBC, "Indices of a Racial Inferiority Feeling Among American Negroes" (unpublished manuscript, January 10, 1938), LOC, Box 168, Folder 2.

30 What is perhaps the most insidious: KBC, "Indices."

31 I have looked at marriage: MKP to KBC, March 21, 1938, LOC, Box 3, Folder 1.

32 Kenneth—I don't think: MKP to KBC, March 24, 1938, LOC, Box 3, Folder 1.

33 It is really very simple: KBC to MKP, March 25, 1938, LOC, Box 3, Folder 1.

34 This morning I am firmly convinced: MKP to KBC, March 28, 1938, LOC, Box 3, Folder 1.

35 We are voting on the May Queen: MKP to KBC, April 5, 1938, Box 3, Folder 1.

36 Will Thursday never come!: MKP to KBC, April 11, 1938, LOC, Box 3, Folder 1.

37 we must sail: "Text of Roosevelt's Fireside Chat Explaining New Recovery Program," *NYT*, April 15, 1938.

38 She was very beautiful: Lewis, discussion.

39 Don't fear: Lewis, discussion.

CHAPTER 4: THE SEED OF A LEGEND

1 Maybe the next generation: Charles H. Houston, "Don't Shout Too Soon," *Crisis* 43, no. 3 (March 1936): 91.

2 He kept hammering at us: Rawn James Jr., *Root and Branch: Charles Hamilton Houston, Thurgood Marshall, and the Struggle to End Segregation* (New York: Bloomsbury, 2010), 54.

3 No pit, no lime; just ashes: Richard Kluger, *Simple Justice: The History of* Brown v. Board of Education *and Black America's Struggle for Equality* (New York: Vintage Books, 1977), 164.

4 It all started with Charlie: James T. Patterson, *Brown v. Board of Education: A Civil Rights Milestone and Its Troubled Legacy* (New York: Oxford University Press, 2001), 12.

5 In the first place: MPC to KBC, June 17, 1938, LOC, Box 3, Folder 2.

6 Please don't be very angry: MPC to KBC, July 9, 1938, LOC, Box 3, Folder 3.

7 tell those Houston people: KBC to MPC, July 11, 1938, LOC, Box 3, Folder 3.

8 Negro-complex: E. Franklin Frazier, "The Pathology of Race Prejudice," *Forum* 77, no. 6 (June 1927): 857.

9 The white psychologist: KBC to MPC, July 11, 1938, LOC, Box 3, Folder 3.

10 It seems that some sort of dragnet: MPC to KBC, July 11, 1938, LOC, Box 3, Folder 3.

11 Keep cool, calm: KBC to MPC, July 11, 1938, LOC, Box 3, Folder 3.

12 I've just built up: MPC to KBC, July 14, 1938, LOC, Box 3, Folder 3.

13 You're the manager: KBC to MPC, July 29, 1938, LOC, Box 3, Folder 3.

14 Both of us seem: MPC to KBC, July 14, 1938, LOC, Box 3, Folder 3.

15 I'm disgusted by the lack: MPC to KBC, August 11, 1938, LOC, Box 3, Folder 3.

16 the awful truth: Dr. Harold H. Phipps to MPC, September 15, 1938, LOC, Box 10, Folder 5.

17 Please answer these questions: Dr. Harold H. Phipps to MPC, September 15, 1938, LOC, Box 10, Folder 5.

18 These things are not learned: Miriam Clark to Katie Phipps, draft, October 1938, LOC, Box 10, Folder 2.

19 One thing that I want: Miriam Clark to MPC, draft, October 1938, LOC, Box 10, Folder 2.

20 Now as for the marriage: Katie Phipps to MPC, October 20, 1938, LOC, Box 10, Folder 5.

21 This letter, I know: KBC to Katie Phipps, draft, n.d., LOC, Box 5, Folder 4.

22 It is with mixed feelings: Dr. Harold H. Phipps to MPC, November 19, 1938, LOC, Box 10, Folder 5.

23 Being back in this workhouse, MPC to KBC, Jan. 4, 1939, LOC, Box 3, Folder 6.

24 Perhaps you aren't interested: MPC to KBC, February 17, 1939, LOC, Box 3, Folder 6.

25 Show me all those: John P. Jackson Jr., *Social Scientists for Social Justice: Making the Case against Segregation* (New York: New York University Press, 2001), 30.

26 Show me which one is you: William E. Cross Jr., *Shades of Black: Diversity in African American Identity* (Philadelphia: Temple University Press, 1991), 8.

27 wishful thinking: Cross, *Shades of Black*, 9.

28 Dr. Meenes decided: MPC to KBC, February 15, 1939, LOC, Box 3, Folder 6.

29 I'm so very excited: MPC to KBC, March 7, 1939, LOC, Box 3, Folder 6.

30 As was expected: MPC to KBC, March 18, 1939, LOC, Box 3, Folder 6.

31 I am sorry—I am trying: KBC to MPC, March 20, 1939, LOC, Box 3, Folder 6.

32 In spite of the hecticness: MPC to KBC, April 13, 1939, LOC, Box 3, Folder 7.

33 Congratulations to you: MPC to KBC, April 13, 1939, LOC, Box 3, Folder 7.

34 You are the sweetest wife: KBC to MPC, April 17, 1939, LOC, Box 3, Folder 7.

35 I hope you get on that study: MPC to KBC, March 18, 1939, LOC, Box 3, Folder 6.

36 Dr. Meenes just came in here: MPC to KBC, April 25, 1939, LOC, Box 3, Folder 7.

37 You are positively the nicest: MPC to KBC, April 29, 1939, LOC, Box 3, Folder 7.

38 The darn thing is so much longer: MPC to KBC, May 4, 1939, LOC, Box 3, Folder 7.

39 To Mr. Kenneth Clark: MPC, "An Investigation of the Development of Consciousness of Distinctive Self in Pre-School Children" (master's thesis, Howard University, May 12, 1939).

40 But I am wondering: Dr. Harold H. Phipps to MPC, May 28, 1939, LOC, Box 10, Folder 5.

CHAPTER 5: NESTING IN HARLEM

1 It is easier to dally: Alain Locke, "Harlem: Dark Weather-Vane," *Survey Graphic* 25, no. 8 (August 1936): 457.

2 Rain pours through the ceiling: Cheryl Lynn Greenberg, *"Or Does It Explode?": Black Harlem in the Great Depression* (1991; repr. New York: Oxford University Press, 1997), 47.

3 On March 19, 1935, several thousands: *Mass Violence in America: The Complete Report of Mayor LaGuardia's Commission on the Harlem Riot of March 19, 1935* (New York: Arno Press, 1969), 122.

4 I do sincerely hope: Dr. Harold H. Phipps to MPC, April 4, 1940, LOC, Box 10, Folder 5.

5 I didn't realize: David W. Southern, *Gunnar Myrdal and Black-White Relations: The Use and Abuse of* An American Dilemma, *1944–1969* (Baton Rouge: Louisiana State University Press, 1987), 8.

6 Howard boys: Southern, *Gunnar Myrdal*, 20.

7 quite a handful: KBC, "Some Factors Influencing the Remembering of Prose

Material," *Archives of Psychology* 36, no. 253 (July 1940): 29.

8   to my wife: KBC, "Some Factors," acknowledgments.

9   Baby responded to sounds: MPC, "Our Little Baby" book, n.d., LOC, Box 8, Folder 1.

10 They were painted: Myla Perkins, *Black Dolls: An Identification and Value Guide, 1820–1991* (Paducah, KY: Collector Books, 1993), 6.

11 negresses in gaudy head kerchief, Perkins, *Black Dolls*, 20.

12 Glazed Nigger Baby: Perkins, *Black Dolls*, 10.

13 This is done to keep it before the white child: "Miss Burrough's (sic) Address," (Indianapolis) *Freeman*, November 14, 1908.

14 These toys are not made: John N. Ingham and Lynne B. Feldman, *African-American Business Leaders: A Biographical Dictionary* (Westport, CT: Greenwood, 1994), 108.

15 Teach your children: Advertisement, *Crisis* 17, no. 6 (April 1919): 309.

16 World's Prettiest: Advertisement, *Crisis* 53, no. 8 (August 1946): 254.

17 Their dolls were dressed: Myla Perkins, telephone conversation with the author, January 25, 2011.

18 Just because colored: Grace M. test sheets, October 8, 1940, LOC, Box 45, Folder 1.

19 I'm black: Kenneth J. test sheets, October 3, 1930 [sic], LOC, Box 45, Folder 3.

20 ARRIVED SAFELY: MPC to KBC, January 7, 1941, LOC, Box 3, Folder 8.

21 Kate behaved beautifully: MPC to KBC, January 8, 1941, LOC, Box 3, Folder 8.

22 'Cause made like that: Rosella B. test sheets, January 6, 1941, LOC, Box 45, Folder 4.

23 it looks pretty: Freddie B. test sheets, January 6, 1941, LOC, Box 45, Folder 4.

24 Looks bad all over: Nathaniel R. test sheets, January 6, 1941, LOC, Box 45, Folder 4.

25 Yes, sir, I'd like to be white: Delores M. test sheets, January 13, 1941, LOC, Box 45, Folder 4.

26 And we have to see: KBC, interview by Wendell B. Harris Jr., March 30, 1981, transcript, 44, HC.

27 We were paid to get: MPC, CUOH, 31.

28 The importance of these results: Untitled draft report, LOC, Box 46, Folder 4.

29 They'll always think: MPC, CUOH, 29.

30 Kenneth, what are you going to do: KBC, CUOH, 126.

CHAPTER 6: STARTING IN THE BASEMENT

1   The policy of the public authorities: Jane Addams, *Twenty Years at Hull-House* (New York: Macmillan, 1938), 98.

2   You can come back, but please, MPC's CUOH, p. 95.

3   You better understand what's going on: Allen, conversation.

4   Miss Brooks, psychology only works: Anne Brooks Goodwyn to KBC, February 22, 1970, LOC, Box 146, Folder 5.

5   I have heard many say: Jervis Anderson, *Bayard Rustin: Troubles I've Seen* (New York: Harper Collins, 1997), 83.

6   the pathological quality: KBC, "Morale among Negroes," in *Civilian Morale*, ed. Goodwin Watson (New York: Houghton-Mifflin, 1942), 232.

7   Dammit, I'm not going: KBC, interview by Tom Jaffee, April 10, 1974, transcript, 5, HC.

8   Bob Hope, Ed Sullivan: Alex Lombard, in discussion with the author, New York City, October 31, 2008.

9   I recommend her: Robert S. Woodworth letter, April 21, 1942, OC.

10 You are, of course, going back: "Mamie Phipps Clark," in *Models of Achievement: Reflections of Eminent Women in Psychology,* ed. Agnes N. O'Connell and Nancy Felipe Russo (New York: Columbia University Press, 1983), 270.

11 She told me he was horrible: KCH, in discussion with the author, Osprey, FL, June 13, 2007.

12 To smash something: James Baldwin, *Notes of a Native Son* (New York: Bantam Books, 1972), 93.

13 Hope it happens again: KBC, "Group Violence: A Preliminary Study of the 1943 Harlem Riot," *Journal of Social Psychology* 19, (1944): 322.

14 Milt Smith and I almost died: KBC in discussion with Lawrence Nyman, New York City, June 19, 1945, transcript p. 10, HC.

15 How are we going to come through: KBC, CUOH, 510.

16 I personally do not desire: MPC to Major D. E. Baier, September 11, 1944, LOC, Box 10, Folder 3.

17 cannot be considered other: Edward Lawson to Major D. E. Baier, September 11, 1944, LOC, Box 10, Folder 3.

18 He had a huge mouth: Allen, conversation.

19 All the people who later: Russia Hughes, in discussion with the author, New York City, October 13, 2007.

20 Kenneth, I've come to the conclusion: KBC, CUOH, 127.

21 I am sorry: Stella Chess, CUOH, November 3, 1990, 5, LOC, Box 154, Folder 2.

22 Each suffers from: KBC, "Candor about Negro-Jewish Relations," *Commentary* 8 (February 1945), 11.

23 Mamie was very strong: Dr. John Moseley, in discussion with the author, New York City, February 16, 1996.

24 Mark and Mamie hit it off terrifically: Hughes, discussion.

25 The only word to describe: *Headlines and Pictures,* April 1946, 33, clipping, OC.

26 dull normal: Gerald Markowitz and David Rosner, *Children, Race, and Power: Kenneth and Mamie Clark's Northside Center* (Charlottesville: University Press of Virginia, 1996), 23.

27 It was almost a deluge: MPC, CUOH, 43.

28 She was a beautiful woman: Cathy Lombard, in discussion with the author, New York City, October 31, 2008.

29 Problem Kids: "Problem Kids," *Ebony* 2, no. 9 *(1947),* 20.

30 The Clarks know: "Problem Kids," 22.

31 My father had dark moods: KCH, discussion, June 13, 2007.

32 It was the army experience: Robert L. Carter, *A Matter of Law: A Memoir of Struggle in the Cause of Equal Rights* (New York: New Press, 2005), 36.

33 We all really felt: Mildred Thompson Stevens, in discussion with the author, New York City, October 20, 2008.

34 I was more attracted: KCH, discussion, June 11, 2007.

35 Haven't I got a lovely wife?: Moseley, discussion, February 16, 1996.

36 Her cooking was nothing special: Allen, conversation.

37 My grandmother probably thought: KCH, discussion, June 13, 2007.

38 No, there was not much: HBC, in discussion with the author, Hastings, NY, January 27, 1995.

39   Kenneth used to surprise me: Moseley, discussion, February 16, 1996.
40   You wouldn't think: Moseley, discussion, February 16, 1996.
41   All of a sudden I'd realize: Hughes, discussion.
42   He would usually do it: HBC, discussion, January 27, 1995.
43   It hurt: KCH, discussion, July 3, 2007.
44   I enjoyed being with: HBC, in discussion with the author, Hastings, NY, January 13, 1995.
45   My mother was dedicated: KCH, discussion, July 3, 2007.
46   I believe that I altered: KBC to Dr. Aaron Karush, September 20, 1948, LOC, Box 14, Folder 4.

CHAPTER 7: THE NAACP COMES KNOCKING

1   Other things being equal: W. E. B. Du Bois, "Does the Negro Need Separate Schools?," *Journal of Negro Education* 4, no. 3 (July 1935): 32.
2   It was a real struggle: Wambly Bald, "Well Balanced," *NYP Week-end Magazine*, December 4, 1949, 2.
3   This is an interracial clinic: Clara Rabinowitz, CUOH, July 18, 1990; LOC, Box 154, Folder 1.
4   It was not a paying job: Dr. Rutherford Stevens, CUOH, December 7, 1990; LOC, Box 154, Folder 3.
5   It was 'our' place: Rabinowitz, CUOH.
6   They would have these showgirls: KCH, discussion, June 13, 2007.
7   And no matter how fancy: Joanne Stern, CUOH, July 16, 1990. LOC, Box 154, Folder 1.
8   It has become the custom: Stella Chess, KBC, and Alexander Thomas, "The Importance of Cultural Evaluation in Psychiatric Diagnosis and Treatment," *Psychiatric Quarterly* 27, no. 1 (January 1953): 109, https://doi.org/10.1007/BF01562479.
9   Cathy, I'm sorry: Cathy Lombard, discussion.
10   She ground her teeth a lot: KCH, discussion, June 13, 2007.
11   She didn't like to make waves: Chess, CUOH.
12   I think she bought into the idea: KCH, in discussion with the author, Osprey, FL, July 14, 2008.
13   We had the white ethnics: HBC, discussion, January 13, 1995.
14   My mother was a practitioner: KCH, in discussion with the author, Osprey, FL, September 9, 2007.
15   Blood, Sweat and Tears: KBC to Ruth Kotinsky, September 1, 1950, LOC, Box 104, Folder 4.
16   Minority-group children are characteristically: KBC, "The Effects of Prejudice and Discrimination," in *Personality in the Making: The Fact-Finding Report of the Midcentury White House Conference on Children and Youth*, ed. Helen Leland Witmer and Ruth Kotinsky (New York: Harper & Bros., 1952), 138.
17   Feelings of inferiority: KBC, "Effects of Prejudice and Discrimination," 139.
18   I must confess: KBC to Albert Deutsch, January 25, 1951, LOC, Box 15, Folder 1.
19   I was angry: KCH, in discussion with the author, Hastings, NY, February 5, 1996.
20   This couldn't have been better: James Moss, "Utilization of Negro Teachers."
21   stamps the colored race: "Majority Opinion of Justice Henry Brown," in *Removing*

a Badge of Slavery: The Record of Brown v. Board of Education, ed. Mark Whitman (Princeton, NJ: Markus Wiener Publishing, 1993), 14.

22 solely because the colored race chooses: "Majority Opinion."

23 Jesus Christ, those damn dolls!: William T. Coleman Jr., *Counsel for the Situation: Shaping the Law to Realize America's Promise* (Washington, DC: Brookings Institution, 2010), 123.

24 They really abused Kenneth: Robert L. Carter, in discussion with the author, New York City, October 21, 2008.

25 Kenneth was an outsider: June Shagaloff Alexander, in discussion with the author, New York City, October 29, 2009.

26 You've got anything else?: Carter, discussion.

27 the Smith-and-Wesson line: Kluger, *Simple Justice*, 323.

28 Yeah, I'm really tired: KBC, interview by Bob Markowitz and Jan Hartman, September 3, 1975, transcript, 6, HC.

CHAPTER 8: JIM CROW ON TRIAL

1   The only way: Ida B. Wells, *The Light of Truth: Writings of an Anti-Lynching Crusader*, ed. Henry Louis Gates Jr. (New York: Penguin Books, 2014), 558.

2   My dolls! My dolls!: KBC to Spottswood Robinson, June 20, 1961, LOC, Box 93, Folder 1.

3   Oh, come on now: KBC, interview by Markowitz and Hartman.

4   Show me the doll: *Briggs v. Elliott*, excerpt from transcript, 87, HC.

5   He was bright, likeable: Jack Greenberg, in discussion with the author, New York City, October 23, 2008.

6   South Carolina School System: "South Carolina School System Goes on Trial Today," *News and Courier* (Charleston), May 28, 1951, 1.

7   the essence of this detrimental effect: *Briggs v. Elliott*, excerpt, 86.

8   This is consistent: *Briggs v. Elliott*, excerpt, 88.

9   For example, I had a young girl: *Briggs v. Elliott*, excerpt, 89.

10 I was forced to the conclusion: *Briggs v. Elliott*, excerpt, 91.

11 perceived Negro as meaning: *Briggs v. Elliott*, transcript, 168, J. Waties Waring Papers, Moorland-Spingarn Research Center, Box 110–25, Folder 761.

12 It is a late day: Waldo E. Martin Jr., ed., *Brown v. Board of Education: A Brief History with Documents* (Boston: Bedford/St. Martin's, 1998), 130.

13 showed beyond a doubt: Martin, *Brown v. Board of Education*, 136.

14 Well, there is nothing she can do: *Brown v. Board of Education*, transcript, 149, National Archives, Washington, DC, Microfilm 1954, 33A3, Roll 1.

15 The best IQ on record: *Brown v. Board of Education*, transcript, 251–52.

16 A sense of inferiority: *Brown v. Board of Education*, transcript, 172.

17 Segregation of white and colored children, Jack Greenberg, *Crusaders in the Courts: How a Dedicated Band of Lawyers Fought for the Civil Rights Revolution* (New York: Basic Books, 1994), 131.

18 It's not right: Ethel B. test sheet, LOC, Box 45, Folder 6.

19 No doubt about it: Richard D. test sheet, LOC, Box 45, Folder 6.

20 They fuss on the street: Clyde C. test sheet, LOC, Box 45, Folder 6.

21 'Cause he white: Glen R. test sheet, LOC, Box 45, Folder 6.

22 In other words, if I may express: *Belton v. Gebhart*, transcript, 81A, National Archives, Washington, DC, Microfilm 1954, 33A3, Roll 3.

23 I think we have clear-cut evidence: *Belton v. Gebhart*, transcript, 171A.

24 To do otherwise is to say: *Removing a Badge of Slavery*, 102–3.

25 —Two bits—four bits—six bits: John A. Stokes, *Students on Strike: Jim Crow, Civil Rights, Brown, and Me* (Washington, DC: National Geographic, 2008), 65.

26 Even though we were only high school students: Stokes, *Students on Strike*, 59.

27 They were out to cut our throats: Kluger, *Simple Justice*, 485.

28 Segregation is like a mist: *Davis v. County School Board of Prince Edward County*, transcript, 2:390, National Archives at Philadelphia.

29 You appear to be of a rather light color: *Davis v. County School Board of Prince Edward County*, transcript, 2:412–13.

30 I think it is very doubtful: *Davis v. County School Board of Prince Edward County*, transcript, 2:916.

31 Boys and girls are taught: *Davis v. County School Board of Prince Edward County*, transcript, 2:920–21.

32 Very well indeed: *Davis v. County School Board of Prince Edward County*, transcript, 2:932.

33 It requires a skilled person: *Davis v. County School Board of Prince Edward County*, transcript, 2:938.

34 It is a large question: *Davis v. County School Board of Prince Edward County*, transcript, 2:954.

35 I think, in the high schools of Virginia: *Davis v. County School Board of Prince Edward County*, transcript, 2:954–55.

36 Will you talk a little bit louder, please?: *Davis v. County School Board of Prince Edward County*, transcript, 2:968.

37 In my opinion, I would say: *Davis v. County School Board of Prince Edward County*, transcript, 2:971–72.

38 That was the last time: "Mamie Phipps Clark," *Models of Achievement*, 270.

39 would severely lessen the interest: Greenberg, *Crusaders in the Courts*, 150.

CHAPTER 9: A TASTE OF VICTORY

1 We are well aware: Malcolm X, *By Any Means Necessary: Speeches, Interviews, and a Letter*, ed. George Breitman (1970; repr., New York: Pathfinder, 1992), 16.

2 Mamie and I: KBC to Diantha Brown, January 23, 1952, LOC, Box 15, Folder 3.

3 I remember my mother laughing: KCH, in discussion with the author, Osprey, FL, September 25, 2007.

4 Mamie, say something: John Heyman, telephone conversation with the author, July 30, 2008.

5 You know, she liked it: KCH, in discussion with the author, Osprey, FL, July 3, 2007.

6 She actually told me: KCH, discussion, February 5, 1996.

7 The first thing I can remember: HBC, discussion, January 13, 1995.

8 I think they wanted their kids: Moseley, discussion, February 17, 1996.

9 She wasn't that verbal: KCH, discussion, July 3, 2007.

10 Mr. and Mrs. Inc. "Mr. and Mrs. Inc.," *Glamour*, February 1951, clipping, OC.

11 That's the first time: "No Cover Charge," George F. Brown column, *Pittsburgh Courier*, October 31, 1953, 19.

12 who is the unusual combination: James Hicks, "Husband and wife medic team win $500 Schaefer Achievement award," *NYAN*, October 31, 1953, 2.

13 Differing and diverse, they make: Lillian Scott, "You Might be the Blame If...," *Chicago Defender*, May 14, 1949, 13.

14 Northside is reaching some: Gertrude Samuels, "Where Troubled Children Are Reborn," *NYT Magazine*, June 13, 1954, 57.

15 It's a matter which we haven't: Samuels, "Troubled Children."

16 She had a very firm hand: Stevens, discussion.

17 In comes Mamie: Cathy Lombard, discussion.

18 It was more like home: HBC, discussion, January 13, 1995.

19 This rules out the possibility: "Grade School Segregation: The Latest Attack on Racial Discrimination," *Yale Law Journal* 61, no. 5 (1952): 737.

20 Oyez, oyez, oyez: Greenberg, *Crusaders in the Courts*, 74.

21 It is our position: Philip B. Kurland and Gerhard Casper, eds., *Landmark Briefs and Arguments of the Supreme Court of the United States: Constitutional Law* (Washington, DC: University Publications of America, 1975), 49:281.

22 I do not know what clearer testimony: Kurland and Casper, *Landmark Briefs and Arguments*, 49:311.

23 The humiliation that these children: Kurland and Casper, *Landmark Briefs and Arguments*, 49:315.

24 Dr. Clark professed to speak: Kurland and Casper, *Landmark Briefs and Arguments*, 49:335.

25 That is a sad result: Kurland and Casper, *Landmark Briefs and Arguments*, 49:336.

26 This is the first indication: Kluger, *Simple Justice*, 656.

27 This pattern clearly facilitates: KBC speech, New York City, February 15, 1954, transcript, 2, HC.

28 I know of no such attempt: William Jansen to KBC, February 24, 1954, LOC, Box 79, Folder 8.

29 The problems so eloquently highlighted: Arthur Levitt to Edward S. Lewis, March 22, 1954, LOC, Box 79, Folder 8.

30 Some City Schools: "Some City Schools Held Segregated," *NYT*, April 25, 1954, clipping, LOC, Box 220, Folder 6.

31 But school segregation is an issue: "On the Way," Abner W. Berry column. *Daily Worker*, April 29, 1954, 9.

32 School Bias Probe: "School Bias Probe Demanded." *New York Age Defender*, May 1, 1954, 1.

33 The entire country should be as interested: "Harlem's 'Segregated' Schools," *Pittsburgh Courier* editorial, July 24, 1954, 14.

34 There is no point to my sitting down: William Jansen to KBC, June 4, 1954, LOC, Box 79, Folder 8.

35 Kenneth, we did it, we did it: KBC, interview by Markowitz and Hartman.

36 To separate them from others: Martin, *Brown v. Board of Education*, 173.

37 Well, Dad, I'm really proud of you: "South of Freedom," Jerry Ludwig column,

Observation Post (City College of New York newspaper), May 28, 1954, clipping, LOC, Box 220, Folder 6.

38 I cannot let the moment: Buell Gallagher to KBC, May 30, 1954, LOC, Box 65, Folder 1.

39 The first three days: KBC to Otto Klineberg, June 7, 1954, LOC, Box 57, Folder 7.

40 Now, apologize: Juan Williams, *Thurgood Marshall: American Revolutionary* (New York: Three Rivers Press, 1998), 229.

41 I'm so excited, like I'm drunk: James McGrath Morris, *Eye on the Struggle: Ethel Payne, the First Lady of the Black Press* (New York: Amistad, 2015), 132.

CHAPTER 10: MASSIVE RESISTANCE

1 We will walk until we are free: Grif Stockley, *Daisy Bates: Civil Rights Crusader from Arkansas* (Jackson: University Press of Mississippi, 2005), 7.

2 This is a powder keg: KBC, "Report of Observations in Milford, Delaware, Area," September 24, 1954, 13, LOC, Box 66, Folder 1.

3 Blood on the White Marble Steps: Reed Sarratt, *The Ordeal of Desegregation: The First Decade* (New York: Harper & Row, 1966), 252–53.

4 The Negro will never be satisfied: Amy Gutmann, *Identity in Democracy* (Princeton, NJ: Princeton University Press, 2003), 130.

5 footnote No. 354A data follows here—Well, gee I won't see my wife again: Marian Knox interview with KBC and James L. Hicks, transcript page 45, July 25, 1975. HC.

6 It was our lives: June Shagaloff Alexander, in discussion with the author, New York City, October 29, 2009.

7 We have natural segregation: "Amsterdam News accuses Jansen of Supporting 'New York Segregation'," *New York Teacher News* (teachers union newspaper), clipping, June 19, 1954, LOC, Box 56, Folder 1.

8 a state of affairs that we all should deplore: Public Education Association, "Status of the Public School Education of Negro and Puerto Rican Children in New York City," 14, LOC, Box 78, Folder 1.

9 a prophet without honor: Ted Poston, "Prejudice and Progress in New York: The Negro and the Schools," *NYP*, April 24, 1956, clipping, LOC, Box 80, Folder 3.

10 We feel that the superintendent: Benjamin Fine, "Critics of Jansen Ask To Query Him," *NYT*, August 5, 1957, 1.

11 Dr. Clark has documented: "A Call for Courage," Helen Henley, *Christian Science Monitor*, July 28, 1955, clipping, LOC, Box 33, Folder 6.

12 Who will be surprised—even shocked: "Book Review" column, Saunders Redding, *Afro-American* (Baltimore), December 10, 1955, clipping, LOC, Box 33, Folder 6.

13 one of the many liberal sociologists: "Discrimination and Science," Bruno Bettelheim, *Commentary*, April 1956, 384.

14 good faith compliance: Martin, *Brown v. Board of Education*, 197–98.

15 Black denoting darkness and terror: Tom P. Brady, *Black Monday: Segregation or Amalgamation... America Has Its Choice* (Winona, MS: Association of Citizens Councils, 1955), 1.

16 You stink: Anonymous to KBC, April 2, 1955, LOC, Box 41, Folder 5.

17 compulsory congregation: Ernest van den Haag, "Social Science Testimony in the

Desegregation Cases—A Reply to Professor Kenneth Clark," *Villanova Law Review* 6, no. 1 (Fall 1960): 71.

18 I have never been: Jeanne Theoharis, *A More Beautiful and Terrible History: The Uses and Misuses of Civil Rights History* (Boston: Beacon Press, 2018), 123.

19 Reverend King is on this train: KBC, "Memorandum on Southern Field Trip," Appendix, 1, HC.

20 I haven't the slightest idea: KBC, "Memorandum on Southern Field Trip," 1.

21 A dollar forty-three!: KBC, "Memorandum on Southern Field Trip," 3.

22 He has the potential for leadership: Woody Klein, ed., *Toward Humanity and Justice: The Writings of Kenneth B. Clark, Scholar of the 1954* Brown v. Board of Education *Decision* (Westport, CT: Praeger, 2004), 100.

23 to buy more plates when needed: KBC, "Some General Observations in Negro Community of Little Rock, Arkansas," 17, LOC, Box 58, Folder 6.

24 Well, maybe if I held the tray: KBC, "Some General Observations," 17.

25 Nobody urged us: HBC, discussion, January 27, 1995.

26 It was clear I was considered: KCH, discussion, February 5, 1996.

27 I wrote a couple of papers: HBC, discussion, January 27, 1995.

28 If things keep going as they are: *Arkansas Democrat*, February 23, 1958, 1.

29 The most exciting day of my life: Sara Slack, " 'New York is Wonderful'-Minniejean (sic) Brown," *NYAN*, March 1, 1958, 1.

30 She had a lot of trouble: KCH, discussion, July 14, 2008.

31 I had none of the skills: Minnijean Brown, in discussion with the author, Little Rock, AR, May 22, 2008.

32 It wasn't all sweetness and light: Brown, discussion.

33 You'd see her jaw tightening: Brown, discussion.

34 I just feel socializing was hard for her: Brown, discussion.

35 I changed my belief: Brown, discussion.

36 So Mamie and I are right back: KBC to Dr. Jesse Orlansky, September 27, 1959, LOC, Box 20, Folder 6.

CHAPTER 11: A DAVID AND GOLIATH BATTLE

1 All over Harlem: James Baldwin, *Notes of a Native Son* (New York: Bantam Books, 1972), 59.

2 were enough to tear you apart: Rabinowitz, CUOH, 4.

3 an insultingly interesting concept: Rabinowitz, CUOH, 74.

4 She never complained: Stern, CUOH, 4.

5 Dr. Bryt practically had that man in tears: Victor Carter, CUOH, 67–68; LOC, Box 154, Folder 4.

6 We just thought they were nuts: Stern, CUOH, 20.

7 They were always fundraising: Stern, CUOH, 11.

8 the greatest thing since, NYP, Aug. 1, 1961, p. 45.

9 inspired research: "NAACP Warns Congress to Act on Rights," (Philadelphia) *Evening Bulletin*, July 16, 1961, 3.

10 We cannot partake: KBC, "The Negro Intellectual in Contemporary America" (speech), Philadelphia, July 16, 1961, transcript, 1, HC.

11 At Northside they used to say: KCH, in discussion with the author, Osprey, FL, September 18, 2007.

12 If it's not illegal: Charles V. Hamilton, *Adam Clayton Powell, Jr.: The Political Biography of an American Dilemma* (New York: Atheneum, 1991), 420.

13 The first words couldn't come out: Boyer, discussion, November 10, 2007.

14 We had a lot of fun: HBC, in discussion with the author, Hastings, NY, February 10, 1995.

15 It was a hell of an education: HBC, discussion, February 10, 1995.

16 Mamie, in her usual wise, calm: KBC to Marion Ascoli, July 25, 1963, LOC, Box 23, Folder 5.

17 with its barbarity: MPC, "Trip Abroad" diary, August 3, 1963, OC.

18 Those who have traveled: KBC, "Implications of Adlerian Theory."

19 The way the Man has us: HARYOU, *Youth in the Ghetto: A Study of the Consequences of Powerlessness and a Blueprint for Change* (New York: HARYOU, 1964), 313, HC.

20 With your brains and my power: KBC, CUOH, 162.

21 See, that's politics: Nat Hentoff, "The Integrationist," *New Yorker*, August 23, 1982, 58.

22 That's fine: Woody Klein, telephone conversation with the author, January 31, 2008.

23 You want to come work for me?: Klein, conversation.

24 Powell Turns on Pressure: Woody Klein, "Powell Turns on Pressure," *New York World-Telegram and Sun*, June 5, 1964, 1.

25 a courageous fighter: "New Battle of Harlem," *NYP* editorial, June 10, 1964, clipping, LOC, Box 220, Folder 8.

26 You can see there is a lot: Martin Arnold, "Threat on Fund Laid to Powell Men," *NYT*, June 15, 1964, 32.

27 Finally, my husband is a man: "Clark's Wife Hits Back at Powell," *NYP*, June 17, 1964, 7.

28 Clark Quits: R.W. Apple Jr., "Clark Quits HARYOU Deploring Politics," *NYT*, July 30, 1964, 1.

29 He didn't understand cynicism: Klein, conversation.

30 I may have the devil's horns: Herbert Krosney, *Beyond Welfare: Poverty in the Supercity* (New York: Holt, Rinehart, and Winston, 1966), 64.

31 He was standing there all alone: MPC, CUOH, 87–88.

CHAPTER 12: JUMP-STARTING HEAD START

1 If this society of yours: Theoharis, *More Beautiful and Terrible History*, 86.

2 lost in a gray world: Edward Zigler and Susan Muenchow, *Head Start: The Inside Story of America's Most Successful Educational Experiment* (New York: Basic Books, 1992), 24.

3 The national media covered: Zigler and Muenchow, *Head Start*, 24.

4 That committee really did all the work: Edward Zigler and Jeanette Valentine, eds., *Project Head Start: A Legacy of the War on Poverty* (New York: Free Press, 1979), 55.

5 Mamie Clark shot down: Zigler and Muenchow, *Head Start*, 20.

6 Once again, Clark led the opposition: Zigler and Muenchow, *Head Start*, 20.

7 We're going to write Head Start: Zigler and Valentine, *Project Head Start*, 82.

8   If it weren't for education: Zigler and Muenchow, *Head Start*, 26.

9   So that what was poor in Niagara Falls: MPC, interview by Gloria Edwards and Caroline Atkinson, 1965, transcript, 12, LOC, Box 132, Folder 1.

10 Frankly, the name change: Eric Pace, "New Name Given to 110th St. Area," *NYT*, September 7, 1965, 41.

11 We can't be antagonistic: MPC, interview by Edwards and Atkinson, transcript, 1.

12 This was a huge thing: KCH, discussion, September 18, 2007.

13 He was so depressed: Jeannette Hopkins, in discussion with the author, Portsmouth, NH, October 15, 2007.

14 I'm not a man: KBC, *Dark Ghetto: Dilemmas of Social Power* (1965; repr., New York: Harper & Row, 1967), 1.

15 It is an indictment, Jervis Anderson, "Look Here!," *New Leader*, September 27, 1965, 28.

16 Whites read and applaud: Sumner Stone, "Stone Hits Dr. Clark with the Powell Record," *NYAN*, September 11, 1965, 5.

17 Powell is an ambassador: Murray Kempton, "Uptown," *New York Review of Books*, October 15, 1965, 14.

18 an investment in negative propaganda: Robert Penn Warren, *Who Speaks for the Negro?* (New York: Random House, 1965), 340–41.

19 I think Ralph Ellison needs: KBC, interview by Harold Isaacs, New York City, January 5, 1962, transcript, 3, HC.

20 She was criticized by some: Elmer Beard, telephone conversation with the author, June 24, 2008.

21 They were such prominent people: Edward Wesson, in discussion with the author, Hot Springs, AR, May 26, 2008.

22 To be the first Negro: KBC, *Dark Ghetto*, 19–20.

23 Bride is escorted: "Donald S. Harris and Kate Clark Are Wed Here," *NYT*, May 2, 1965, 93.

24 That is, if he can stay in his classrooms: Ted Poston, "Kenneth Clark: Civil Rights Front-Runner," *NYP* magazine, March 22, 1964, 2.

25 But I think he pulls too many punches: M.A. Farber, "New College Magazine Aimed at Ending Negro 'Indifference',", *NYT*, April 16, 1966, 13.

26 Love you madly: MPC to KBC, October 5, 1971, LOC, Box 403, Folder 4.

CHAPTER 13: BLACK POWER

1   If America don't come around: Robert H. Brisbane, *Black Activism: Racial Revolution in the United States, 1954–1970* (Valley Forge, PA: Judson Press, 1974), 168.

2   We want Black Power!: Shirley Sherrod, *The Courage to Hope: How I Stood Up to the Politics of Fear* (New York: Atria Books, 2012), 73.

3   It is a desperate retreat: "It's Continuing White Resistance To Change in Negro Status," KBC column, *Boston Globe*, October 23, 1966, 7.

4   Brain Trust: "Brain Trust Here to Study Problems of the Deprived," *NYP*, March 8, 1967, clipping, LOC, Box 221, Folder 2.

5   the greatest purveyor of violence: Taylor Branch, *At Canaan's Edge: America in the King Years, 1965–68* (New York: Simon and Schuster, 2006), 592.

6   He wasn't the kind of person: George Dalley, in discussion with the author, Washington, DC, May 21, 2012.

7   I must again in candor say: KBC, Kerner Commission testimony, transcript, 1228, LOC, Box 201, Folder 4.

8   Dr. Clark was prophetic: "Expert Views Slums," Drew Pearson column, WP, March 10, 1968, B7.

9   Dr. Kenneth B. Clark Lays It On Line: Ethel Payne, "Says Black Elected Aides Must Enter Total Process," Chicago Daily Defender, September 15, 1969, 2.

10 Kenneth really saw there had to be something: Roger Wilkins, in discussion with the author, Washington, DC, May 25, 2012.

11 He was a leader of leaders: Dalley, discussion.

12 We're gonna get you: KBC, interview by Jim Warren, July 12, 1979, transcript, 24, HC.

13 The Other: Sally Hammond, "The Other Dr. Clark," NYP, January 26, 1970, 37.

14 Dr. Mamie Phipps Clark deserves: "Conversation Piece," Betty Granger Reid column, NYAN, February 7, 1970, 5.

15 You have to cry out: Lawrence Van Gelder, "Dismay in Nation," NYT, April 5, 1968, 1.

16 Black people know that they need to get guns: Richard D. Kahlenberg, Tough Liberal: Albert Shanker and the Battles Over Schools, Unions, Race, and Democracy (New York: Columbia University Press, 2007), 92.

17 Listen, I don't represent children: Kahlenberg, Tough Liberal, 125.

18 The Mason-Dixon line: I.F. Stone, "The Mason Dixon Line Moves to New York," November 4, 1968, 1.

19 The Jewish community felt: Dalley, discussion.

20 We have invaded W.A.S.P. territory: MPC, Trip Abroad diary, July 30, 1969, OC.

CHAPTER 14: OPENING A GATEWAY TO HARLEM

1   Until twenty million black people: Imani Perry, Looking for Lorraine: The Radiant and Radical Life of Lorraine Hansberry (Boston: Beacon Press, 2018), 169.

2   Even from my pessimism: Roger Wilkins, A Man's Life: An Autobiography (New York: Simon and Schuster, 1982), 286.

3   benign neglect: Adam Clymer, "Daniel Patrick Moynihan Is Dead; Senator From Academia Was 76," NYT, March 27, 2003, 1.

4   You not only showed me such gross disrespect: Lisa Paisley-Cleveland, CUOH, November 11, 1990, 11, LOC, Box 154, Folder 2.

5   This is a non-negotiable item: Board minutes, December 3, 1970, Northside Center for Child Development Papers, Manuscripts and Archives Division, New York Public Library.

6   It is my firm personal conviction: MPC, statement, February 4, 1971, LOC, Box 403, Folder 5.

7   Kenneth Clark is hardly a minor figure: "The Clark Study," Washington Evening Star, editorial, March 27, 1970, clipping, LOC, Box 222, Folder 1.

8   I have some concerns: David Pike, "Detroit Educator Hugh Schott Chosen to Head Schools," Washington Daily News, September 1, 1970, clipping, LOC, Box 296, Folder 3.

9   educational racists: Lyle Denniston, "Clark Defends Plan, Asks School Action," October 29, 1970, B1.

10 He's just another racist: Lawrence Feinberg, "Clark Held Racist in Cassell Speech," WP, November 20, 1970, A11.

11 If only the parents could take Scott: "'Do Something for the Children!'" William Raspberry, column, WP, November 28, 1970, clipping, LOC, Box 296, Folder 4.

12 I told him I thought it was dangerous: Hopkins, discussion.

13 This form of psychotechnological medication: KBC, "The Pathos of Power: A Psychological Perspective," American Psychologist 26, no. 12 (December 1971): 1056, https://doi.org/10.1037/h0032217.

14 I'll tell you: KBC, CUOH, 374, HC.

15 Why the hell do you want: KBC, CUOH, 374, HC.

16 Kenneth Clark Asks: Boyce Rensberger, "Kenneth Clark Asks New Drugs to Curb Hostility of Leaders," NYT, September 5, 1971, 1.

17 Dr. Clark Wants to Prevent Holocaust: Drugs Prescribed for World Leaders: Stuart Auerback, WP, September 5, 1971, 1.

18 You're sick! Incurably sick!: "Clark's 'peace pill' proposal—a year later," Jim Warren, APA Monitor, September/October 1972, 6.

19 drivel: "Behaviorists Criticized By Agnew," WP, November 18, 1971, clipping, LOC, Box 223, Folder 1.

20 every bit as dreadful: Maurice Carroll, "Social Science Lab Notes," NYT, September 28, 1974, 27.

21 I am an unreconstructed integrationist: Julia Malone, "How U.S. schools look to integrationist," Christian Science Monitor, June 4, 1973, 1.

22 Nigger, go home: U.S. Civil Rights Commission, Five Communities: Their Search for Equal Education (Washington, DC: U.S. Government Printing Office, 1972), 20.

23 It's Not the Distance, It's the Niggers: NAACP Legal Defense and Education Fund, It's Not the Distance, "It's the Niggers.": Comments on the Controversy over School Busing (Washington, DC: U.S. Department of Health, Education and Welfare, 1972).

24 The Big Town: "The Big Town Turns Out To Toast Ken Clark!" NYAN, March 10, 1973.

25 But he has held his ground: "Ken Clark's Lonely Road," James A. Wechsler, column, NYP Magazine, February 14, 1975, 5.

26 There was a sense of discouragement: Dalley, discussion.

27 During the past year I have become aware: KBC to Gunnar Myrdal, January 7, 1975, LOC, Box 304, Folder 3.

28 Ken's challenge: Dalley, discussion.

29 one of the most persistent civil rights leaders: American Civil Liberties Union newsletter, November–December 1975, 6, clipping, LOC, Box 225, Folder 3.

30 glorious defeats: KBC, "A Few Remarks" (speech), New York City, October 14, 1975, transcript, 2, HC.

CHAPTER 15: QUIET COURAGE

1 Sometimes as I sit communing: Mary McLeod Bethune, "My Last Will and Testament," *Ebony*, August 1955.

2 Needless to say: KBC to Reverend Leon H. Sullivan, November 20, 1975, LOC, Box 140, Folder 6.

3 It was difficult: Angela Jones, "Hilton Clark, following in father's footsteps," *NYAN*, May 31, 1980.

4 We're not going with the white-washers: KBC, City College seminar, June 3, 1975, transcript, 7, LOC, Box 306, Folder 4.

5 an irascible egghead: "Segregation harmful to majorities too," Roy Wilkins, column, *Staten Island Advance*, June 26, 1979, clipping, LOC, Box 147, Folder 3.

6 Then I was a Negro: KBC, "New York City's Biracial Public Schools," *Integrated Education*, May/June 1975, 154.

7 fit the description of several: "Dr. Kenneth Clark Detained And Searched For Drugs In Germany," *NYAN*, November 20, 1976, clipping, LOC, Box 226, Folder 2.

8 I guess we knew a lot of people: Judith Cummings, "Harlem Center Aids Disturbed Children," *NYT*, November 1, 1976.

9 Kenneth, stop this: KBC, CUOH, 329.

10 Mother, you know how much: KCH, discussion, June 11, 2007.

11 She hated public speaking: KCH, discussion, September 18, 2007.

12 You're very persistent: Henry Allen, "Kenneth Clark, Social Psychologist As Persistent Paradox," *WP*, March 7, 1979, (story begins on page B1, but quote's on B3.) B1.

13 stays angry and keeps working: John Walter, "Kenneth Clark 'stays angry and keeps working' for blacks," *Washington Star*, March 7, 1979, E1.

14 Administratively, it was a mess: KCH, discussion, September 18, 2007.

15 Mamie has almost given up: KBC to Genevieve Klein, March 10, 1981, LOC, Box 155, Folder 1.

16 Black people are tired: Angela Jones, "Hilton Clark, following in father's footsteps," *NYAN*, May 31, 1980, 10.

17 Polls show: "Polls Show Blacks See Return of Racism," *Pittsburg Courier*, January 26, 1980, 1.

18 What Do Blacks Think: "What Do Blacks Think of Themselves?" KBC and MPC, *Ebony*, November 1980, 176–82.

19 She had a chest X-ray: KCH, discussion, September 25, 2007.

20 Kenneth, I couldn't have got a piddling form: KBC, CUOH, 494.

21 As you probably suspect: KBC to David Gibbons, October 14, 1982, LOC, Box 144, Folder 4.

22 He just refused to accept the idea: KCH, discussion, September 25, 2007.

23 I think he makes us comfortable: Jay Nordlinger, "A Long Way from '78," *National Review*, June 6, 2003, https://www.nationalreview.com/2003/06/long-way-78-jay-nordlinger/.

24 The moral there is: "Kenneth Clark, Social Psychologist," Allen, *WP*, March 7, 1979, B1.

25 I didn't know it was meant: Leighla Whipper Ford, in discussion with the author, Kingston, NY, April 26, 1994.
26 I remember it as a very touching time: Hughes, discussion.
27 It was just like talk, talk, talk: KCH, discussion, September 25, 2007.
28 Kenneth, we can't complain: KBC, CUOH, 493.
29 Look, you've got to keep on: KBC, CUOH, 492.
30 No, you can't do that!: KBC, CUOH, 495.

EPILOGUE: STRUGGLING ON

1   If you can't run, walk: Morris, *Eye on the Struggle*, 192.
2   With Mamie gone, the living was gone: John Heyman, telephone conversation with the author, July 30, 2008.
3   I would say he was clinically depressed: Stephen Berger, telephone conversation with the author, Oct. 5, 2007.
4   We call this resegregation: KBC, "American Racism: The Default of Public Education" (speech), New York City, September 7, 1988, transcript, HC.
5   It was awful to see this man: Shagaloff Alexander, discussion, October 29, 2009.
6   Integrate NYC: Hari Sreenivasan and Laura Fong, "New York City Students Are Fighting for School Integration," PBS NewsHour Weekend, June 29, 2019, https://pbs.org /newshour/show/new-york-city-students-are-fighting-for-school-integration.
7   The mission is to have real integration: Sreenivasan and Fong, "New York City Students."
8   I mean I cannot see that it's changed: Perry, *Looking for Lorraine*, 160.
9   I don't want to be colored: Mary Ellen Goodman, *Race Awareness in Young Children* (Cambridge, MA: Addison-Wesley, 1952), 38.
10 because it is Black: *A Girl Like Me*, directed by Kiri Davis (Brooklyn, NY: Reel Works Teen Filmmaking, 2005).
11 First, times may be changing: Joseph Hraba and Geoffrey Grant, "Black Is Beautiful: A Reexamination of Racial Preference and Identification," *Journal of Personality and Social Psychology* 16, no. 3 (1970): 400, https://doi.org/10.1037/h0030043.
12 The Clarks saw Negroness as a stigma: William E. Cross Jr., *Shades of Black: Diversity in African-American Identity* (Philadelphia: Temple University Press), 1991, 37.
13 Because she's a lot darker: "Kids' Test Answers on Race Brings [sic] Mother to Tears," CNN, May 18, 2010, https://ac360.blogs.cnn.com/2010/05/18/kids-test -answers-on-race-brings-mother-to-tears/.

ACKNOWLEDGMENTS

I thank three remarkable teachers who by their character and instruction inspired me to write this book: the late William Rowley and novelist William Kennedy, both of the State University of New York at Albany, and the late John M. Reilly, also of the Albany campus's English Department and later at Howard University.

This book is partly the product of about a hundred interviews I conducted, most of them with the cooperation of elderly Black friends, relatives, and colleagues of the Clarks, people who welcomed me in their homes and offered insights into the couple's lives that otherwise would have been lost in the mists of time.

I also want to thank my friends and colleagues who read parts of the manuscript or encouraged it in other ways: Ian Vasquez, Jim Leonard, Paul Jerome, Ronald Sheehy, Paul Regnier, Morgan Desmond, Cindy Hart, John Runfola, Art Silvergleid, Pamela Newkirk, and Carole Slipowitz. Also A.J. Williams-Myers of SUNY New Paltz; Esme Bahn of Howard University's Moorland-Spingarn Research Center; Gary Mormino and Raymond Arsenault, both of the University of South Florida St. Petersburg; and Blake J. Wintory of Little Rock, Arkansas.

I tip my hat to three authors whose books proved invaluable in researching the Clarks' lives: David McCullough for *The Path Between the Seas*, which describes the daily lives of Black migrants in

Colon, Panama, during the construction of the Panama Canal after the turn of the last century; Gerald Markowitz and David Rosner for *Children, Race, and Power*, which tells the story of the Clarks' founding of Northside Center for Child Development in Harlem; and Edward Zigler and Susan Muenchow for *Head Start*, their history of the successful War on Poverty project. Richard Kluger's *Simple Justice* and Jack Greenberg's *Crusaders in the Courts* provided great insight into the *Brown v. Board of Education* litigation. The Columbia (University) Center for Oral History Research transcribed interviews with both of the Clarks that proved invaluable.

I have nothing but praise for the hard-working, professional staffs of the Moorland-Spingarn Research Center at Howard University; the Manuscripts Division of the Library of Congress, also in Washington, D.C.; the Special Collections Department of the University of Arkansas Libraries in Fayetteville, Arkansas; the Manuscripts and Archives Division of the New York Public Library; and the Schomburg Center for Research in Black Culture, also in New York City.

Without the empathy, guidance, and determination of my literary agent, Rachel Sussman of Chalberg & Sussman, and my editor, Anna Michels of Sourcebooks, the Clarks' story might never have seen the light of day.

I end with thanks to three more women who made this book possible. The late Russia Hughes, personal assistant to Kenneth Clark, kindly paved the way for my interviews with him and mailed me copies of his voluminous writings and correspondence even before they were available to the public. Kate Clark Harris, the Clarks' daughter, opened her garage door and let me scour the contents of boxes stuffed with Clark family letters, documents, and photographs. She patiently sat for long interviews that yielded intimate glimpses of her parents' daily lives and careers. And finally, I thank my wife, Barbara Sloane Spofford, who served as my editor, adviser, critic, and muse. Her patience, encouragement, and assistance were vital to preparing this story for readers.

INDEX

Note: Illustrations are indicated by italics.

A

ABC television network, 277
ACT (Associated Community Teams), 213–214, 219–222
Adler, Alfred, 51
AJC (American Jewish Committee), 136
"Alice-in-Wonderland" prediction, 244–245
Ali, Muhammad, 276
Allen, Anita, 261
Almond, James Lindsay, Jr., 161, 164
Alston, Myra and Charles, 124
American Dilemma, An (Myrdal), 88
American Jewish Committee (AJC), 136
American Psychological Association speech, 263–266
American Public Health Association, 112–113
Armed Forces Institute, U.S., 113
Ascoli, Marian, 121–123, 131–132, 207–210
Associated Community Teams (ACT), 213–214, 219–222

B

Baier, D. E., 111–112
Baker, Ella, 178–179, 181, 192
Baldwin, James, 218, 236
Banks, Alida, 53
Bartlett, Frederick, 89
Bates, Daisy, 200–201
Bates, L. C., 200
Bernard, Viola, 122
Betchman, H. B., 147, 148
Bettelheim, Bruno, 138, 194
Black dolls, history of, 93–94
Black English, 262
Black inferiority complex, 50–52, 56–57, 102
Black nationalism, 216–217
Black Power, 238–243

Black student activism, 210–211
Black student protests of 1968, 249–250
Bond, Julian, 235, 246
Bowles, Bryant, 189, 190
Brady, Tom P., 195
Briggs v. Elliott, 145–153, 177
Brooke, Edward, 244
Brotherhood Reception, 268
Brown, H. Rap, 239, 243
Brown, Minnijean, 199–201, 202–205
Brown, Oliver, 153–154
Brown, Sterling, 16
Brown v. Board of Education
    arguments and ruling on, 176–178, 182–184
    Clarks' findings submitted as evidence in, 174–176
    court decision on how to desegregate (*Brown II*), 190–191, 194–195
    reaction and aftermath, 187–191, 195–196, 199–205, 291–292
Brown v. Board of Education of Topeka (federal court case), 153–155
Bryt, Albert, 208–209
Bunche, Ralph, 35, 38, 39, 40, 87, 88, 184
busing policies, 266–269
Butler Medal, 248
Byrnes, James, 149

C

Carmichael, Stokely, 238–239, 242, 243, 250
Carnegie Corporation, 87–88
Carter, Jimmy, 279
Carter, Robert, 139–143, 149, 150, 153, 154, 161, 163–165, 175, 176–177
Carter, Victor, 21, 122–123, 173
Cassell, Charles, 262, 263
CCI (Commission on Community Interrelations), 115
Chein, Isidor, 175
Chess, Stella, 113, 114, 122, 131, 173, 208
City College of New York, 104–105, 107, 109–110, 123, 237, 271
civil rights movement, 196–199, 210–211, 238–243
Clark, Arthurton, 25–27, 54
Clark Associates, 272–276, 273
Clark, Hilton, 109, 112, 126–127, *168*, 169, 201, 202, 216–217, 236, 273
Clark, Kate, 91–92, 123, 126–127, 139, *168*, 168–170, 201–202, 235–236
Clark, Kenneth, *174*. *See also* doll test
    books by, 193–194, 230–235, 266
    childhood and early life, 25–34, *28*
    college education, 34–40, 43–44, 47–49, 50–52, 54, 78, 89–92

    dark moods, 120–121
    early career, 68–70, 86–89, 104–107
    family and social life, 123–127, 167–170, *168*
    final illness and death, 289–290
    home in Hastings, 134–135, 138–139, 167–170, *260*
    Jewish community, ties to, 115, 136
    Kerner Commission testimony on causes of race riots, 244–245
    legacy, 290–295
    in mourning after Mamie's death, 287–289
    overwork, 166–167, 217, 233, 247–248
    public stature and reputation, 119–120, 170–172, 191–192, 234–235, 247–248
    racial politics and identity, views on, 56–57
    retirement, 269–271
    romance and marriage to Mamie, 16–25, *24*, 40–45, 47, 49–50, 52–61, 65–66, 71–74
    St. Nicholas Place apartment, 79, 85
    Sugar Hill apartment, 107–108
    teaching career, 40–42, 104–106, 107, 109–110
    vacationing trips, 217–218, 233–234, 253–254
Clark, Mamie, *174. See also* doll test
    childhood and early life, 3–16, *9*
    college education, 22–23, 49, 52–53, 65–66, 74–77, 81–82, 100, 103, 108–109, 111
    early career, 66–68, 73–74, 111–114
    family and social life, 123–127, 167–170
    final illness and death, 282–286
    home in Hastings, 134–135, 138–139, 167–170, *260*
    legacy, 290–295
    Northside Center. *see* Northside Child Development Center
    Project Head Start and, 224–228
    public speaking, difficulty with, 214–215, 233, 278–279
    public stature and reputation, 170–173, 248, 277
    receives first letter from Kenneth, 5, 15–16, 40
    retirement, 278–279
    romance and marriage to Kenneth, 16–25, *24*, 40–45, 47, 49–50, 52–61, 65–66, 71–74
    St. Nicholas Place apartment, 79, 85
    Sugar Hill apartment, 107–108
    testifies in NAACP's suit, 161, 164–165
Clark, Miriam, 21, 25–30, 31, 32–33, 49–50, 71–74, 125, 134
"Clark Plan," 262–263
Coleman, William, 142, 174
coloring test, 95–96, 151
Columbia University, 43–44, 47–49, 50–52, 54, 78, 89–92, 100, 103, 108–109, 111,

236, 248, 249–250
Commission on Community Interrelations (CCI), 115
Conyers, John, 246
Cooke, Robert, 225–226
Cook, Stuart, 175
Cross, William E., Jr., 294
cultural deprivation, 226

D

Dark Ghetto (Clark), 230–235, 237
Data Black, 280–282
Davis, John W., 177–178
Davis, Kiri, 293
Davis v. County School Board of Prince Edward County, 160–165
Declining Significance of Race, The (Wilson), 279
DeLaine, J. A., 146, 147
Depression, 32–33, 83–84
desegregation. *See* school desegregation, fight for
Dobie, Armistead M., 164
dolls, Black, history of, 93–94
doll test, vii–xiii, *xi*, 92–103, 136, 281–282
    Clarks' findings based on, 102–103
    Clarks' legacy and, 292–295
    Mamie's thesis as basis for, viii, 85–86
    Northside Center and, *118*, 120
    use in legal fight against school segregation, 145–148, 150–153, 157, 158, 162–163, 174–178
Drew, Charles, 35
Du Bois, W. E. B., 99–100
Dudley, Edward, 219–220
Dumpson, James, 210
Dunbar, Leslie, 270

E

Ebony magazine articles, 120, 281–282
educational reform. *See* school reform
Ellison, Ralph, 124, 167, 184, 233
English, Horace B., 154

F

Faubus, Orval, 199
Field Foundation, 237, 240, 270
Figg, Robert, 149, 151–152
Ford Foundation, 240

Frankfurter, Felix, 178
Franklin, John Hope, 284
Frazier, E. Franklin, 52–53, 54–55, 69, 75, 84, 167–168
Freedom Riders, 211
Frelinghuysen, 73–74
Freud, Sigmund, 51

G

Gardner, Adella, 55, 57–58
Garrett, Henry, 91, 100, 103, 108, 161, 162–165
Garvey, Marcus, 28–29
Gaspard, Elaine, 230
George Washington High School, 31–33
Gibson, Kenneth, 247
Great Depression, 32–33, 83–84
Greenberg, Jack, 153, 154, 157
Greenwald, H. J., 293

H

Hamer, Fanny Lou, 236
Hamilton, Charles V., 271
Hampton Institute, 105–106
Hanson, Bea, 26, 27–28
Harlem, 28–31, 32, 83–85. *See also* Northside Child Development Center
Harlem Neighborhood Association, 212
Harlem race riots, 84, 110, 223–224
Harlem Renaissance, 30
Harlem Youth Opportunities Unlimited (HARYOU), 212–222
Harris, Abram, 38
Harris, Donald, 235–236
Harris, Gilbert, 10
Harris, Kate. *See* Clark, Kate
HARYOU (Harlem Youth Opportunities Unlimited), 212–222
Hastie, William, 68
Hastings-on-Hudson, New York, 134–135, 138–139, 167–170, *260*
Hatcher, Richard, 247
Head Start, 224–228
Height, Dorothy, 239, 242
Hicks, James L., 190
Hill, Oliver, 160, 161
Hilltop (school newspaper), 35, 37, 38, 42–43
Holt, Louisa, 154–155
Hope, Bob, 171
Hopson, Darlene Powell, 293

Horowitz, Eugene, 75–76
Horowitz, Ruth, 75, 76
Hot Springs, Arkansas, 3–4, 6–8, 96–99, 126–127, 233
Houston and Houston law firm, 66–68
Houston, Charles Hamilton, 35, 66–67
Howard University, 14–16, 33–43, 49, 52–57, 65–66, 74–77, 81–82, 249
Howard University's Charter Day speech, 56–57
Hughes, Langston, 112
Huxman, Walter, 155

I

inferiority complex, racial, 50–52, 56–57, 102
Intergroup Committee on New York Public Schools, 179

J

Jack, Hulan, 179–180, 230
Jackson, Barry, 228, 230
Jackson, Jesse, 284
Jackson, Wagner, 187–188
Jansen, William, 180, 182, 192, 193
Javits, Jacob, 248
Jewish Board of Guardians, 211–212
Jewish community, 115, 136, 211–212, 252
Johns, Barbara, 159–160
Johnson, Lady Bird, 224
Johnson, Lyndon, 224, 227, 244
Johnson, Mordecai, 35, 38, 40, 53
Joint Center for Political and Economic Studies, 247, 279
Jones, J. Raymond, 213, 229
Jordan, Vernon, 268

K

Kappa Alpha Psi, 37
Kennedy, John F., 212
Kerner Commission, 244–245
Kheel, Theodore, 241
King, Coretta Scott, 197–198, 284
King, Martin Luther, Jr., 196–199, 238, 241–243, 250
Klineberg, Otto, 49, 50–52, 78, 87, 135
Ku Klux Klan, 10, 267

L

Langston High School, 10–12, 15, 233
Lanier, R. O'Hara, 105

Lawrence, Jacob and Gwen, 167
Lee, Alfred McClung, 175, 187
Levitt, Arthur, 180–181
Lewis, Hylan, 41, 55, 57, 59–61, 124, 167–168, 197, 198
Lewis, Joe, 130
Lewis, John, 235
Lewis, Leighla, 41, 55, 57, 59–61
Lindsay, John, 248, 252
Lipchitz, Jacques, 167
Little Rock Nine, 199–201
Local 1199, 257–258
Locke, Alain, 16, 84, 135, 167–168
Logan, Wenonah and Arthur, 124
Luca, Mark, 117

M
MacLean, Malcolm, 105–106
Malcolm X, 216–217
MARC (Metropolitan Applied Research Center), 240–243, 247, 249, 252, 269–271
Marshall, Thurgood, 67, 68, 139–146, 149–150, 154, 174–178, 182–184, 190–191, 194–195
McCoy, Rhody, 252
McKissick, Floyd, 242
Meenes, Max, 52, 68, 75, 77, 81–82
Melecio, Apolonio, 230
Meredith, James, 238
Metropolitan Applied Research Center. *See* MARC
Midcentury White House Conference on Children and Youth, 135–138
Miller, Dean Kelly, 38
Montgomery bus boycott, 196–198
Montgomery, Eugene, 146–147
Moore, T. Justin, 161, 162–163, 165
Moseley, Louise and John, 124
Moynihan, Daniel P., 256
Murphy, Gardner, 49, 78, 81–82, 107
Museum of Modern Art, 277
Myrdal, Alva, 87, 254
Myrdal, Gunnar, 80, 86–89, 254

N
NAACP, 99, 275
    awards Spingarn Medal to Kenneth, 211
    Brown v. Board of Education and, 174–178, 182–184, 187–191
    New York City school desegregation and, 178–182, 192–193

state-level school segregation lawsuits and, 139–165
National Association for the Advancement of White People, 189
National Conference of Negro Elected Officials, 245–247
New Lincoln School, 126, 133, 134, 203
New York City schools, desegregation of, 178–182, 192–193
New York City teachers' strike of 1968, 250–253
New York Public Library, 277
New York State Board of Regents, 261, 267–269
Nixon, Richard, 246, 256, 267
Northside Child Development Center
    Clarks' founding of, 116–119, *118*
    Clarks' leadership of, 132–133, 172–173
    clientele and staff, 129–130, 172
    funding issues/fundraising, 121–123, 130, 209–210, 276–277, 278
    gateway-to-Harlem project, 228–230, 237, 248–249, 257, 258–260
    Mamie's retirement from, 278–279
    move to 110th Street, 128–133
    move to Schomburg Plaza, 258–260
    public/media interest in, 120, 170–172
    tensions between Clarks and chief benefactor Ascoli, 131–132, 207–210
    union shop at, 257–258
nuclear disarmament, 264–266
Nyquist, Ewald, 267, 268–269

O

Office of War Information, U.S., 106–107
One Hundred Black Men, 247
Oppenheim, D. B., 293

P

Palisades Interstate Park Commission, 277
Parker, John J., 149, 152
Parks, Gordon, 120
Parks, Rosa, 196
Pathos of Power (Clark), 266
Phipps, Harold, 5–12, 7, 14–15, 44, 49–50, 66, 71–74, 174
Phipps, Harold, Jr., 9, 9, 49
Phipps, Katie, 8–9, 12–13, 44, 49–50, 66, 71–74
Phipps, Mamie. *See* Clark, Mamie
Plessy v. Ferguson, 141, 183
"Policy Framework for Racial Justice, A" (Clark and Franklin), 284
Powell, Adam Clayton, Jr., 104–105, 107, 213–214, 219–222, 231, 232
Prashker, Herbert, 257, 258
Prejudice and Your Child (Clark), 193–194

Project Head Start, 224–228

R
race riots, 84, 110, 223–224, 243–245
racial inferiority complex, 50–52, 56–57, 102
Randolph, A. Philip, 239, 241
Rangel, Charles, 268
Reagan, Ronald, 283–284
Redding, Louis, 157
Richards, Ruby, 130
Riverdale Children's Association, 113–114
Robertson, Archibald, 161
Robinson, Spottswood, 160, 161
Rockefeller, Nelson, 248–249
Rose, Arnold, 87
Rosenwald Fund, viii, 86
Rosenwald, Julius, viii, 122
Rustin, Bayard, 239, 241

S
Schomburg, Arthur, 31, 259
Schomburg Plaza, 258–260
school desegregation, fight for. See also Brown v. Board of Education
    busing policies, 266–269
    Houston and Houston law firm and, 66–68
    Little Rock Nine, 199–201
    NAACP recruits Kenneth as consultant in, 139–142
    NAACP's state-level lawsuits, 139–165
    in New York City, 178–182, 192–193
    reemergence of issue, 291
school reform, 261–263
Schultz, George, 267
Scott, Hugh, 262, 263
Seitz, Collins, 157, 158–159
Shagaloff, June, 190–191
Shanker, Albert, 251, 252
Shriver, Sargent, 225, 227
Simons, William, 262
Smith, Alfred, 5, 14, 50
Smith, Jesse Rufus, 8
Smith, Katie. See Phipps, Katie
Smith, Mamie, 8
social psychology, 47–49
Spingarn Medal, 211, 260

Stokes, Carl, 243
Stone, C. Sumner "Chuck," 232
Student Afro-American Society at Columbia, 236
Student Nonviolent Coordinating Committee, 238–239, 242
student protests, 210–211, 249–250
Stylus literary magazine, 41, 42–43
Summer Olympics of 1976, 277–278
Sumner, Francis, 23, 37–38, 39, 41, 51, 75, 77, 81
Supreme Court ruling on school segregation. *See Brown v. Board of Education*
Sutton, Percy, 245–246, 280–281

T
teachers' strike of 1968, 250–253
Thomas, Alexander, 131
Timmerman, George Bell, 149
Trager, Helen, 152
Truman, Harry, 135, 137
"Two Cities" project, 269–271

U
Union of Concerned Parents, 252
Unitarian Service Committee, 197
Urban Development Corporation, 248–249

V
Vietnam War, 241–242, 256
Vinson, Fred, 178

W
Wagner, Robert F., 179–180, 181, 212, 228–229
Wallace, George, 266–267
War Department, U.S., 111–112
Waring, J. Waties, 149, 152–153
War on Poverty, 212, 224
Warren, Earl, 178, 194–195
Washington, D.C. school reform, 261–263
Weaver, Robert C., 268
Wertham, Fredric, 157–158
Wesley, Charles, 39
White Citizens' Council, 195
White House Conference on Children and Youth, 135–138
Wilkins, Roy, 235, 239, 242, 244, 275
Wilson, William Julius, 279, 284
Works Progress Administration, 68–69

World War II, 106, 110–116

Y
Yeshiva University, 208
Young Lords, 249
Young, Whitney, 235, 239, 242
Youth in the Ghetto (Clark), 218–219

ABOUT THE AUTHOR

© Kelly Nash

Tim Spofford grew up in the all-white mill town of Cohoes, New York, hearing stories of recently arrived Black families evicted in the middle of the night—stories with the ring of historical truth given that the surrounding cities included Black residents.

Spofford taught writing and journalism in schools and colleges and has a doctor of arts in English from the State University at Albany. As an education writer for seven years at the *Albany Times Union* in New York's capital city, he often interviewed Kenneth Clark, a member of the state Board of Regents.

Spofford's first book, *Lynch Street*, reconstructs the fatal shootings in May 1970 at Jackson State, a Black college in Mississippi. He's published articles in the *New York Times*, *Newsday*, *Mother Jones*, *Columbia Journalism Review*, and other publications. He lives with his wife, Barbara, in St. Petersburg, Florida, and Lee, Massachusetts.